Visual Reference

Microsoft®
Excel 2000
At a Glance

Microsoft Press

PUBLISHED by **Microsoft Press**
A Division of Microsoft Corporation
One Microsoft Way
Redmond, Washington 98052-6399

Library of Congress Cataloging-in-Publication Data
Microsoft Excel 2000 At a Glance. Perspection
     p.   cm.
   Includes index.
   ISBN 1-57231-942-9
    1. Microsoft Excel for Windows.   2. Business—computer programs.   3. Electronic spreadsheets
  I. Perspection, Inc.
HF5548.4.M523M51579   1999
005.369—dc21

98-31456
CIP

Printed and bound in the United States of America.

1 2 3 4 5 6 7 8 9 WCWC 4 3 2 1 0 9

Distributed in Canada by ITP Nelson, a division of Thomson Canada limited.

A CIP catalog record for this book is available from the British Library.

Microsoft Press books are available through booksellers and distributors worldwide. For further information about international editions, contact your local Microsoft Corporation office. Or contact Microsoft Press International directly at fax (425) 936-7329. Visit our Web site at mspress.microsoft.com.

For Perspection, Inc.
Writer: Elizabeth Eisner Reding
Managing Editor: Steven M. Johnson
Series Editor: Jane E. Pedicini
Production Editor: David W. Beskeen
Developmental Editor: Mary-Terese Cozzola
Technical Editors: Nicholas Chu; Craig Fernandez

For Microsoft Press
Acquisitions Editors: Kim Fryer; Susanne Forderer
Project Editor: Jenny Moss Benson

Contents

Start Excel.
See page 6

Detect and repair problems.
See page 17

Use the Office Clipboard.
See page 37

1 About This Book 1
    No Computerese! 1
    What's New 2
    Useful Tasks... 2
    ...And the Easiest Way to Do Them 2
    A Quick Overview 2
    A Final Word (or Two) 3

2 Getting Started with Excel 5
    Starting Excel 6
    Viewing the Excel Window 7
    Working with the Excel Window 8
    Starting a New Workbook 9
    Opening a Workbook 10 **New**2000
    Moving Around the Workbook 12
    Working with Menus and Toolbars 14 **New**2000
    Working with Dialog Boxes and Wizards 16
    Detecting and Repairing Problems 17 **New**2000
    Getting Help 18 **New**2000
    Saving a Workbook 20 **New**2000
    Printing a Worksheet 22
    Closing a Workbook and Quitting Excel 24

3 Basic Workbook Skills 25
    Making Cell Entries 26
    Selecting Cells 27 **New**2000
    Entering Labels on a Worksheet 28
    Entering Values on a Worksheet 30
    Entering Values Quickly with AutoFill 32 **New**2000
    Editing Cell Contents 33
    Clearing Cell Contents 34
    Undoing and Redoing an Action 35
    Understanding How Excel Pastes Data 36
    Storing Cell Contents 37 **New**2000

"How do I use AutoCorrect to correct text?"

See page 44

Use functions to create equations.
See page 62

Adjust columns and rows.
See page 72

Copying Cell Contents 38

Moving Cell Contents 40

Inserting and Deleting Cells 42

Correcting Text with AutoCorrect 44

Checking Your Spelling 46

4 Working with Formulas and Functions 47

Creating a Simple Formula 48

Editing a Formula 50

Understanding Relative Cell Referencing 52

Using Absolute Cell References 53

Using Labels for Cell References 54

Naming Cells and Ranges 56

Simplifying a Formula with Ranges 58

Displaying Calculations with AutoCalculate 59

Calculating Totals with AutoSum 60

Performing Calculations Using Functions 61

Creating Functions 62

5 Modifying Worksheets and Workbooks 63

Selecting and Naming a Worksheet 64

Inserting and Deleting a Worksheet 65

Moving and Copying a Worksheet 66

Selecting a Column or Row 68

Inserting a Column or Row 69

Deleting a Column or Row 70

Hiding a Column or Row 71

Adjusting Column Width and Row Height 72

Freezing a Column or Row 74

Previewing Page Breaks 75

Setting Up the Page 76

Adding a Header or Footer 77

Customizing Worksheet Printing 78

Setting a Print Area 80

Change a font style.
See page 86

Insert media clips.
See page 106

Insert AutoShapes.
See page 126

6   **Formatting a Worksheet** **81**

Formatting Text and Numbers 82

Designing Conditional Formatting 84

Copying Cell Formats 85

Changing Fonts 86

Changing Data Alignment 88

Controlling Text Flow 90

Changing Data Color 91

Adding Color and Patterns to Cells 92

Adding Borders to Cells 94

Formatting Data with AutoFormat 96

Modifying an AutoFormat 97

Creating and Applying a Style 98

Modifying a Style 100

Changing Languages 102   **New**2000

7   **Inserting Graphics and Related Materials** **103**

Inserting Pictures 104

Inserting Media Clips 106   **New**2000

Stylizing Text with WordArt 108

Editing WordArt Text 110

Applying WordArt Text Effects 112

Inserting an Organization Chart 114

Modifying an Organization Chart 116

Creating and Reading a Cell Comment 118

Editing and Deleting a Cell Comment 119

Modifying Graphic Images 120

8   **Drawing and Modifying Objects** **121**

Drawing Lines and Arrows 122

Drawing AutoShapes 124

Inserting AutoShapes from the Clip Gallery 126   **New**2000

Drawing a Freeform Object 128

Create 3-D objects.
See page 140

Editing a Freeform Object 130
Moving and Resizing an Object 132
Rotating and Flipping an Object 134
Choosing Object Colors 136
Adding Object Shadows 138
Creating a 3-D Object 140
Aligning and Distributing Objects 142
Arranging and Grouping Objects 144
Changing Object View Settings 146

9 Creating Charts and Maps 147
Understanding Chart Terminology 148
Choosing the Right Type of Chart 149
Creating a Chart .... 150 **New** 2000
Editing a Chart 152
Selecting a Chart 153
Changing a Chart Type 154
Moving and Resizing a Chart 155
Pulling Out a Pie Slice 156
Adding and Deleting a Data Series 158
Enhancing a Data Series 160
Enhancing a Chart 162
Drawing on a Chart 164
Formatting Chart Elements 166
Creating a Map 167
Modifying a Map 168

10 Analyzing Worksheet Data 169
Understanding List Terminology 170
Creating a List 171
Understanding a Data Form 172
Adding Records Using a Data Form 173
Managing Records Using a Data Form 174

Create a chart.
See page 150

Create a map.
See page 167

Analyze data using a
PivotTable.
See page 182

*"How can I add
menus and menu
items to Excel?"*

See page 198

Record a macro.
See page 215

Sorting Data in a List 176
Displaying Parts of a List with AutoFilter 178
Creating Complex Searches 179
Entering Data in a List 180
Adding Data Validation to a Worksheet 181
Analyzing Data Using a PivotTable 182 **New**2000
Updating a PivotTable 184
Modifying a PivotTable and PivotChart 185 **New**2000
Charting a PivotTable 186 **New**2000
Auditing a Worksheet 188

11 **Tools for Working More Efficiently 189**
Customizing Your Excel Work Environment 190
Viewing Multiple Workbooks 192
Changing Your Worksheet View 193
Creating a Toolbar 194
Customizing a Toolbar 196
Adding Menus and Menu Items 198 **New**2000
Creating Groups and Outlines 199 **New**2000
Saving Time with Templates 200
Creating a Template 201
Working with Templates 202
Tracking Changes 204
Protecting Your Data 206

12 **Building More Powerful Worksheets 207**
Generating Multiple-Page Reports 208
Creating Scenarios 210
Looking at Alternatives with Data Tables 212
Asking "What If" with Goal Seek 213
Understanding How Macros Automate Your Work 214
Recording a Macro 215
Running a Macro 216

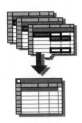

Share information among
documents.
See page 226

*"How do I open a
workbook as a
Web page?"*

See page 244

Have a Web discussion.
See page 252

Understanding Macro Code 217
Debugging a Macro Using Step Mode 218
Editing a Macro 219
Understanding Excel Program Add-Ins 220

13 Tools for Working Together 221
Sharing Workbooks 222
Merging Workbooks 224
Sharing Information Among Documents 226
Exporting and Importing Data 228 **New**2000
Linking and Embedding Files 230
Linking Data 232
Consolidating Data 234
Getting Data from Queries 236 **New**2000
Getting Data from Another Program 238
Converting Excel Data into Access Data 240

14 Linking Excel to the Internet 241
Creating a Web Page 242 **New**2000
Opening a Workbook as a Web Page 244 **New**2000
Previewing a Web Page 245 **New**2000
Inserting an Internet Link 246
Getting Data from the Web 248
Copying a Web Table to a Worksheet 250 **New**2000
Understanding Office Server Extensions 251 **New**2000
Having a Web Discussion 252 **New**2000
Scheduling and Holding an Online Meeting 254 **New**2000
Sending Workbooks Using E-Mail 256 **New**2000
Accessing Office Information on the Web 258 **New**2000

Index 259

Acknowledgments

The task of creating any book requires the talents of many hardworking people pulling together to meet almost impossible demands. For their effort and commitment, we'd like to thank the outstanding team responsible for making this book possible: the writer, Elizabeth Reding; the developmental editor, Mary-Terese Cozzola; the technical editors, Nicholas Chu and Craig Fernandez; the production team, Gary Bellig and Tracy Teyler; and the indexer, Michael Brackney.

At Microsoft Press, we'd like to thank Kim Fryer and Susanne Forderer for the opportunity to undertake this project, and Jenny Benson for project editing and overall help when needed most.

Perspection

Perspection

Perspection, Inc., is a software training company committed to providing information to help people communicate, make decisions, and solve problems. Perspection writes and produces software training books, and develops interactive multimedia applications for Windows-based and Macintosh personal computers.

Microsoft Excel 2000 At a Glance incorporates Perspection's training expertise to ensure that you'll receive the maximum return on your time. With this staightforward, easy-to-read reference tool, you'll get the information you need when you need it. You'll focus on the skills that increase productivity while working at your own pace and convenience.

We invite you to visit the Perspection World Wide Web site. You can visit us at:

http://www.perspection.com

You'll find descriptions of all of our books, additional content for our books, information about Perspection, and much more.

About This Book

IN THIS SECTION

No Computerese!

New2000 **What's New**

Useful Tasks...

...And the Easiest Way to Do Them

A Quick Overview

A Final Word (or Two)

Microsoft Excel 2000 At a Glance is for anyone who wants to get the most from their computer and their software with the least amount of time and effort. You'll find this book to be a straightforward, easy-to-read reference tool. With the premise that your computer should work for you, not you for it, this book's purpose is to help you get your work done quickly and efficiently so that you can get away from the computer and live your life.

No Computerese!

Let's face it—when there's a task you don't know how to do but you need to get it done in a hurry, or when you're stuck in the middle of a task and can't figure out what to do next, there's nothing more frustrating than having to read page after page of technical background material. You want the information you need—nothing more, nothing less—and you want it now! And the information should be easy to find and understand.

That's what this book is all about. It's written in plain English—no technical jargon and no computerese. There's no single task in the book that takes more than two pages. Just look up the task in the index or the table of contents, turn to the page, and there it is. Each task introduction gives you information that is essential to performing the task, suggesting situations in which you can use the task, or providing examples of the benefit you gain from completing the procedure. The task itself is laid out step by step and accompanied by a graphic that adds visual clarity. Just read the introduction, follow the steps, look at the illustrations, and get your work done with a minimum of hassle.

You may want to turn to another task if the one you're working on has a "See Also" in the left column. Because there's a lot of overlap among tasks, we didn't want to keep repeating ourselves; you might find more elementary or more advanced tasks laid out on the pages referenced. We wanted to bring you through the tasks in such a way that they would make sense to you. We've also added some useful tips here and there and offered a "Try This" once in a while to give you a context in which to use the task. But, by and large, we've tried to remain true to the heart and soul of the book, which is that information you need should be available to you *at a glance*.

What's New

If you're looking for what's new in Excel 2000, just look for our new icon: **New**2000. We've inserted it throughout this book. You will find the new icon in the table of contents so you can quickly and easily identify new or improved features in Excel. You will also find the new icon on the first page of each section. There it will serve as a handy reminder of the latest improvements in Excel as you move from one task to another.

Useful Tasks...

Whether you use Excel for work, play, or some of each, we've tried to pack this book with procedures for everything we could think of that you might want to do, from the simplest tasks to some that are more challenging.

...And the Easiest Way to Do Them

Another thing we've done in *Microsoft Excel 2000 At a Glance* is document the easiest way to accomplish a task. Excel often offers many ways to accomplish a single result, which can be daunting or delightful, depending on the way you like to work. If you tend to stick with one favorite and familiar approach, we think the methods described in this book are the way to go. If you like trying out alternative techniques, go ahead! The intuitiveness of Excel invites exploration, and you're likely to discover ways of doing things that you think are easier or that you like better. If you do, that's great! It's exactly what the creators of Excel had in mind when they provided so many alternatives.

A Quick Overview

You don't have to read this book in any particular order. It's designed so that you can jump in, get the information you need, and then close the book and keep it nearby until you need it again. But that doesn't mean we scattered the information about with wild abandon. If you were to read the book from front to back, you'd find a logical progression from the simple tasks to the more complex ones. Here's a quick overview.

First, we assume that Excel 2000 is already installed on your computer. If it's not, the Setup Wizard makes installation so simple that you won't need our help anyway. So, unlike most computer books, this one doesn't start out with installation instructions and a list of system requirements. You've already got that under control.

Sections 2 through 5 of the book cover the basics: starting and quitting Excel; working with menus, toolbars, and dialog boxes; entering text labels and numbers; creating simple formulas; modifying worksheets and workbooks; and printing and saving workbooks.

Sections 6 through 9 describe tasks that are useful for enhancing the look of a worksheet: formatting worksheets; adding and modifying pictures; drawing shapes; inserting comments; and creating charts and geographic maps.

Section 10 addresses a task that is a little more technical but really useful: analyzing worksheet data.

Sections 11 helps you to fine-tune Excel so you can work more efficiently, including customizing your environment, changing your view, and working with templates.

Sections 12 through 14 cover topics that significantly power up your work, such as linking and consolidating data, using add-ins, collaborating with others, importing and exporting data, and working with the Internet.

A Final Word (or Two)

We had three goals in writing this book. We want our book to help you:

- ◆ Do all the things you want to do with Excel 2000.

- ◆ Discover how to do things you didn't know you wanted to do with Excel 2000.

- ◆ Enjoy doing your work with Excel 2000.

Our "thank you" for buying this book is the achievement of those goals. We hope you'll have as much fun using *Microsoft Excel 2000 At a Glance* as we've had writing it. The best way to learn is by doing, and that's what we hope you'll get from this book.

Jump right in!

2

Getting Started with Excel

IN THIS SECTION

Starting Excel

Viewing the Excel Window

Working with the Excel Window

Starting a New Workbook

New2000 **Opening a Workbook**

Moving Around the Workbook

New2000 **Working with Menus and Toolbars**

Working with Dialog Boxes and Wizards

New2000 **Detecting and Repairing Problems**

New2000 **Getting Help**

New2000 **Saving a Workbook**

Printing a Worksheet

Closing a Workbook and Quitting Excel

If you're spending too much time rewriting financial reports, drawing charts, and searching for your calculator, you're probably eager to start using Microsoft Excel 2000. This book teaches you to use Excel's most popular features so you can become productive immediately.

Excel is a *spreadsheet program*, a type of software you can use to record, analyze, and present quantitative information. With Excel, you can track and analyze sales, organize finances, create budgets, and accomplish a variety of business tasks in a fraction of the time it would take using pen and paper.

The file you create and save in Excel is called a *workbook*. It contains a collection of *worksheets*, which are the "pages" that look similar to an accountant's ledger sheets, but you can use Excel to perform calculations and other tasks automatically.

Using Excel, you can create a variety of documents that can be used for analysis and record keeping, such as:

◆ Monthly sales and expense reports

◆ Charts displaying annual sales data

◆ An inventory of products

◆ A payment schedule for an equipment purchase

Starting Excel

Before you can begin using Excel, you need to start the program. The easiest way to start Excel is to use the Start menu, which you open by clicking the Start button on the taskbar. When Excel starts, it displays a new workbook so that you can begin working immediately. If you have installed Excel as part of the Microsoft Office 2000 suite of programs, you can open a new workbook and start Excel at the same time using the New Office Document command, also located on the Start menu.

TIP

Use the Office Shortcut Bar to start Excel. *If the Office Shortcut Bar is displayed on your computer screen, you can click the Start A New Document button on the Office Shortcut Bar. If the Office Shortcut Bar is not displayed, click the Start button, point to Programs, point to Office Tools, and then click Microsoft Office Shortcut Bar to display it.*

Start Excel from the Start Menu

1. Click the Start button on the taskbar.

2. Point to Programs.

3. Click Microsoft Excel.

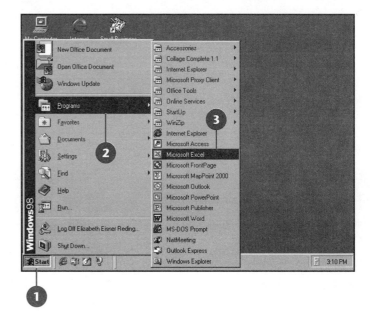

Start Excel and a New Workbook from Microsoft Office

1. Click the Start button on the taskbar, and then click New Office Document.

2. Click the General tab.

3. Click the Blank Workbook icon.

4. Click OK.

Click to display other workbook solutions.

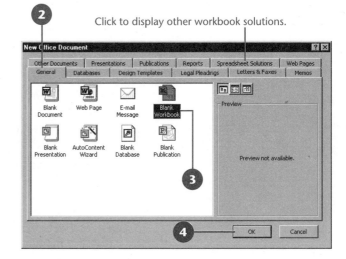

Viewing the Excel Window

When you start Excel, the Excel program window opens with a blank workbook—ready for you to begin working.

Menu bar
All Excel commands are organized on menus on the *menu bar*.

Name box
The address of the currently selected (or active) cell appears in the *Name box*.

Active cell
The active cell is the currently selected cell (its address appears in the Name box); you enter data in the active cell.

Status bar
The *status bar* shows information about selected commands or procedures.

Title bar
The *title bar* contains the name of the active workbook.

Formula bar
Any data contained in the active cell appears on the *formula bar*.

Toolbars
Frequently used Excel commands are available through *toolbar buttons*, which are organized on *toolbars*.

Mouse pointer
The mouse pointer takes this shape when Excel is ready to perform a new task. The mouse pointer is context-sensitive; its shape changes depending on the action you are performing.

Office Assistant
The Office Assistant automatically appears. You can ask the Office Assistant questions about Excel tasks, and it provides helpful information.

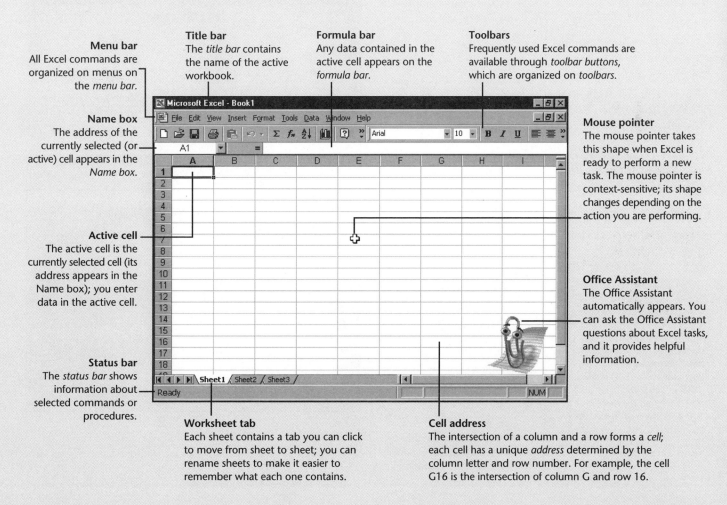

Worksheet tab
Each sheet contains a tab you can click to move from sheet to sheet; you can rename sheets to make it easier to remember what each one contains.

Cell address
The intersection of a column and a row forms a *cell*; each cell has a unique *address* determined by the column letter and row number. For example, the cell G16 is the intersection of column G and row 16.

Working with the Excel Window

You can open more than one workbook window at a time. That means that if you are working with one workbook and need to check or work with data in another, you don't need to close the current file. You can view open windows one at a time, or arrange all of them on the screen at once, and then click one window at a time to work in it. You can also move and resize each window to suit your needs.

TIP

Quick Office document switching. *Each open Office 2000 document displays its own button on the Windows taskbar. You can quickly click the buttons on the taskbar to switch between the open Office documents.*

Switch Between Workbook Windows

1. Click the Window menu to display the list of open workbook windows.

2. Click the name of the workbook you want to switch to.

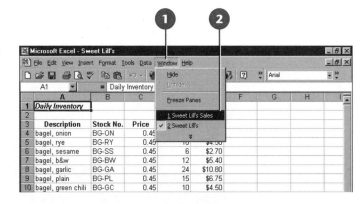

Resize and Move Windows

◆ Minimize a window

To reduce a window to a button on the taskbar, click the Minimize button.

◆ Maximize a window

To maximize a window to fit the screen, click the Maximize button.

◆ Resize a window

To change the size of the window, position the mouse pointer over a window edge, and then drag the sizing handle.

◆ Move a window

To change a window's location, drag the title bar of the workbook window to a different location.

Title bar   Minimize button   Maximize button

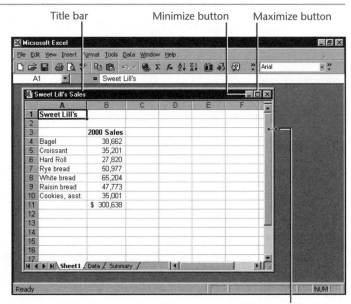

Sizing handle

Starting a New Workbook

When you start Excel, the program window opens with a new workbook so that you can begin working in it. You can also start a new workbook whenever Excel is running, and you can start as many new workbooks as you want. Each new workbook displays a default name ("Book1," "Book2," and so on), numbered according to how many new workbooks you have started during the work session until you save it with a more meaningful name.

SEE ALSO

See "Viewing the Excel Window" on page 7 for information on the Excel workbook window.

SEE ALSO

See "Saving a Workbook" on page 20 for more information on saving and naming a workbook.

Start a New Workbook from the File Menu

1. Click the File menu, and then click New.

2. Click the General tab.

3. Click the Workbook icon.

4. Click OK.

A blank workbook is opened.

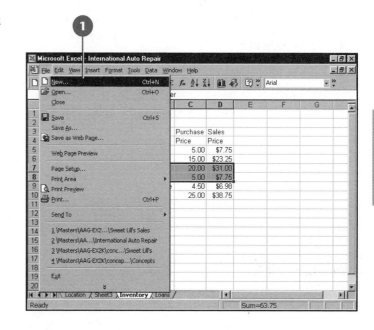

Click to display other workbook solutions.

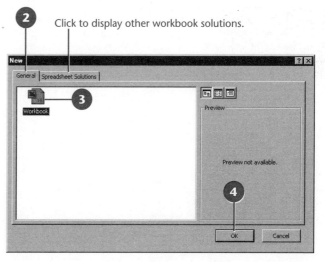

Opening a Workbook

When you want to use a workbook you have previously created, you must first open it. You can open an Excel workbook and start Excel simultaneously, or you can open an Excel workbook file or file created in another spreadsheet program after you start Excel. If you can't remember the workbook's name or location, Excel even helps you find files.

> **TIP**
>
> **Change the default file location of the Open dialog box.** *Click the Tools menu, click Options, click the General tab, and then enter a new location in the Default File Location box.*

> **TIP**
>
> **Recently opened files appear on the File menu.** *If you have recently opened and closed a workbook file, you can click the File menu and then click the filename at the bottom of the File menu to open the file.*

Open a Workbook from the Excel Window

1. Click the Open button on the Standard toolbar.

2. Click one of the icons on the Places bar for quick access to frequently used folders.

3. If the file is located in another folder, click the Look In drop-down arrow, and select the drive or folder containing the file you want to open.

4. If necessary, click the Files Of Type drop-down arrow, and then click the type of file you want to open (click Microsoft Excel Files to see workbook files).

5. Click the name of the workbook file.

6. Click Open.

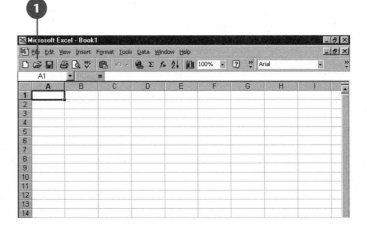

Click to move back to a recently visited folder.

Click another file type to open a file created in another program.

TIP

Can't find a file created in another spreadsheet program? *If the name of the spreadsheet program you want to open doesn't appear in the Files Of Type list, use the Excel setup program to install the necessary filters.*

TIP

Change the number of recently opened files that appear on the File menu. *Click the Tools menu, click Options, click the General tab, and then change the number in the Recently Used File List box.*

TIP

Find a file when you're not sure of its name. *In the Open dialog box, click the Look In drop-down arrow, and select the drive where the file might be located. If you know any characters contained in the file name, type them in the File Name box. Click the Tools button, click Find, click to select the Search Subfolders check box, and then click Find Now.*

SEE ALSO

See "Opening a Workbook as a Web Page" on page 244 for information on opening an Excel Web page.

Open a Recently Opened Workbook from the Start Menu

1. Click the Start button on the taskbar.

2. Point to Documents. The Documents menu displays a list of recently opened documents.

3. Click the Excel workbook you want to open.

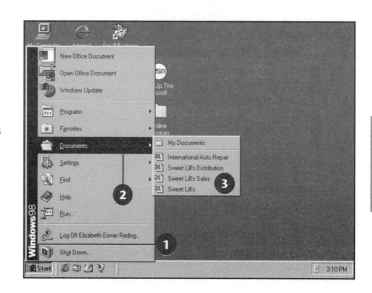

Open an Office File from the Start Menu

1. Click the Start button on the taskbar, and then click Open Office Document.

2. If necessary, click the Files Of Type drop-down arrow, and then click the type of file you want to open.

3. Click the Look In drop-down arrow, if necessary, and select the drive and folder containing the workbook file you want to open.

4. Click the name of the file.

5. Click Open.

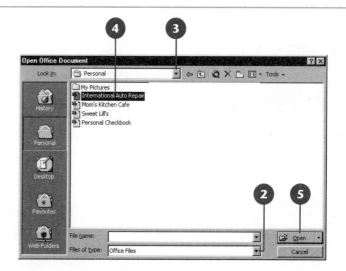

Moving Around the Workbook

You can move around a worksheet or workbook using your mouse or the keyboard. You might find that using your mouse to move from cell to cell is most convenient, while using various keyboard combinations is easier for covering large areas of a worksheet quickly. However, there is no one right way; whichever method feels the most comfortable is the one you should use.

TIP

Microsoft IntelliMouse users can roll from cell to cell with IntelliMouse. *If you have the new Microsoft IntelliMouse—with the wheel button between the left and right buttons—you can click the wheel button and move the mouse in any direction to move quickly around the worksheet.*

Use the Mouse to Navigate

Using the mouse, you can navigate to:

◆ Another cell

◆ Another part of a worksheet

◆ Another worksheet

To move from one cell to another, point to the cell you want to move to, and then click.

When you click the wheel button, the pointer changes shape. Drag the pointer in any direction to move to a new location quickly.

To see more sheet tabs without changing the location of the active cell, click a sheet scroll button.

To move from one worksheet to another, click the tab of the sheet you want to move to.

To see other parts of the worksheet without changing the location of the active cell, click the horizontal or vertical scroll buttons, or drag the scroll bars.

TIP

Change move cell selection after pressing Enter. *When you press Enter, the active cell moves down one cell. To change the direction, click the Tools menu, click Options, click the Edit tab, click the Direction drop-down arrow, select a direction, and then click OK.*

TIP

Zoom on roll with IntelliMouse. *Instead of scrolling when you roll with the IntelliMouse, you can zoom in or out. To turn on this feature, click the Tools menu, click Options, click the General tab, click to select the Zoom On Roll With IntelliMouse check box, and then click OK.*

SEE ALSO

See "Moving and Copying a Worksheet" on page 66 for more information on changing the order of worksheets within a workbook.

SEE ALSO

See "Viewing the Excel Window" on page 7 for more information on the Excel worksheet.

Use the Keyboard to Navigate

Using the keyboard, you can navigate to:

◆ Another cell

◆ Another part of a worksheet

Refer to the table for keyboard shortcuts for navigating around a worksheet.

KEYS FOR NAVIGATING IN A WORKSHEET	
Press This Key	**To Move**
Left arrow	One cell to the left
Right arrow	One cell to the right
Up arrow	One cell up
Down arrow	One cell down
Enter	One cell down
Tab	One cell to the right
Shift+Tab	One cell to the left
Page Up	One screen up
Page Down	One screen down
End+arrow key	In the direction of the arrow key to the next cell containing data or to the last empty cell in current row or column
Home	To column A in the current row
Ctrl+Home	To cell A1
Ctrl+End	To the last cell in the worksheet containing data

2

Working with Menus and Toolbars

All Excel commands are organized on menus on the menu bar, and each menu contains a list of related commands. A *short menu* displays often used commands, and an *expanded menu* displays all commands available on that menu. A menu command followed by an ellipsis (...) indicates that a dialog box opens, so you can provide additional information. An arrow to the right of a command indicates that a submenu opens, displaying related commands. An icon to the left means a toolbar button is available for that command. Toolbars contain buttons you can click to carry out commands you use frequently. A keyboard combination to the right of a menu command indicates a *shortcut key* is available for the command.

Choose a Command Using a Menu

① Click a menu name on the menu bar to display a list of commands.

② If necessary, click the double-headed arrow to expand the menu and display more commands, or wait until the expanded list of commands appears.

③ Click the command you want, or point to the arrow to the right of the menu command to display a submenu of related commands, and then click the command.

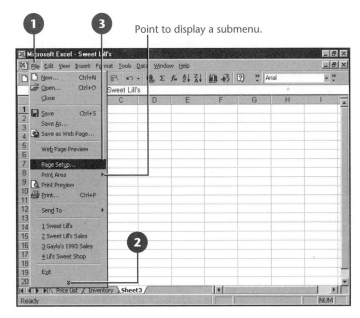

Point to display a submenu.

Choose a Command Using a Toolbar Button

① If you're not sure what a toolbar button does, point to it to display a ScreenTip.

② To choose a command, click the button or click the More Buttons drop-arrow, and then click the button.

When you select a button from the More Buttons drop-arrow, the button appears on the toolbar, showing only the buttons you use most often.

The Standard and Formatting toolbars are displayed within a single bar.

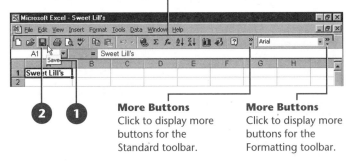

More Buttons
Click to display more buttons for the Standard toolbar.

More Buttons
Click to display more buttons for the Formatting toolbar.

Move and reshape a toolbar. *A toolbar that appears at the top or on the edge of a window is* docked*; if it appears somewhere else on the screen, it is* floating. *To move a toolbar to another location, click a blank area of the toolbar (not a button), and then drag the toolbar to a new location. To change the shape of a floating toolbar, position the mouse pointer over the edge of the toolbar, and then drag to reshape it.*

Choose a Command Using a Shortcut Key

◆ To choose a command using a shortcut key, press and hold the first key, and then press the other key. For example, press and hold the Ctrl key, and then press S to perform the Save command.

Shortcut keys

The commands and buttons on menus and toolbars respond to your work habits. *As you select menu commands or toolbar buttons, those commands and toolbar buttons are promoted to the short menu and shared toolbar if they were not already there.*

Display or Hide a Toolbar

1. Click the View menu, and then point to Toolbars.

2. Click the unchecked toolbar you want to display or the checked toolbar you want to hide.

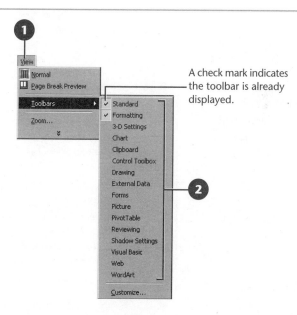

A check mark indicates the toolbar is already displayed.

Working with Dialog Boxes and Wizards

A *dialog box* is a special window that opens when Excel needs additional information from you in order to complete a task. You indicate your choices by selecting a variety of option buttons and check boxes; in some cases, you type the necessary information in the boxes provided. Some dialog boxes consist of a single window, while others contain *tabs* that you click to display more sets of options. *Wizards* are special dialog boxes that guide you through a task; they are powerful tools that make complicated tasks, such as creating a chart or analyzing data, easy.

Select Dialog Box and Wizard Options

A dialog box may contain one or more of these components.

◆ Check boxes

◆ Drop-down lists

◆ Option buttons

◆ Spin boxes

◆ Tabs

◆ Text boxes

After you select the options you want or enter the necessary information:

◆ Click OK to complete the command and close the dialog box.

◆ Click Cancel or press the Esc key to cancel the command and close the dialog box.

Navigating Through a Wizard Dialog Box

Because a wizard guides you through a series of dialog boxes, there are additional options.

◆ Click Back to move backward through the dialog boxes and change your selections.

◆ Click Next to continue to the next dialog box in the series.

◆ Click Finish to complete the wizard.

Tabs
Click a tab to select specific task-related options.

Spin box
Click the up arrow or down arrow of a spin box to change a quantity or measurement, or type the value in the corresponding text box.

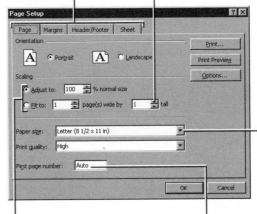

Drop-down list
Click the drop-down arrow of a list box to open a list of available choices, and click the item you want.

Option buttons
Click one option button to activate the feature you want. You can choose only one option button at a time.

Text box
Type necessary information directly into a text box.

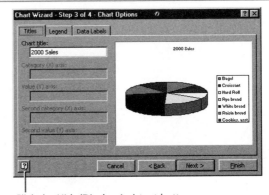

Click the Hide/Display Assistant button to get additional information.

Detecting and Repairing Problems

Excel can automatically detect and repair problems with itself. When you start Excel, it determines if essential files are missing and where they are found and repairs them. Sometimes problems arise after you start Excel. The Detect And Repair feature scans for noncritical Excel file discrepancies and then fixes the problems wherever possible. If you access a feature or file, such as a template, not currently installed, Excel will install the feature or file on first use. You can also use the maintenance mode to repair a program, add or remove program features, or remove a program.

TIP

Allow time for repairs. *The Detect And Repair feature can take an hour or more to complete, depending on your computer's processor speed.*

Detect and Repair Problems

1. Click the Help menu, and then click Detect And Repair.

2. Click Start.

   Make sure the Microsoft Office CD is in your CD-ROM drive.

3. Click Repair Office, and then click Reinstall Office or Repair errors in your Office installation.

4. Click Finish.

Perform Maintenance on Office Programs

1. Double-click the Setup icon on the Office CD in Windows Explorer.

2. Click one of the following maintenance buttons.

   ◆ Repair Office to repair or reinstall Office

   ◆ Add Or Remove Features to determine which and when features are installed or removed

   ◆ Remove Office to delete Office

3. Follow the wizard instructions to complete the maintenance option.

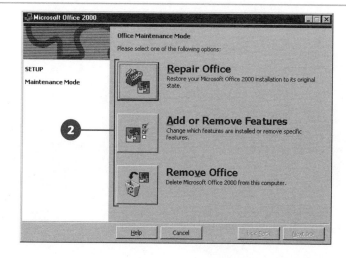

Select to restore program shortcuts to the Start menu.

Getting Help

Excel provides an extensive online Help system to guide you in completing tasks. You can get help any time in Excel using the Help menu, the Help pointer, or the *Office Assistant*—an animated Help feature that displays helpful tips while you are working in Excel. You can "ask" the Office Assistant how to accomplish a task or learn helpful information about Excel.

Get Help Using the Help Pointer

1. Click the Help button on the title bar of a dialog box, or click the Help menu, and then click What's This.

2. Click the Help pointer on any area of the worksheet or an item in a dialog box to display a Help definition box.

3. Click the mouse button or press Esc to close the definition box.

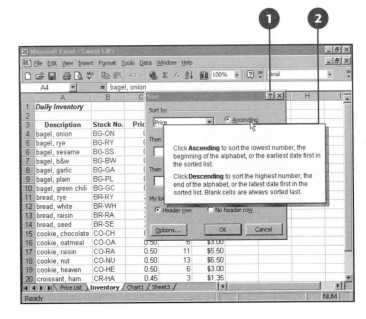

Show or Hide the Office Assistant

1. Click the Help menu.

2. Click Show The Office Assistant to turn it on, or click Hide The Office Assistant to turn it off.

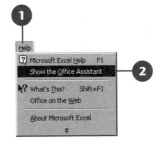

Use the Office Assistant to get a tip. *If a light bulb appears over the Office Assistant, Excel has a tip to help guide you through your current task. Click the light bulb to read the tip.*

Office Assistant provides interactive help. *If you see a Show Me link in Help, click the link to display a demonstration of how to perform the task.*

See "Accessing Office Information on the Web" on page 258 for information on getting updated information on Office programs.

Transition options for Lotus 1-2-3 users. *If you are a former Lotus 1-2-3 user, click the Tools menu, click Options, click the Transition tab, and then select the Help, navigation, and formula options you want to use.*

Ask for Help from the Office Assistant

1. Click the Office Assistant or click the Help button on the Standard toolbar.

2. Type your question.

3. Click Search.

4. Click the button for the topic you're interested in.

5. Read the topic or click a hyperlink to another topic.

6. Click the Close button.

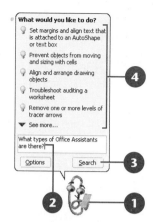

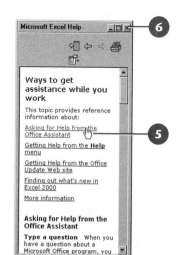

Get Help for Lotus 1-2-3 Users

1. Click the Help menu, and then click Lotus 1-2-3 Help.

2. Click a Lotus 1-2-3 menu command.

3. Click a Help Options option button.

4. Click OK.

5. Read the procedure.

6. Click Close.

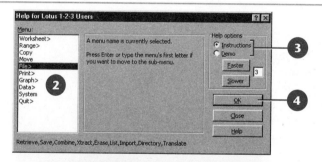

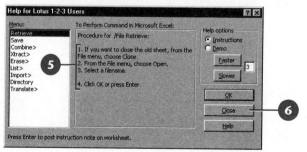

Saving a Workbook

When you create a new Excel workbook, the title bar displays a default title, such as Book1 or Book2. When you save a workbook for the first time, you need to give it a meaningful name and specify where you want to store it. Once you have saved a workbook, you should continue to save it as you work so that changes you make are saved in the file. If you want to make changes to a previously saved workbook but keep the original version intact, you need to save the changed workbook with a different name; then you will have the original workbook and one with the changes. If necessary, you can also change the file format so you can use the workbook file with a different program.

Save a Workbook for the First Time

1 Click the Save button on the Standard toolbar.

2 Click one of the icons on the Places bar (quick access to frequently used folders) to select a location to save the workbook file.

3 If you want to save the file in another folder, click the Save In drop-down arrow, and then select the drive and folder in which you want to store the workbook file.

4 Type the filename for the new workbook name.

5 Click Save.

The new name appears in the title bar of the workbook.

Click to return to a recently visited folder.

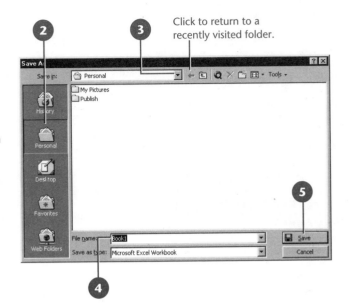

TIP

Save an Excel 2000 workbook for an Excel 97 user. *In the Save As dialog box, click the Save As Type drop-down arrow, and then select a previous version of Excel available in the list.*

SEE ALSO

See "Understanding Excel Program Add-Ins" on page 220 for more information on saving workbooks automatically at a specific time interval.

TIP

Create a new folder in the Save As and Open dialog boxes. *In the Save As or Open dialog box, click the Create New Folder button, type the name of the folder in the Name box, and then click OK.*

TIP

Perform common file management tasks in the Save As and Open dialog boxes. *In the Save As or Open dialog box, click the Tools menu, and then click a file management command.*

Tools ▾

Save an Existing Workbook with a Different Name and in a Different Format

1 Click the File menu, and then click Save As.

2 Click one of the icons on the Places bar for quick access to frequently used folders.

3 If you want to save the file in another folder, click the Save In drop-down arrow, and then select the drive and folder in which you want to save the workbook file.

4 Type the new filename.

5 Click the Save As Type drop-down arrow.

6 Select the file format you want.

7 Click Save.

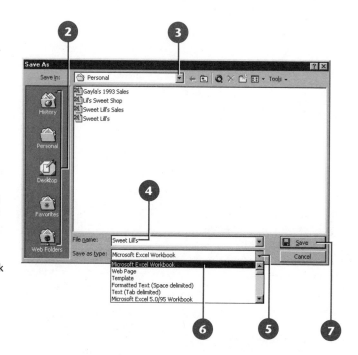

Printing a Worksheet

You should always preview your work before sending it to the printer. A *print preview* is a miniature view of the entire worksheet that shows you how your worksheet will look when it is printed. You can print a copy of your worksheet quickly to review it by clicking the Print button on the Standard or Print Preview toolbar. Or use the Print dialog box to specify several print options, such as choosing a new printer, selecting the number of pages in the worksheet you want printed, and specifying the number of copies.

Print Preview button

SEE ALSO

See "Generating Multiple-Page Reports" on page 208 for information on creating customized reports using the Report Manager.

Preview a Worksheet

1 Click the Print Preview button on the Standard toolbar.

2 Click the Zoom button on the Print Preview toolbar, or click the Zoom pointer anywhere on the worksheet to enlarge a specific area of the page.

3 If you do not want to print from print preview, click the Close button to return to the worksheet.

4 If you want to print, click the Print button on the Print Preview toolbar to open the Print dialog box.

5 Specify the printing options you want, and then click Print.

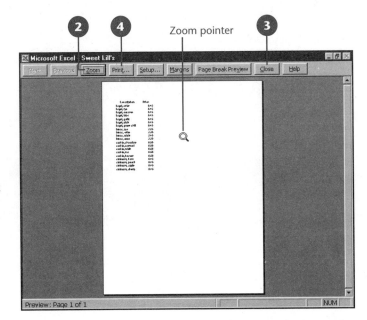

Zoom pointer

Print a Copy of a Worksheet Quickly

1 Click the Print button on the Standard toolbar.

Excel prints the selected worksheet with the current Print dialog box settings.

The ScreenTip displays the name of your printer.

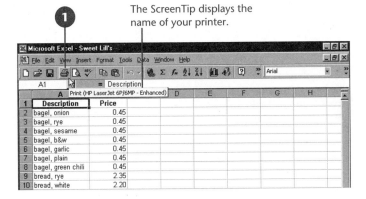

TIP

Preview your work from the Print dialog box. *Click the Preview button in the Print dialog box. After previewing, you can click the Print button on the Print Preview toolbar to print the worksheet or click the Close button on the Print Preview toolbar to return to your document.*

TIP

Change printer properties. *Click the File menu, click Print, and click Properties to change general printer properties for paper size and orientation, graphics, and fonts.*

TIP

What happens when you collate copies? *When you select the Collate check box, Excel prints multiple copies of a worksheet by complete sets. For two copies of a two-page document, the Collate option prints pages 1 and 2, and then prints pages 1 and 2 again.*

Specify Print Options Using the Print Dialog Box

1. Click the File menu, and then click Print.

2. To choose another (installed) printer, click the Name drop-down arrow, and then select the printer you want to use.

3. To print selected pages (rather than all pages), click the Page(s) option button, and then click the From and To up or down arrows to specify the page range you want.

4. To print more than one copy of the print range, click the Number Of Copies up or down arrow to specify the number of copies you want.

5. To change the worksheet print area, click one of the Print What option buttons that correctly identifies the area to be printed.

6. Click OK.

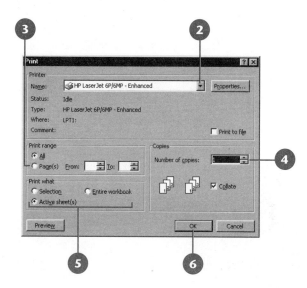

2

Closing a Workbook and Quitting Excel

After you finish working on a workbook, you can close it. Closing a workbook makes more computer memory available for other processes. Closing a workbook is different from quitting Excel: after you close a workbook, Excel is still running. When you're finished using Excel, you can quit the program. To protect your files, always quit Excel before turning off your computer.

Close button

Close a Workbook

1. Click the File menu and then click Close, or click the Close button on the worksheet window title bar.

   If you have made any changes to the workbook since last saving it, the Office Assistant asks if you want them saved.

2. Click Yes to save any workbook changes; click No to close the workbook without saving any changes; or click Cancel to return to the workbook without closing it.

Quit Excel

1. Click the Close button on the Excel program window title bar, or click the File menu, and then click Exit.

   If any files are open and you have made any changes since last saving, a dialog box opens asking if you want to save changes.

2. Click Yes to save any workbook changes, or click No to ignore any changes.

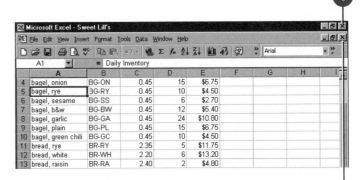

Clicking this button closes only the worksheet window.

3

Basic Workbook Skills

IN THIS SECTION

Making Cell Entries

New2000 **Selecting Cells**

Entering Labels and Values on a Worksheet

New2000 **Entering Values Quickly with AutoFill**

Editing Cell Contents

Clearing Cell Contents

Undoing and Redoing an Action

Understanding How Excel Pastes Data

New2000 **Storing Cell Contents**

Copying and Moving Cell Contents

Inserting and Deleting Cells

Correcting Text with AutoCorrect

Checking Your Spelling

Creating a Microsoft Excel workbook is as simple as entering data in the cells of an Excel worksheet. Cells contain either labels or values (or a combination of label and values), and entries can be modified using the keyboard or mouse. In addition, you can use several Excel tools to simplify data entry and correct spelling errors. Cell contents can be moved or copied into other cells, another feature that increases your efficiency and decreases the amount of time you spend typing.

Regardless of how carefully you plan, it's often necessary to add or remove cells. When you work with pencil and paper, the only way to increase the size and depth of your work is to erase and rewrite, often having to re-create the entire worksheet to make room for the new cells. With Excel, you can automate these tasks. Excel even lets you choose where to shift existing cells when you make insertions or deletions so that the worksheet looks just the way you want.

Making Cell Entries

There are three basic types of cell entries: labels, values, and formulas. A *label* is text in a cell that identifies the data on the worksheet so readers can interpret the information. Excel does not use labels in its calculations. For example, the label *Description* identifies the kinds of daily inventory listed in this worksheet. A *value* is a number you enter in a cell. Excel knows to include values in its calculations. To enter values easily and quickly, you can format a cell, a range of cells, or a column with a specific number-related format. For example, if you need to enter *$6.93* in a cell, you can format the cell as currency with a dollar sign and two places to the right of the decimal. So instead of entering *$6.93*, you enter *693* and then press Enter.

To perform a calculation in a worksheet, you enter a formula in a cell. A *formula* is a calculation that contains cell references, values, and arithmetic operators. The result of a formula appears in the worksheet cell where you entered the formula. For example, cell E4 in the figure displays *6.75*; however, the cell actually contains the formula *=C4*D4* (that is, "the value of this cell equals the product of cell C4's contents multiplied by cell D4's contents"). The contents of the cell appears on the formula bar. Entering cell references rather than actual values in a formula has distinct advantages. When you change the data in the worksheet (for example, changing the contents of cell C4 from .45 to .55) or copy the formula to other cells (copying this formula to the cell below), Excel automatically adjusts the cell references in the formula and returns the correct results.

The formula entered in cell E4 appears here.

The result of the formula you entered appears in this cell.

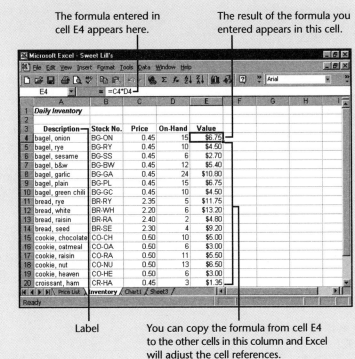

Label

You can copy the formula from cell E4 to the other cells in this column and Excel will adjust the cell references.

Selecting Cells

In order to work with a cell— to enter data in it, edit or move it, or perform an action—you *select* the cell so it becomes the active cell. When you want to work with more than one cell at a time—to move or copy them, use them in a formula, or perform any group action—you must first select the cells as a *range*. A range can be *contiguous* (where selected cells are adjacent to each other) or *noncontiguous* (where the cells may be in different parts of the worksheet and are not adjacent to each other). As you select a range, you can see the range reference in the Name box. A *range reference* contains the cell address of the top-left cell in the range, a colon (:), and the cell address of the bottom-right cell in the range.

TIP

Deselect a range. *To deselect a range, click anywhere in the worksheet.*

Select a Contiguous Range

1. Click the first cell you want to include in the range.

2. Drag the mouse to the last cell you want to include in the range.

   When a range is selected, the top-left cell is surrounded by the cell pointer while the additional cells are highlighted in color.

Name box
The reference of the currently selected cell or range appears here.

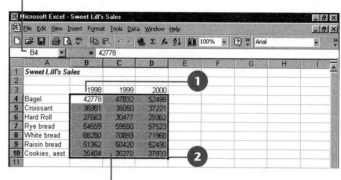

See-Through selection
Shows the text and styles behind the highlighting

Select a Noncontiguous Range

1. Click the first cell you want to include in the range.

2. Drag the mouse to the last contiguous cell, and then release the mouse button.

3. Press and hold the Ctrl key, and then click the next cell or drag the pointer over the next group of cells you want in the range.

4. Repeat steps 3 and 4 until all the cells are selected.

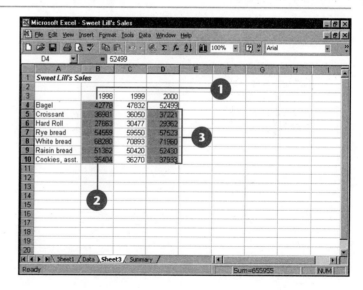

Entering Labels on a Worksheet

Labels turn a worksheet full of numbers into a meaningful report by identifying the different types of information it contains. You use labels to describe the data in worksheet cells, columns, and rows. You can enter a number as a label (for example, the year 2000), so that Excel does not use the number in its calculations. To help keep your labels consistent, you can use Excel's *AutoComplete* feature, which automatically completes your entries based on previously entered labels.

Enter a Text Label

1. Click the cell where you want to enter a label.

2. Type a label. A label can include uppercase and lowercase letters, spaces, punctuation, and numbers.

3. Press Enter, or click the Enter button on the formula bar.

Click to cancel an entry.

What you type in the cell appears here.

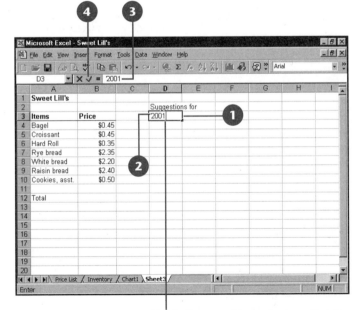

Enter a Number as a Label

1. Click the cell where you want to enter a number as a label.

2. Type ' (an apostrophe). The apostrophe is a *label prefix* and does not appear on the worksheet.

3. Type a number value. Examples of numbers that you might use as labels include a year, a social security number, or a telephone number.

4. Press Enter, or click the Enter button on the formula bar.

Excel will not use this number in a calculation because it is formatted as a label.

TIP

Long labels might appear truncated. *When you enter a label that is wider than the cell it occupies, the excess text appears to spill into the next cell to the right—unless there is data in the adjacent cell. If that cell contains data, the label will appear truncated—you'll only see the portion of the label that fits in the cell's current width. Click the cell to see its entire contents displayed on the formula bar.*

TIP

Excel doesn't recognize the entry. *The AutoComplete option may not be turned on. To turn on the feature, click the Tools menu, click Options, click the Edit tab, click to select Enable AutoComplete For Cell Values check box, and then click OK.*

SEE ALSO

See "Adjusting Column Width and Row Height" on page 72 for information on changing the width of a column.

SEE ALSO

See "Entering Data in a List" on page 180 for information on entering labels using PickList.

Enter a Label Using AutoComplete

1 Type the first few characters of a label.

If Excel recognizes the entry, AutoComplete completes it.

2 To accept the suggested entry, press Enter or click the Enter button on the formula bar.

3 To reject the suggested completion, simply continue typing.

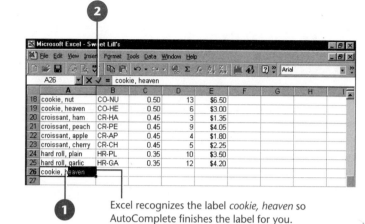

Excel recognizes the label *cookie, heaven* so AutoComplete finishes the label for you.

Entering Values on a Worksheet

You can enter values as whole numbers, decimals, percentages, or dates. You can enter values using the numbers on the top row of your keyboard, or the numeric keypad on the right. When you enter a date or the time of day, Excel automatically recognizes these entries (if entered in an acceptable format) as numeric values and changes the cell's format to a default date or time format.

TIP

Use the numeric keypad to enter numbers. *Before using the numeric keypad, make sure NUM appears in the lower-right corner of the status bar. If NUM is not displayed, you can turn this feature on by pressing the Num Lock key on the numeric keypad. You can then use the numeric keypad like a calculator to enter numbers on your worksheet.*

Enter a Value

1. Click the cell where you want to enter a value.

2. Type a value. To simplify your data entry, type the values without commas and dollar signs, and apply a numeric format to them later.

3. Press Enter, or click the Enter button on the formula bar.

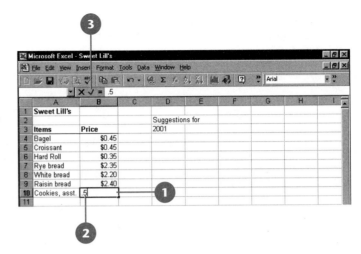

Enter a Date or Time

1. To enter a date, type the date using a slash (/) or a hyphen (-) between the month, day, and year in a cell or on the formula bar.

   To enter a time, type the hour based on a 12-hour clock, followed by a colon (:), followed by the minute, followed by a space, and ending with an "a" or a "p" to denote A.M. or P.M.

2. Press Enter, or click the Enter button on the formula bar.

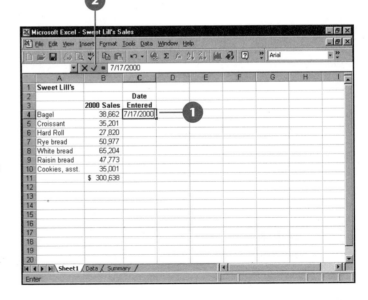

Simplify data entry. *Enter values as simply as possible to make data entry quicker. For example, to enter the value "10.00" simply type "10". Use the Cells command on the Format menu to format your cell entries with decimal places, commas, dollar signs, and other formatting attributes.*

See "Formatting Text and Numbers" on page 82 for more information on changing the appearance of data on the worksheet.

Year 2000 dates settings for administrators. *Excel 2000 has added two new administrator settings that make the year 2000 transition easier. The first setting allows users to set their own rules for the range of years a two-digit year should fall under. The second setting ensures that if a user enters a date with a full four-digit year, the cell is formatted to show all four digits of the year. These settings are accessible through the System Policy Editor. See your system administrator for more details.*

Change Date or Time Format

1. Click the cell that contains the date format you want to change.

2. Click the Format menu, and then click Cells.

3. Click the Number tab.

4. Click Date.

5. Click the date or time format.

6. Click OK.

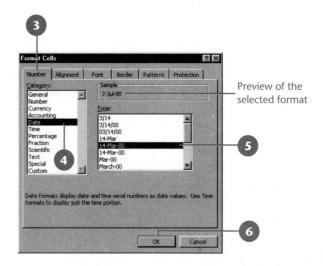

Preview of the selected format

Set Dates for Year 2000

1. Click the Start menu, point to Settings, and then click Control Panel (for those running Windows 98 or Windows NT 5.0 or later).

2. Double-click the Regional Settings icon.

3. Click the Date tab.

4. Enter years the way you want to interpret two-digit numbers.

5. Click OK.

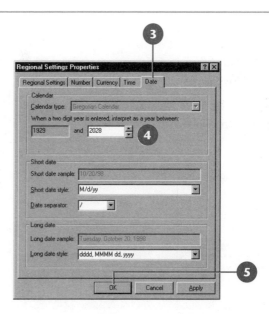

3

Entering Values Quickly with AutoFill

AutoFill is a feature that automatically fills in data based on the data in adjacent cells. Using the fill handle, you can enter data in a series, or you can copy values or formulas to adjacent cells. A single cell entry can result in a repeating value or label, or the results can be a more complex series such as days of the week, months of the year, or consecutive numbering.

TIP

Additional AutoFill commands. *Right-click a cell and drag the fill handle for additional fill commands, such as Fill Formats, Fill Values, Fill Days, Fill Months, or Fill Years.*

SEE ALSO

See "Creating a Simple Formula" on page 48 for information on copying a formula using the fill handle.

Enter Repeating Data Using AutoFill

1. Select the first cell in the range you want to fill.

2. Enter the starting value to be repeated.

3. Position the pointer on the lower-right corner of the selected cell. The pointer changes to the fill handle (a black plus sign).

4. Drag the fill handle over the range in which you want the value repeated.

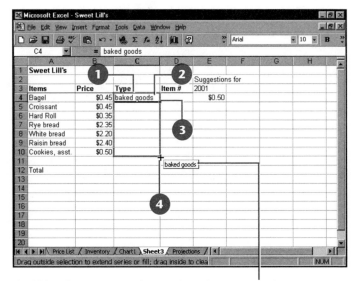

The fill handle ScreenTip indicates what is being repeated.

Create a Complex Series Using AutoFill

1. Select the first cell in the range you want to fill.

2. Enter the starting value for the series, and then press Enter.

3. Hold down Ctrl as you drag the fill handle (a black plus sign with a smaller plus sign) located in the lower-right corner of the selected cell over the range.

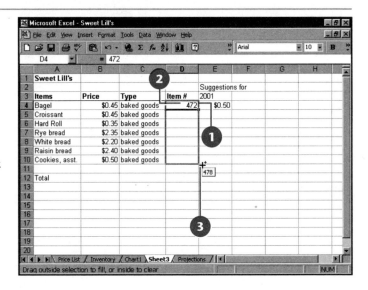

Editing Cell Contents

No matter how much you plan, you can count on having to make changes on a worksheet. Sometimes it's because you want to correct an error or see how your worksheet results would be affected by different conditions, such as higher sales, fewer units produced, or other variables. You edit data just as easily as you enter it, using the formula bar or directly editing the active cell.

TIP

Edit cell contents using the formula bar. *Click the cell you want to edit, click to place the insertion point on the formula bar, and then edit the cell contents.*

TIP

Change editing options. *Click the Tools menu, click Options, click the Edit tab, change the editing options you want, and then click OK.*

Edit Cell Contents

1. Double-click the cell you want to edit. The insertion point appears in the cell.

   The status bar now displays Edit instead of Ready.

2. If necessary, use the Home, End, and arrow keys to position the insertion point within the cell contents.

3. Use any combination of the Backspace and Delete keys to erase unwanted characters, and then type new characters as needed.

4. Click the Enter button on the formula bar to accept the edit, or click the Cancel button to cancel it.

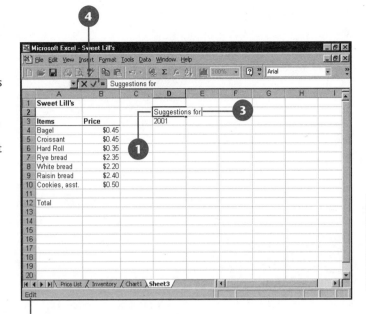

The mode indicator changes to Edit.

Clearing Cell Contents

You can clear a cell to remove its contents. Clearing a cell does not remove the cell from the worksheet; it just removes from the cell whatever elements you specify: data, comments (also called *cell notes*), or formatting instructions. When clearing a cell, you must specify whether to remove one, two, or all three of these elements from the selected cell or range.

TIP

Deleting a cell removes the cell from the worksheet.
When you choose Delete from the Edit menu or from the shortcut menu, you must choose to move the remaining cells left or up, or to remove the entire row or column.

Clear the Contents of a Cell

1 Select the cell or range you want to clear.

2 Click the right mouse button, and then click Clear Contents on the shortcut menu, or press Delete.

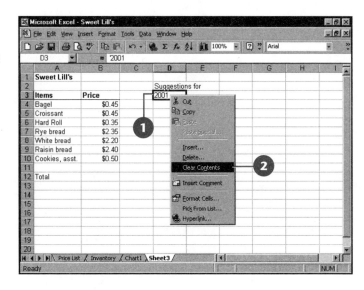

Clear Cell Contents, Formatting, and Comments

1 Select the cell or range you want to clear.

2 Click the Edit menu, and then point to Clear.

3 Click All.

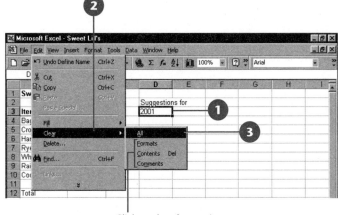

Click to clear formatting, contents, or comments individually.

Undoing and Redoing an Action

You may realize you've made a mistake shortly after completing an action or a task. The Undo feature lets you "take back" one or more previous actions, including data you entered, edits you made, or commands you selected. For example, if you were to enter a number in a cell and then decide the number was incorrect, you could undo the entry instead of selecting the data and deleting it. A few moments later, if you decide the number you deleted was correct after all, you could use the Redo feature to restore it to the cell.

TIP

Display the Redo button. *If the Redo button does not appear on the toolbar, click the More Buttons drop-down arrow, and then click Redo. Once a button is used, it remains on the toolbar.*

Undo an Action

◆ Click the Undo button on the Standard toolbar to undo the last action you completed.

◆ Click the Undo drop-down arrow on the Standard toolbar to see a list of recent actions that can be undone. As you point to an action you want to undo, Excel selects that action and all actions above it.

Click an action. Excel reverses the selected action and all actions above it.

Undo button   Undo drop-down arrow

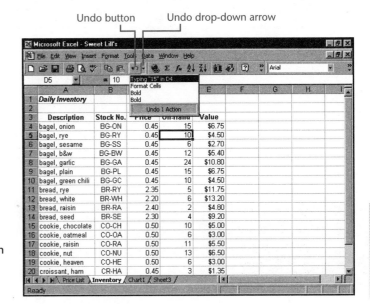

Redo an Action

◆ Click the Redo button on the Standard toolbar to restore your last undone action.

◆ Click the Redo drop-down arrow to see a list of recently undone actions that can be restored. As you point to an action you want to repeat, Excel selects that action and all actions above it.

Click the action you want to restore. All actions above it will be restored as well.

Redo button   Redo drop-down arrow

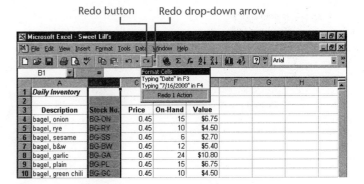

3

Understanding How Excel Pastes Data

If you want to use data that has already been entered on your worksheet, you can cut or copy it and then paste it in another location. When you cut or copy data, the data is stored in an area of memory called the *Windows Clipboard*. When pasting a range of cells from the Windows Clipboard, you only need to specify the first cell in the new location. After you select the first cell in the new location and then click the Paste button, Excel automatically places all the selected cells in the correct order. Depending on the number of cells you select before you cut or copy, Excel pastes data in one of the following ways:

◆ **One to one**

A single cell in the Windows Clipboard is pasted to one cell location.

◆ **One to many**

A single cell in the Windows Clipboard is pasted into a selected range of cells.

◆ **Many to one**

Many cells are pasted into a range of cells, but only the first cell is identified. The entire contents of the Windows Clipboard will be pasted starting with the selected cell. Make sure there is enough room for the selection; if not, the selection will copy over any previously occupied cells.

◆ **Many to many**

Many cells are pasted into a range of cells. The entire contents of the Windows Clipboard will be pasted into the selected cells. If the selected range is larger than the selection, the data will be repeated in the extra cells. To turn off the selection marquee and cancel your action, press the Esc key.

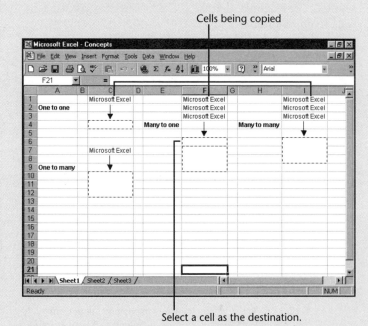

Cells being copied

Select a cell as the destination.

Storing Cell Contents

With Office 2000, you can use the *Office Clipboard* to store multiple pieces of information from several different sources in one storage area shared by all Office programs. Unlike the Windows Clipboard, which only stores a single piece of information at a time, the Office Clipboard allows you to copy up to twelve pieces of text or pictures from one or more documents. When you copy multiple items, you see the Office Clipboard, showing all the items you stored there. You can paste these pieces of information into any Office program, either individually or all at once.

SEE ALSO

See "Copying Cell Contents" on page 38 and "Moving Cell Contents" on page 40 for information on copying and moving cell contents using the Windows Clipboard.

Copy Data to the Office Clipboard

1. Click the View menu, point to Toolbars, and then click Clipboard.

2. Select the data you want to copy.

3. Click the Copy button on the Office Clipboard or Standard toolbar.

   The data is copied into the first empty position on the Office Clipboard toolbar.

4. Click the Close button on the Office Clipboard toolbar.

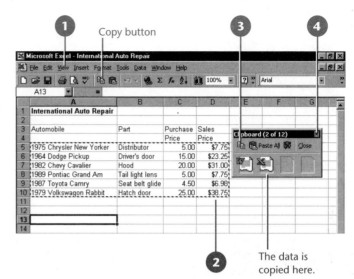

Copy button

The data is copied here.

Paste Data from the Office Clipboard

1. Click the View menu, point to Toolbars, and then click Clipboard.

2. In the Excel worksheet, click the first cell where you want to paste data.

3. Click the Office Clipboard toolbar item you want to paste.

4. Click the Close button on the Office Clipboard toolbar.

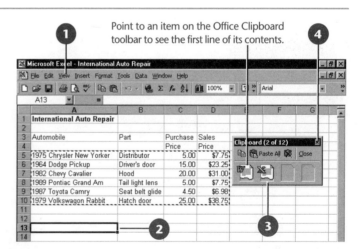

Point to an item on the Office Clipboard toolbar to see the first line of its contents.

3

Copying Cell Contents

You can copy and move data on a worksheet from one cell or range to another location on any worksheet in your workbook. When you *copy* data, a duplicate of the selected cells is placed on the Windows Clipboard. To complete the copy or move, you must *paste* the data stored on the Windows Clipboard in another location. With the Paste Special command, you can control what you want to paste and even perform mathematical operations. To copy or move data without using the Windows Clipboard, you can use a technique called *drag-and-drop*. Drag-and-drop makes it easy to copy or move data short distances on your worksheet.

Copy Data Using the Windows Clipboard

① Select the cell or range that contains the data you want to copy.

② Click the Copy button on the Standard toolbar.

The data in the cells remains in its original location and an outline of the selected cells, called a *marquee*, shows the size of the selection. If you don't want to paste this selection, press Esc to remove the marquee.

③ Click the first cell where you want to paste the data.

④ Click the Paste button on the Standard toolbar.

The data remains on the Clipboard, available for further pasting, until you replace it with another selection.

⑤ If you don't want to paste this selection anywhere else, press the Esc key to remove the marquee.

If the Copy button is not displayed, click the More Buttons drop-down arrow.

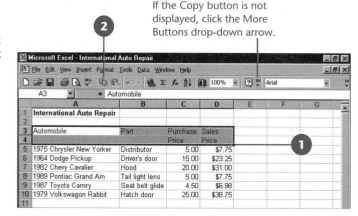

When you copy cells, the data remains in its original location.

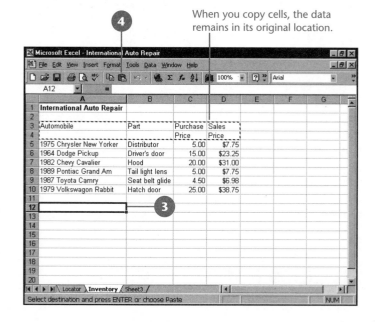

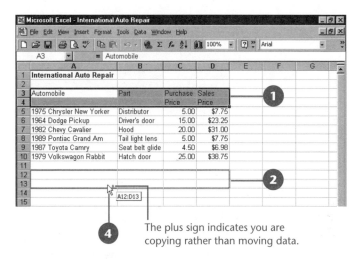

TIP

Use the Alt key to drag and drop to a different worksheet. *Once cells are selected, press and hold the Alt key, and then drag the selection to the appropriate sheet tab. Release the Alt key and drag the selection to the desired location on the new worksheet.*

TIP

The Windows Clipboard changes when you copy or cut information. *The contents of the Windows Clipboard changes each time you copy or cut data. The most recent selection is available only until you copy or cut another selection.*

TIP

Perform math with pasted cells. *With the Paste Special command, you can combine the current cell contents and the information on the Windows Clipboard using mathematical operations.*

SEE ALSO

See "Storing Cell Contents" on page 37 for information on using the Office Clipboard to paste multiple items.

Copy Data Using Drag-and-Drop

1. Select the cell or range that contains the data you want to copy.

2. Move the mouse pointer to an edge of the selected cell or range until the pointer changes to an arrowhead.

3. Press and hold the mouse button and the Ctrl key.

4. Drag the selection to the new location, and then release the mouse button and the Ctrl key.

The plus sign indicates you are copying rather than moving data.

Paste Data with Special Results

1. Select the cell or range that contains the data you want to copy.

2. Click the Copy button on the Standard toolbar.

3. Click the first cell where you want to paste the data.

4. Click the Edit menu, and then click Paste Special.

5. Click the option buttons with the paste results and mathematical operations you want.

6. Click OK.

Moving Cell Contents

Unlike copied data, moved data no longer remains in its original location. Perhaps you typed data in a range of cells near the top of a worksheet, but later realized it should appear near the bottom of the sheet. Moving data lets you change its location without having to retype it. When you *move* data, you are cutting the data from its current location and pasting it elsewhere. *Cutting* removes the selected cell or range content from the worksheet and places it on the Windows Clipboard.

TIP

Use the Office Clipboard to cut multiple items. *When the Office Clipboard toolbar is displayed, selections you cut can be placed on this clipboard. You can move data to the Office Clipboard, and then paste it at a later time.*

Move Data Using the Windows Clipboard

1. Select the cell or range that contains the data you want to move.

2. Click the Cut button on the Standard toolbar.

   An outline of the selected cells, called a *marquee*, shows the size of the selection. If you don't want to paste this selection, press Esc to remove the marquee.

3. Click the top-left cell of the range where you want to paste the data.

4. Click the Paste button on the Standard toolbar.

   The marquee disappears. The data is still on the Clipboard and still available for further pasting until you replace it with another selection.

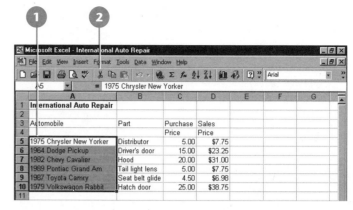

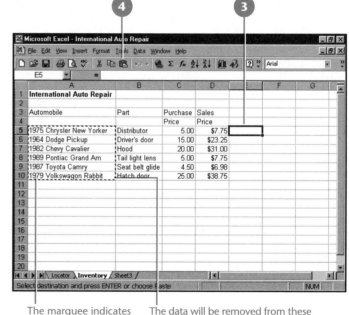

The marquee indicates the selection.

The data will be removed from these cells after you paste the selection in its new location.

TIP

Reposition the mouse pointer to use drag-and-drop. *If the mouse pointer changes to a thick plus sign, reposition the pointer on the edge of the selected range until the pointer changes to an arrowhead.*

TIP

Different mouse pointer for moving data using drag-and-drop. *The mouse pointer for moving data using drag-and-drop looks identical to the pointer for copying, except that it does not contain the plus sign.*

SEE ALSO

See "Copying Cell Contents" on page 38 for information on using drag-and drop to copy cells.

TIP

Open the Office Clipboard automatically. *The Office Clipboard automatically appears when two different selections are consecutively copied or cut.*

Move Data Using Drag-and-Drop

1 Select the cell or range that contains the data you want to move.

2 Move the mouse pointer to an edge of the cell until the pointer changes to an arrowhead.

3 Press and hold the mouse button while dragging the selection to its new location, and then release the mouse button.

Paste Cells from Rows to Columns or Columns to Rows

1 Select the cells that you want to switch.

2 Click the Copy button on the Standard toolbar.

3 Click the top-left cell of where you want to paste the data.

4 Click the Edit menu, and then click Paste Special.

5 Click to select the Transpose check box.

6 Click OK.

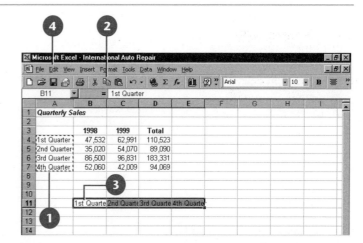

Inserting and Deleting Cells

You can *insert* new, blank cells anywhere on the worksheet in order to enter new data or data you forgot to enter earlier. Inserting cells moves the remaining cells in the column or row in the direction of your choice, and Excel adjusts any formulas so they refer to the correct cells. You can also *delete* cells if you find you don't need them; deleting cells shifts the remaining cells to the left or up—just the opposite of inserting cells. When you delete a cell, Excel removes the actual cell from the worksheet.

SEE ALSO

See "Inserting a Column or Row" on page 69 and "Deleting a Column or Row" on page 70 for more information about changing worksheet columns and rows.

Insert a Cell

1 Select the cell or cells where you want to insert the new cell(s).

For example, to insert two blank cells at the position of C10 and C11, select cells C10 and C11.

2 Click the Insert menu, and then click Cells.

3 Click the option you want.

◆ If you want the contents of cells C10 and C11 to move to cells D10 and D11, click the Shift Cells Right option button.

◆ If you want the contents of cells C10 and C11 to move to cells C12 and C13, click the Shift Cells Down option button.

Either way, two blank cells will be at the position of C10 and C11.

4 Click OK.

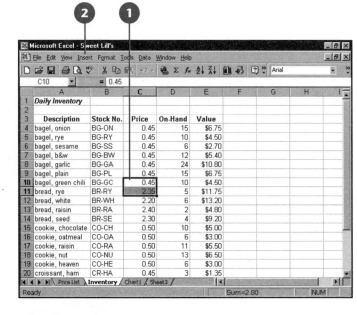

Delete a Cell

1. Select the cell or range you want to delete.

2. Click the Edit menu, and then click Delete.

3. Click the option you want.

   ◆ If you want the remaining cells to move left, click the Shift Cells Left option button.

   ◆ If you want the remaining cells to move up, click the Shift Cells Up option button.

4. Click OK.

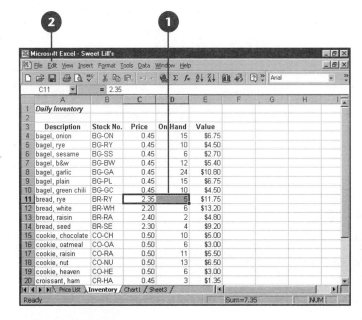

Correcting Text with AutoCorrect

Excel's *AutoCorrect* feature automatically corrects misspelled words as you type them. AutoCorrect comes with hundreds of text and symbol entries you can edit or remove.

Add words and phrases to the AutoCorrect dictionary that you misspell, or add often-typed words and save time by just typing their initials. You could use AutoCorrect to automatically change the initials *EPA* to *Environmental Protection Agency*, for example. Use the AutoCorrect Exceptions dialog box to control how Excel handles capital letters.

SEE ALSO

See "Checking Your Spelling" on page 46 for information about turning on AutoCorrect.

Add an AutoCorrect Entry

1. Click the Tools menu, and then click AutoCorrect.

2. Type a misspelled word or an abbreviation.

3. Type the replacement entry.

4. Click Add.

5. Repeat steps 2 through 4 for each entry you want to add.

6. Click OK.

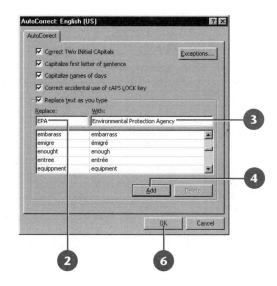

Edit an AutoCorrect Entry

1. Click the Tools menu, and then click AutoCorrect.

2. Select the AutoCorrect entry you want to change. You can either type the first few letters of the entry to be changed in the Replace box, or scroll to the entry and then click to select it.

3. Type the replacement entry.

4. Click Replace. If necessary, click Yes to redefine entry.

5. Click OK.

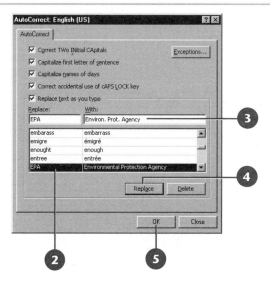

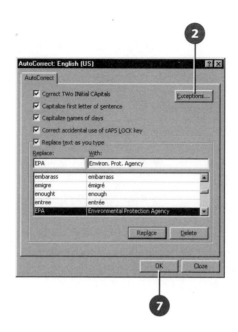

TIP

Prevent automatic corrections. *Click the Tools menu, click AutoCorrect, click to clear the Replace Text As You Type check box, and then click OK.*

TIP

Delete an AutoCorrect entry. *Click the Tools menu, click AutoCorrect, select the AutoCorrect entry you want to delete, and then click Delete.*

TIP

Don't capitalize the first letter of a sentence. *Click the Tools menu, click AutoCorrect, click to clear the Capitalize First Letter Of Sentence check box, and then click OK.*

Change AutoCorrect Exceptions

1. Click the Tools menu, and then click AutoCorrect.

2. Click Exceptions.

3. Click the First Letter or INitial CAps tab.

   The First Letter list contains words that end with a period (.) but whose following word is never capitalized. The INitial CAps list contains words that have multiple capital letters; adding words to this list means that Excel will not try to correct them.

4. Type the entry you want to add.

5. Click Add.

6. Click OK.

7. Click OK.

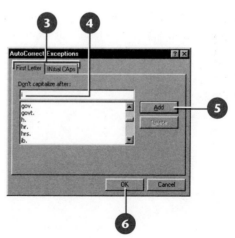

Checking Your Spelling

A worksheet's textual inaccuracies can distract the reader, so it's important that your text be error-free. Excel provides a spelling checker so that you can check the spelling in an entire worksheet. You can even avoid future spelling errors on a worksheet by enabling the AutoCorrect feature to automatically correct words as you type.

Spelling button

SEE ALSO

See "Correcting Text with AutoCorrect" on page 44 for more information on minimizing spelling errors.

SEE ALSO

See "Entering Labels on a Worksheet" on page 28 for more information on entering data accurately and efficiently.

Check Spelling

1. Click the Spelling button on the Standard toolbar.

   The Spelling dialog box will open if it comes upon a word it doesn't recognize.

2. If the suggested spelling is unacceptable or you want to use the original word, click Ignore or Ignore All.

3. If the suggested spelling is acceptable, click Change or Change All.

4. If you want to add a word to the custom dictionary, click Add.

5. When complete, click OK.

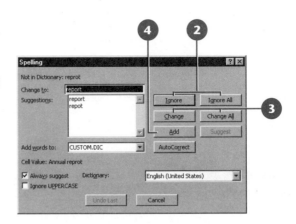

Turn On AutoCorrect

1. Click the Tools menu, and then click AutoCorrect.

2. Click to select the Replace Text As You Type check box.

3. Click OK.

2. If checked, AutoCorrect is already turned on.

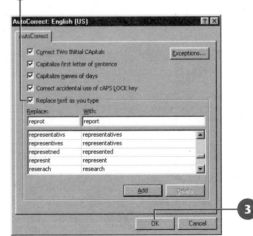

Working with Formulas and Functions

IN THIS SECTION

Creating a Simple Formula

Editing a Formula

Understanding Relative Cell Referencing

Using Absolute Cell References

Using Labels for Cell References

Naming Cells and Ranges

Simplifying a Formula with Ranges

Displaying Calculations with AutoCalculate

Calculating Totals with AutoSum

Performing Calculations Using Functions

Creating Functions

Once you enter the data on a worksheet, you'll want to add formulas to calculate values. You can create your own formulas or insert built-in formulas, called *functions*, for more complex computations. You don't need extensive accounting skills to build powerful worksheets. As long as you know the type of result you want, such as asset depreciation or an investment's net present value, you can use the Paste Function feature to find the appropriate function. Once you locate the function, either use it as is or plug it into a larger formula. The Paste Function feature also helps you complete all necessary variables so your results are accurate. Because Excel automatically recalculates formulas, your worksheets remain accurate and up-to-date no matter how often the data changes.

Cell references within formulas generally change when that formula is copied to a new location. Sometimes, however, you'll want cell references to remain the same. Excel gives you the option of controlling how cell references are treated when they're copied.

Creating a Simple Formula

A *formula* calculates values to return a result. On an Excel worksheet, you create a formula using values (such as *147* or *$10.00),* arithmetic operators (shown in the table), and cell references. An Excel formula always begins with the equal sign (=). By default, only formula results are displayed in a cell, but you can change the view of the worksheet to display formulas instead of results.

Enter a Formula

1 Click the cell where you want to enter a formula.

2 Type = (an equal sign). If you do not begin a formula with an equal sign, Excel will display, not calculate, the information you type.

3 Enter the first argument. An *argument* can be a number or a cell reference. If it is a cell reference, you can type the reference or click the cell on the worksheet.

4 Enter an arithmetic operator.

5 Enter the next argument.

6 Repeat steps 4 and 5 as needed to complete the formula.

7 Click the Enter button on the formula bar, or press Enter.

Notice that the result of the formula appears in the cell (if you select the cell, the formula itself appears on the formula bar).

ARITHMETIC OPERATORS		
Symbol	**Operation**	**Example**
+	Addition	=E3+F3
-	Subtraction	=E3-F3
*	Multiplication	=E3*F3
/	Division	=E3/F3

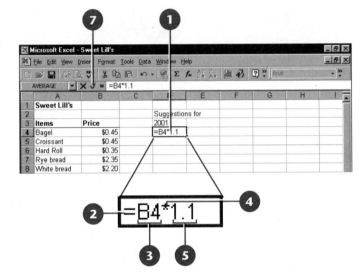

Use the order of precedence to create correct formulas. *Excel calculates formulas containing more than one operator according to the order of precedence: exponentiation, multiplication and division, and finally, addition and subtraction. So, in the formula 5 + 2 * 3, Excel performs multiplication first and addition next for a result of 11. Excel calculates operations within parentheses first. The result of the formula (5 + 2) * 3 is 21.*

Create a formula by pointing. *Once you've entered the equal sign (=), point to cells rather than typing their addresses to build the formula.*

See "Understanding Excel Program Add-Ins" on page 220 for information on additional tools for creating different types of formulas.

Display Formulas in Cells

1. Click the Tools menu, and then click Options.

2. Click the View tab.

3. Click to select the Formulas check box.

4. Click OK.

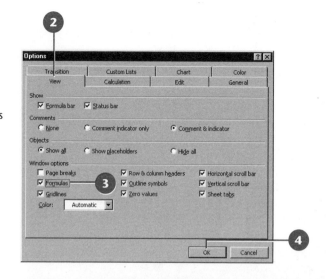

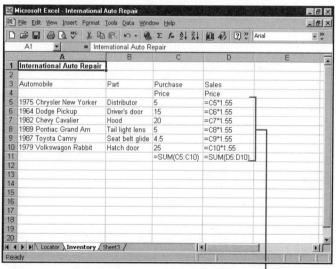

The formulas appear here.

Editing a Formula

You edit formulas just as you do other cell contents, using the formula bar or working in the cell. You can select, cut, copy, paste, delete, and format cells containing formulas just as you do cells containing labels or values. Using AutoFill, you can quickly copy formulas to adjacent cells. If you need to copy formulas to different parts of a worksheet, use the Windows Clipboard.

SEE ALSO

See "Entering Data in a List" on page 180 for information on copying formulas and data formats in a list quickly using List AutoFill.

TRY THIS

Copy a formula down a column. *If you're creating a worksheet that contains several similar calculations, such as a budget, use the fill handle to copy a formula down a column, and watch how each formula adjusts to refer to the correct cells.*

Edit a Formula Using the Formula Bar

1. Select the cell that contains the formula you want to edit.

2. Press F2 to change to Edit mode.

3. If necessary, use the Home, End, and arrow keys to position the insertion point within the cell contents.

4. Use any combination of the Backspace and Delete keys to erase unwanted characters, and then type new characters as needed.

5. Click the Enter button on the formula bar, or press Enter.

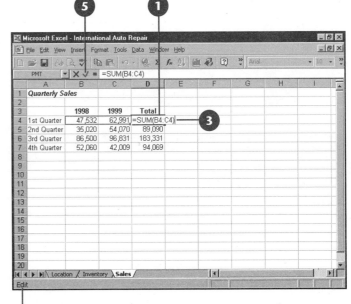

The mode indicator changes to Edit.

Copy a Formula Using AutoFill

1. Select the cell that contains the formula you want to copy.

2. Position the pointer (fill handle) on the lower-right corner of the selected cell.

3. Drag the mouse down until the adjacent cells where you want the formula pasted are selected, and then release the mouse button.

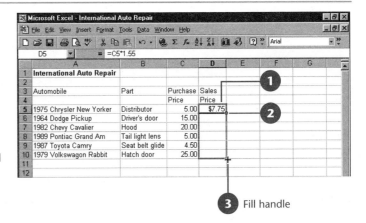

Fill handle

TIP

Display the Copy button. *If the Copy button does not appear on the Standard toolbar, click the More Buttons drop-down arrow, and then click the Copy button.*

SEE ALSO

See "Editing Cell Contents" on page 33 for more information on editing the contents of a cell.

SEE ALSO

See "Copying Cell Contents" on page 38 and "Moving Cell Contents" on page 40 for more information on copying and moving cell contents.

TIP

Use Paste Special to copy only formulas. *Select the cells containing the formulas you want to copy, click where you want to paste the data, click the Edit menu, click Paste Special, click the Formulas option button, and then click OK.*

Copy a Formula Using the Windows Clipboard

1. Select the cell that contains the formula you want to copy.

2. Click the Copy button on the Standard toolbar.

3. Select one or more cells where you want to paste the formula.

4. Click the Paste button on the Standard toolbar.

5. If you don't want to paste this selection anywhere else, press Esc to remove the marquee.

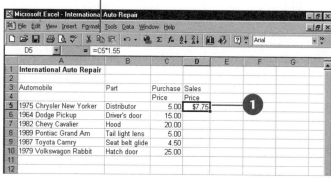

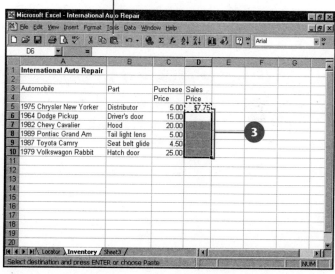

Understanding Relative Cell Referencing

By default, cell addresses in formulas change when you copy or move them to new locations. When you paste or drag a formula to a new location, the cell references in the formula adjust automatically relative to their new locations and calculate the same formula with the information in the new cells. For example, when you copy the formula =D3+D4 in cell D5 to cell E5, the cell references change automatically so the formula becomes =E3+E4. This automatic adjustment is called *relative addressing*. Relative addressing can save you the trouble of creating new formulas for each row or column in a worksheet filled with repetitive information.

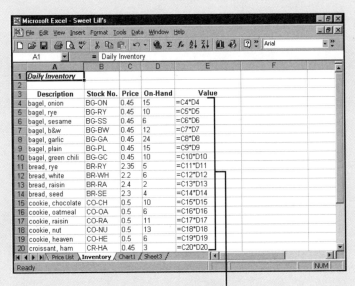

Each formula is identical, but the cell references are modified according to row.

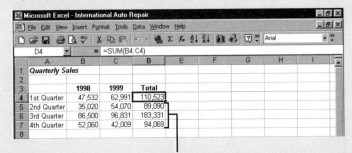

These formulas are identical to the one in D4, but their cell references have adjusted relative to their new location.

Using Absolute Cell References

When you want a formula to consistently refer to a particular cell, even if you copy or move the formula elsewhere on the worksheet, you need to use an absolute cell reference. An *absolute cell reference* is a cell address that contains a dollar sign ($) in either the row or column coordinate, or both, to indicate that the reference should not adjust to a new cell location.

TRY THIS

Edit a cell reference in a formula. *Select a cell with an absolute reference, and then press the F4 key several times to cycle through choices of which coordinates should be absolute.*

Use an Absolute Reference

1. Click a cell where you want to enter a formula.

2. Type = (an equal sign) to begin the formula.

3. Select a cell, and then type + (an arithmetic operator).

4. Select another cell, and press F4 to make that cell reference absolute.

5. If necessary, continue entering the formula.

6. Click the Enter button on the formula bar, or press Enter.

Even if you move or copy this formula to another location, this cell reference will not change.

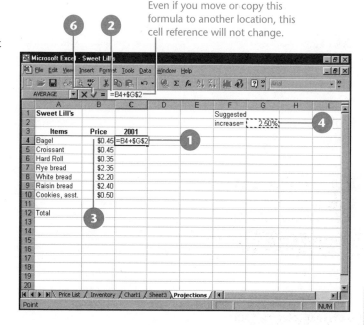

Using Labels for Cell References

Many worksheets use labels above columns and to the left of rows. You can use the labels on your worksheet instead of cell addresses to reference cells. You can point to cells to add their labels to a formula. However, before you can point to a cell to use its label, you have to define a label range. A *label range* is the group of row and column labels that you want to use in your formulas. When you define a label range, Excel assigns the row and column labels to the cells.

TIP

What happens when you zoom in on a label? *When you zoom the view of the worksheet to 39 percent or less, Excel adds a blue border around the labels you have created. The blue border does not print.*

Define Label Ranges

1. Select the range containing the row labels you want to reference to cells.

2. Click the Insert menu, point to Name, and then click Label.

   The selected range appears in the Add Label Range box and the Row Labels option is selected.

3. Click Add.

4. Click OK.

5. Select the range containing the column labels you want to reference to cells and repeat steps 2 through 4.

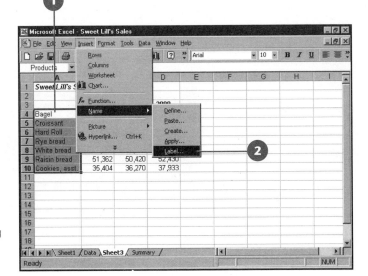

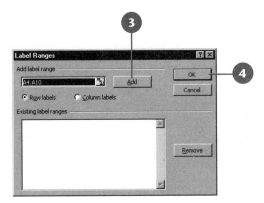

TIP

What happens when you change a label reference?

If you change the name of a reference label, Excel automatically makes the same change to every formula in which the name is used.

TIP

Label names are relative.

When you use a label name in a formula or function, Excel sees it as a relative reference. You can copy the formula to other cells, or use AutoFill to copy it and the references change.

SEE ALSO

See "Naming Cells and Ranges" on page 56 and "Simplifying a Formula with Ranges" on page 58 for information on using named ranges.

Remove a Label Range

1. Click the Insert menu, point to Name, and then click Label.

2. Click to select the existing label range you want to remove.

3. Click Remove.

4. Click OK.

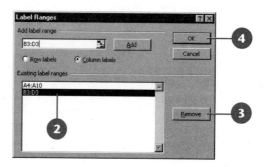

Naming Cells and Ranges

To make working with ranges easier, Excel allows you to name them. The name *Sales*, for example, is easier to remember than the range reference B4:D10. Named ranges can be used to navigate large worksheets. Named ranges can also be used in formulas instead of typing or pointing to specific cells. If the cell or range you want to name has labels, you can have Excel automatically name the cell or range for you. If you have already entered a cell or range address in a formula or function, you can apply a name to the address instead of re-creating it.

Name a Cell or Range

1. Select the cell or range you want to name.

2. Click the Name box on the formula bar.

3. Type a name for the range. A range name can include uppercase or lowercase letters, numbers, and punctuation, but no spaces. Try to use a simple name that reflects the type of information in the range, such as *Sales98*.

4. Press Enter. The range name will appear in the Name box whenever you select the range.

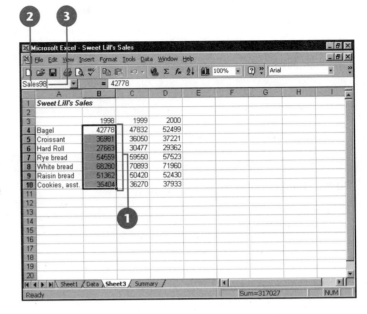

Select a Named Cell or Range

1. Click the Name box drop-down arrow on the formula bar.

2. Click the name of the cell or range you want to use.

   The range name appears in the Name box, and all cells included in the range are highlighted on the worksheet.

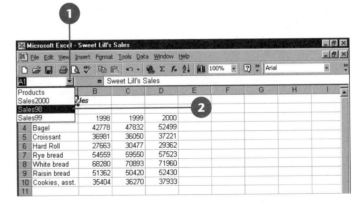

TIP

Should I select the Ignore Relative/Absolute option? *When you select this option, Excel replaces the reference with the name whether the address is absolute or relative. When you deselect this option, Excel only replaces absolute references.*

TIP

Should I select the Use Row And Column Names option? *When you select this option, Excel uses the range row and column headings to refer to the range you've selected (if a cell does not have its own name but is part of a named range).*

TIP

Delete a name range. *Click the Insert menu, point to Name, click Define, select the range name, and then click Delete.*

SEE ALSO

See "Simplifying a Formula with Ranges" on page 58 for information on using cell and range names.

Let Excel Name a Cell or Range

1 Select the cells containing the labels and the cells you want to name.

2 Click the Insert menu, point to Name, and then click Create.

3 Click to select the check box with the position of the labels in relation to the cells.

Excel automatically tries to determine the position of the labels, so you might not have to change any options.

4 Click OK.

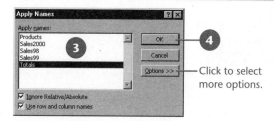

Apply a Name to a Cell or Range Address

1 Select the cells in which you want to apply a name.

2 Click the Insert menu, point to Name, and then click Apply.

3 Click the names you want to apply.

4 Click OK.

Click to select more options.

Simplifying a Formula with Ranges

You can simplify formulas by using ranges and range names. For example, if 12 cells on your worksheet contain monthly budget amounts, and you want to multiply each amount by 10 percent, you can insert one range address in a formula instead of inserting 12 different cell addresses, or you can insert a range name. Using a range name in a formula helps to identify what the formula does; the formula =1997 SALES * .10, for example, is more meaningful than =D7:O7*.10.

SEE ALSO

See "Naming Cells and Ranges" on page 56 for more information on selecting and naming a range.

SEE ALSO

See "Creating a Simple Formula" on page 48 for more information on creating a formula.

Use a Range in a Formula

1. Type an equal sign (=), and then type a function (such as SUM).

2. Click the first cell of the range, and then drag to select the last cell in the range. Excel enters the range address for you.

3. Complete the formula, and then click the Enter button on the formula bar, or press Enter.

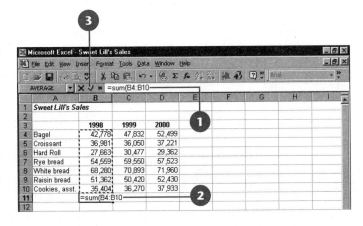

Use a Range Name in a Formula

1. Type an equal sign (=), and then type the function you want to use.

2. Press F3 to display a list of named ranges.

3. Click the name of the range you want to insert.

4. Click OK.

5. Complete the formula, and then click the Enter button on the formula bar, or press Enter.

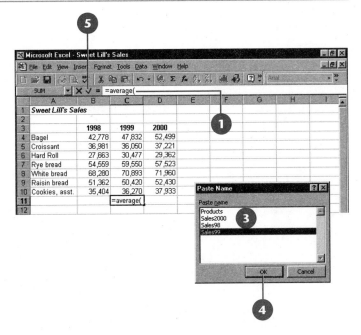

Displaying Calculations with Auto-Calculate

You can simplify your work using a feature called AutoCalculate when you don't want to insert a formula, but you want to see the results of a simple calculation quickly. *Auto-Calculate automatically displays the sum, average, maximum, minimum, or count of the selected values on the status bar. Auto-Calculate results do not appear on the worksheet when printed but are useful for giving you quick answers while you work.*

TRY THIS

Modify AutoCalculate.
Right-click AutoCalculate on the status bar and change its calculation method.

Calculate a Range Automatically

1 Select the range of cells you want to calculate.

The sum of the selected cells appears on the status bar next to SUM=.

2 If you want to change the type of calculation AutoCalculate performs, right-click anywhere on the status bar to open the AutoCalculate palette.

3 Click the type of calculation you want.

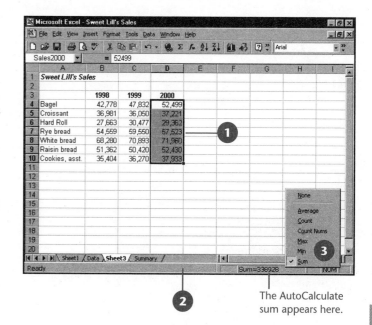

The AutoCalculate sum appears here.

4

Calculating Totals with AutoSum

A range of cells can be added easily using the AutoSum button on the Standard toolbar. AutoSum suggests the range to sum, although this range can be changed if it's incorrect. Subtotals can be calculated for data ranges using the Tools menu and the Subtotals dialog box. This dialog box lets you select where the subtotals occur, as well as the function type.

TRY THIS

Modify the AutoSum range. *Select a range, click the AutoSum button on the Standard toolbar, and then use your mouse to modify the automatically selected range.*

SEE ALSO

See "Understanding Excel Program Add-Ins" on page 220 for information on Excel's Conditional Sum Wizard.

Calculate Totals with AutoSum

1. Click the cell you want to display the calculation.

2. Click the AutoSum button on the Standard toolbar.

3. Click the Enter button on the formula bar, or press Enter.

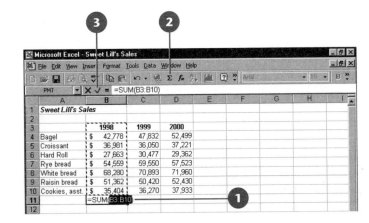

Calculate Subtotals and Totals

1. Click anywhere within the data to be subtotaled.

2. Click the Data menu, and then click Subtotals.

    If a message box appears, read the message, and then click the appropriate button.

3. Click to select the appropriate check boxes to specify how the data is subtotaled.

4. Click OK.

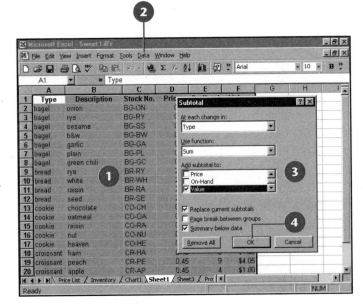

Performing Calculations Using Functions

Functions are predesigned formulas that save you the time and trouble of creating commonly used or complex equations. Excel includes hundreds of functions that you can use alone or in combination with other formulas or functions. Functions perform a variety of calculations, from adding, averaging, and counting to more complicated tasks, such as calculating the monthly payment amount of a loan. You can enter a function manually if you know its name and all the required arguments, or you can easily insert a function using the Paste Function feature.

SEE ALSO

See "Creating Functions" on page 62 for more information on entering a function using the Paste Function feature.

Enter a Function

1 Click the cell where you want to enter the function.

2 Type = (an equal sign), type the name of the function, and then type ((an opening parenthesis). For example, to insert the SUM function, type **=SUM(**.

3 Type the argument or select the cell or range you want to insert in the function.

4 Click the Enter button on the formula bar, or press Enter.

Excel will automatically add the closing parenthesis to complete the function.

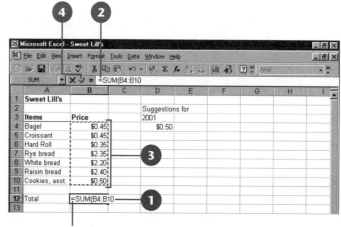

A function always begins with an equal sign.

COMMONLY USED EXCEL FUNCTIONS		
Function	**Description**	**Sample**
SUM	Displays the sum of the argument	=SUM(*argument*)
AVERAGE	Displays the average value in the argument	=AVERAGE(*argument*)
COUNT	Calculates the number of values in the argument	=COUNT(*argument*)
MAX	Determines the largest value in the argument	=MAX(*argument*)
MIN	Determines the smallest value in the argument	=MIN(*argument*)
PMT	Determines the monthly payment of a loan	=PMT(*argument*)

Creating Functions

Trying to write a formula that calculates various pieces of data, such as calculating payments for an investment over a period of time at a certain rate, can be difficult and time-consuming. The *Paste Function* feature simplifies the process by organizing Excel's built-in formulas, called functions, into categories so they are easy to find and use. A function defines all the necessary components (also called arguments) you need to produce a specific result; all you have to do is supply the values, cell references, and other variables. You can even combine one or more functions if necessary.

Paste Function button

Enter a Function Using Paste Function

1. Click the cell where you want to enter the function.

2. Click the Paste Function button on the Standard toolbar.

3. Click a function category you want to use.

4. Click a function you want to use.

5. Click OK.

6. Enter the cell addresses in the text boxes. Type them or click the Collapse Dialog button to the right of the text box, select the cell or range using your mouse, and then click the Expand Dialog button.

   In many cases, the Paste Function might try to "guess" which cells you want to include in the function.

7. Click OK.

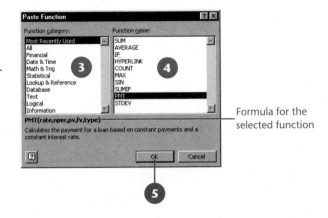

Formula for the selected function

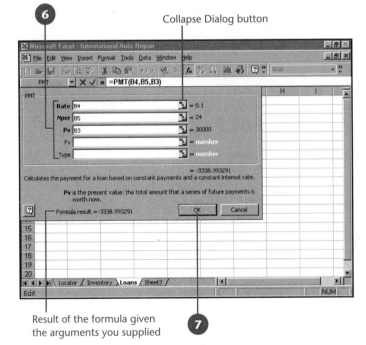

Collapse Dialog button

Result of the formula given the arguments you supplied

IN THIS SECTION

Selecting and Naming a Worksheet

Inserting and Deleting a Worksheet

Moving and Copying a Worksheet

Selecting a Column or Row

Inserting a Column or Row

Deleting a Column or Row

Hiding a Column or Row

Adjusting Column Width and Row Height

Freezing a Column or Row

Previewing Page Breaks

Setting Up the Page

Adding a Header or Footer

Customizing Worksheet Printing

Setting a Print Area

5

Modifying Worksheets and Workbooks

Making changes in a workbook is inevitable—it's just not possible to think of everything you'll want to include right from the start. In addition to editing the data in a workbook, you can modify the workbook itself as you work.

You can reorganize a workbook by adding, deleting, moving, and renaming worksheets. On any worksheet, you can insert and delete cells, rows, and columns, and adjust column width and row height so that you can structure the worksheet exactly the way you want. It's easy to make changes because Excel updates cell references in existing formulas as necessary whenever you modify a worksheet and recalculates formulas automatically to ensure that the results are always up-to-date.

You can also modify the look of your printouts by adjusting a variety of print settings, including page orientation, margins, headers and footers, and other elements that enhance the readability of your worksheets and workbooks.

Selecting and Naming a Worksheet

By default, each new workbook you open contains three worksheets. You can easily switch from sheet to sheet to record and modify information that is related but separate, such as budget information for separate months. Whichever sheet you are working on is the *active* sheet. Each sheet is named consecutively—Sheet1, Sheet2, and Sheet3. You can give a sheet a more meaningful name; the size of the sheet tab adjusts to accommodate the name's length.

Select a Worksheet

1. Click the sheet tab of the worksheet you want to make active.

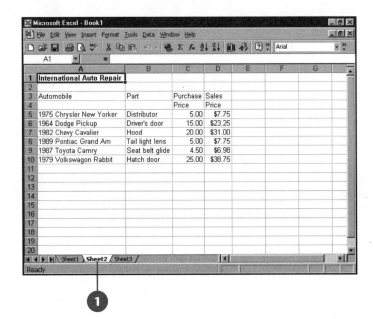

Name a Worksheet

1. Double-click the sheet tab of the worksheet you want to name.

2. Type a new name. The current name, which is selected, is automatically replaced when you begin typing.

3. Press Enter.

Inserting and Deleting a Worksheet

You can add or delete sheets in a workbook. If, for example, you are working on a project that requires more than three worksheets, you can insert additional sheets in one workbook rather than use multiple workbooks. If, on the other hand, you are using only one or two sheets in a workbook, you can delete the unused sheets to save disk space.

TIP

Hide a worksheet. *Click the sheet tab you want to hide, click the Format menu, point to Sheet, and then click Hide. To unhide a worksheet, click the Format menu, point to Sheet, click Unhide, select the worksheet you want to unhide, and then click OK.*

SEE ALSO

See "Moving and Copying a Worksheet" on page 66 for information on reorganizing sheets in a workbook.

Insert a Worksheet

1. Click the sheet tab of the worksheet to the right of where you want to insert the new sheet.

2. Click the Insert menu, and then click Worksheet.

   A new worksheet will be inserted to the left of the selected worksheet.

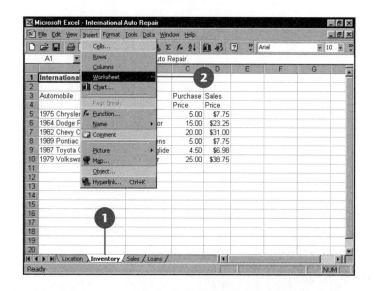

Delete a Worksheet

1. Click the sheet tab of the worksheet you want to delete, or click any cell on the sheet.

2. Click the Edit menu, and then click Delete Sheet.

3. Click OK to confirm the deletion.

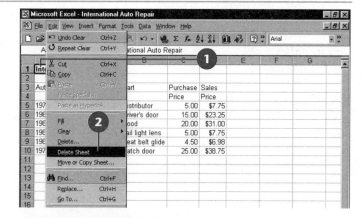

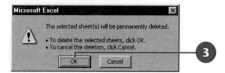

Moving and Copying a Worksheet

After adding several sheets to a workbook, you might want to reorganize them. You might want to arrange sheets in chronological order or in order of their importance in a particular project. You can easily move or copy a sheet within a workbook or even to a different open workbook. Copying a worksheet is easier and often more convenient than having to reenter similar information on a new sheet.

TIP

Give your worksheet a background. *Click the tab of sheet on which you want to insert a background, click the Format menu, point to Sheet, and then click Background. Select the picture you want to use as a background, and then click Insert.*

Move a Worksheet Within a Workbook

1. Click the sheet tab of the worksheet you want to move, and then press and hold the mouse button.

2. When the mouse pointer changes to a small sheet, drag it to the right of the sheet tab where you want to move the worksheet.

3. Release the mouse button.

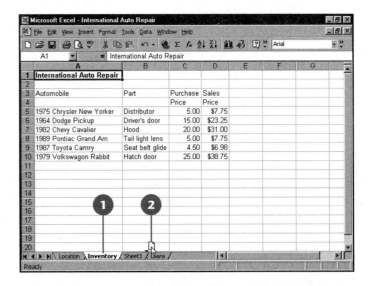

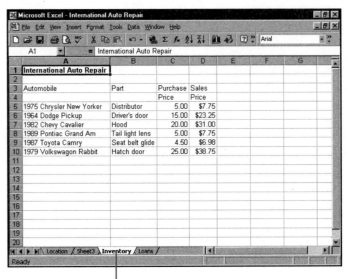

The sheet moves to a new location.

TIP

Use the Create A Copy check box to move a worksheet. *Click to clear the Create A Copy check box in the Move Or Copy dialog box to move a worksheet rather than copy it.*

TIP

The workbook I want to copy to doesn't show up in the To Book drop-down list. *In order to copy or move a sheet to a different workbook, you must first open the other workbook, and then switch back to the workbook of the sheet you want to copy or move.*

TIP

Use groups to affect multiple worksheets. *Click a sheet tab, press and hold the Shift key, and click another sheet tab to group worksheets. Right-click a grouped sheet tab, and then click Ungroup Sheet on the shortcut menu.*

SEE ALSO

See "Copying Cell Contents" on page 38 and "Moving Cell Contents" on page 40 for additional information on copying and moving data in cells.

Copy a Worksheet

1. Click the sheet tab of the worksheet you want to copy.

2. Click the Edit menu, and then click Move Or Copy Sheet.

3. If you want to copy the sheet to another open workbook, click the To Book drop-down arrow, and select the name of that workbook.

   The sheets of the selected workbook appear in the Before Sheet box.

4. Click a sheet name in the Before Sheet list. The copy will be inserted to the left of this sheet.

5. Click to select the Create A Copy check box.

6. Click OK.

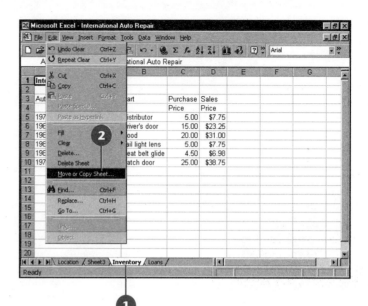

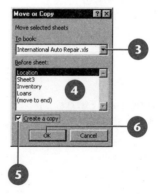

5

Selecting a Column or Row

You can select one or more columns or rows in a worksheet in order to apply formatting attributes, insert or delete columns or rows, or perform other group actions. The *header buttons* above each column and to the left of each row indicate the letter or number of the column or row. You can select multiple columns or rows even if they are *non-contiguous*—that is, not next to one another in the worksheet.

SEE ALSO

See *"Moving and Copying a Worksheet" on page 66 for* information on reorganizing sheets in a workbook.

Select a Column or Row

1. Click the column or row header button of the column or row you want to select.

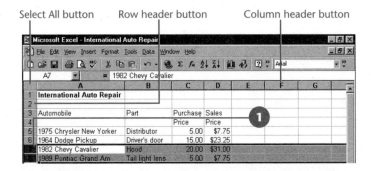

Select All button · Row header button · Column header button

Select Multiple Columns or Rows

1. Drag the mouse over the header buttons of any contiguous columns or rows you want to select.

2. To select noncontiguous columns or rows, press and hold the Ctrl key while clicking each additional column or row header button.

2. Press and hold the Ctrl key to add a column to the selection.

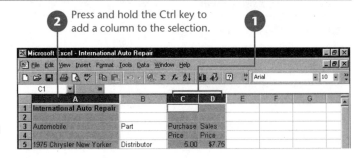

Select an Entire Worksheet

1. Click the Select All button.

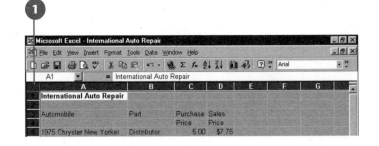

Inserting a Column or Row

You can insert blank columns and rows between columns and rows on a worksheet without disturbing any existing data. Excel repositions existing cells to accommodate the new columns and rows and adjusts any existing formulas so that they refer to the correct cells. When you insert one or more columns, they are inserted to the *left* of the selected column. When you add one or more rows, they are inserted *above* the selected row.

TIP

The Insert menu changes depending on what you select. *Clicking a column header button selects an entire column; then only the Columns command is available on the Insert menu. Clicking a row header button selects an entire row; then only the Rows command is available on the Insert menu.*

Insert a Column or Row

1. To insert a column, click anywhere in the column to the right of the location of the new column you want to insert.

   To insert a row, click anywhere in the row immediately below the location of the row you want to insert.

2. Click the Insert menu, and then click Columns or Rows.

   A new column is inserted to the left of the selected column; a new row is inserted above the selected row.

Row header button   Column header button

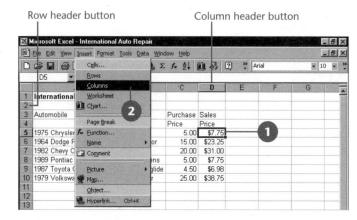

Insert Multiple Columns or Rows

1. To insert multiple columns, drag to select the column header buttons for the number of columns you want to insert.

   To insert multiple rows, drag to select the row header buttons for the number of rows you want to insert.

2. Click the Insert menu, and then click Columns or Rows.

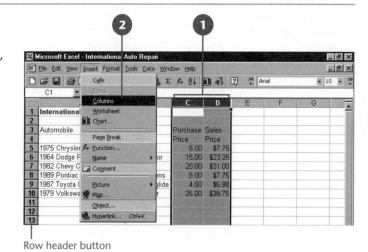

Row header button

5

Deleting a Column or Row

At some time, you may want to remove an entire column or row from a worksheet rather than deleting or editing individual cells. You can delete columns and rows just as easily as you insert them. Remaining columns and rows move to the left or up to join the other remaining cells.

TRY THIS

Verify your formulas after deleting a row. *After deleting a column or row, check the formulas on your worksheet and you'll see they have adjusted to the new worksheet structure.*

SEE ALSO

See "Inserting and Deleting Cells" on page 42 for more information about using the Delete command.

Delete a Column

1. Click the column header button of the column(s) you want to delete.

2. Click the Edit menu, and then click Delete.

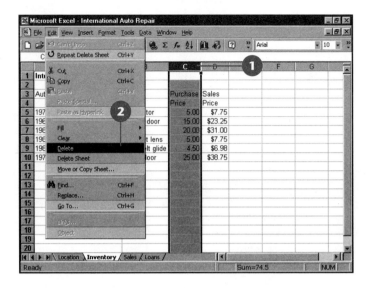

Delete a Row

1. Click the row header button of the row(s) you want to delete.

2. Click the Edit menu, and then click Delete.

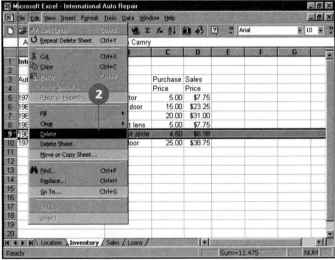

Hiding a Column or Row

Not all the data on a worksheet should be available to everyone. You can hide sensitive information without deleting it by hiding selected columns or rows. For example, if you want to share a worksheet with others, but it includes employee salaries, which are confidential, you can simply hide the salary column. Hiding columns and rows does not affect calculations in a worksheet; all data in hidden columns and rows is still referenced by formulas as necessary. Hidden columns and rows do not appear in a printout either. When you need the data, you can unhide the sensitive information.

SEE ALSO

See "Inserting a Column or Row" on page 69 or "Deleting a Column or Row" on page 70 for information on changing columns and rows on a worksheet.

Hide a Column or Row

1. Click the column or row header button of the column or row you want to hide. (Drag to select multiple header buttons to hide more than one column or row.)

2. Click the Format menu, point to Column or Row, and then click Hide.

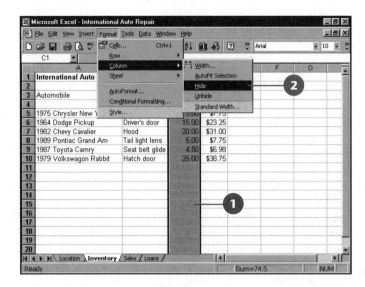

Unhide a Column or Row

1. Drag to select the column or row header buttons on either side of the hidden column or row.

2. Click the Format menu, point to Column or Row, and then click Unhide.

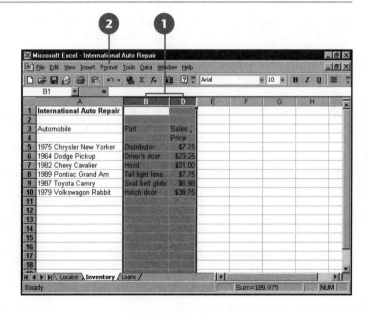

5

Adjusting Column Width and Row Height

As you build your worksheet, you'll want to change the default width of some columns or the default height of some rows to accommodate long strings of data or larger font sizes. You can manually change column widths or row heights, or you can use the *AutoFit* feature to have Excel automatically adjust column or row size to fit data you have entered. Changing the width of a column or the height of a row will enhance the readability of your worksheet.

SEE ALSO

See "Formatting Data with AutoFormat" on page 96 for more information about formatting data quickly.

Change Column Width Using AutoFit

1. Position the mouse pointer on the right edge of the header button of the column you want to adjust. The pointer changes to a double-headed arrow.

2. Double-click the mouse button.

The column width adjusts to fit the longest cell entry in the column.

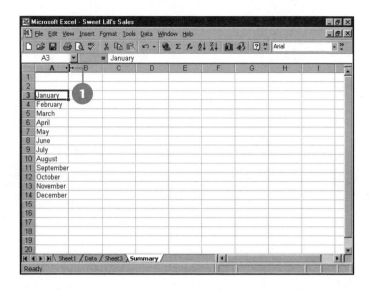

Change Row Height Using AutoFit

1. Position the mouse pointer on the bottom edge of the header button of the row you want to adjust. The pointer changes to a double-headed arrow.

2. Double-click the mouse button.

The row height adjusts to fit the largest font size.

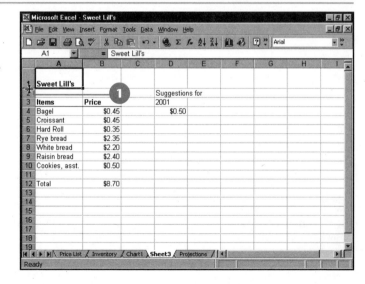

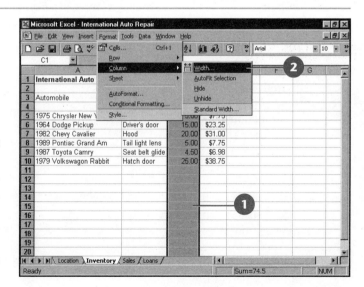

TIP

Correctly position the mouse pointer when adjusting a column's width. *Place the mouse pointer between the header buttons of the column to be resized and the column to its right.*

TIP

Correctly position the mouse pointer when adjusting a row's height. *Place the mouse pointer between the header button of the row to be resized and the row below it.*

TIP

Standard column width and row height. *By default, each column in each worksheet is 8.43 points wide, and each row is 12.75 points high. Select the column you want to set to the standard width, click the Format menu, point to Column, click Standard Width, and then click OK.*

TIP

What is a point? *A point is a measurement unit used to size text and space on a worksheet. One inch equals 72 points. Apply different point sizes to your column width, row height, and text to determine which size is best for your worksheet.*

Adjust Column Width or Row Height Using the Mouse

1. Position the mouse pointer on the right edge of the column header button or the bottom edge of the row header button for the column or row you want to change.

2. When the mouse pointer changes to a double-headed arrow, drag the pointer to a new width or height.

Change Column Width or Row Height Using the Menu

1. Click anywhere in the column or row you want to adjust.

2. Click the Format menu, point to Column, and then click Width. Or click the Format menu, point to Row, and then click Height.

3. Type a new column width or row height in points.

4. Click OK.

Freezing a Column or Row

Large worksheets can be difficult to work with, especially on low-resolution or small monitor screens. If you scroll down to see the bottom of the list, you can no longer see the column names at the top of the list. Instead of repeatedly scrolling up and down, you can temporarily fix, or *freeze*, those column or row headings so that you can see them no matter where you scroll in the list. When you freeze a row or column, you are actually splitting the screen into one or more *panes* (window sections) and freezing one of the panes. You can split the screen into up to four panes and can freeze up to two of these panes. You can edit the data in a frozen pane just as you do any Excel data, but the cells remain stationary even when you use the scroll bars; only the unfrozen part of the screen scrolls.

Freeze a Column or Row

1. Select the column to the right of the columns you want to freeze, or select the row below the rows you want to freeze.

   To freeze both, click the cell to the right and below the column and row you want to freeze.

2. Click the Window menu, and then click Freeze Panes.

   ◆ When you freeze a pane horizontally, all the rows *above* the active cell freeze. When you freeze a pane vertically, all the columns to the *left* of the active cell freeze.

   ◆ When you freeze a pane, it has no effect on how a worksheet looks when printed.

Unfreeze a Column or Row

1. Click the Window menu.

2. Click Unfreeze Panes.

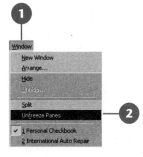

Previewing Page Breaks

If you want to print a worksheet that is larger than one page, Excel divides it into pages by inserting *automatic page breaks*. These page breaks are based on paper size, margin settings, and scaling options you set. You can change which rows or columns are printed on the page by inserting *horizontal* or *vertical page breaks*. In *page break preview*, you can view the page breaks and move them by dragging them to a different location on the worksheet.

TIP

Remove a page break.
Select the column or row next to the page break, click the Insert menu, and then click Remove Page Break.

Insert a Page Break

1. To insert a vertical page break, click the column header button to the right of the location where you want to insert a page break.

   To insert a horizontal page break, click the row header button below the location where you want to insert a page break.

   To start a new page, click the cell below and to the right of the location where you want a new page.

2. Click the Insert menu, and then click Page Break.

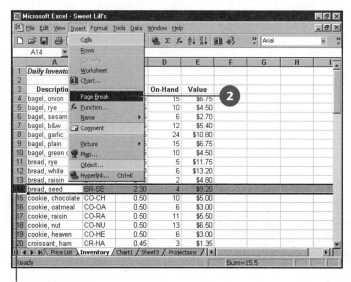

Page break inserted here

Preview and Move a Page Break

1. Click the View menu, and then click Page Break Preview.

2. Move a page break to a new location by placing the pointer over the blue page break and dragging it to a new location.

3. When you're done, click the View menu, and then click Normal.

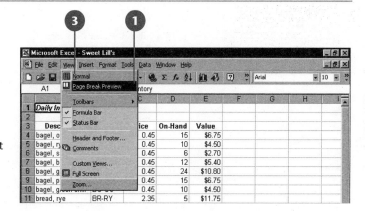

Setting Up the Page

You can set up the worksheet page so that it is printed just the way you want. With the Page Setup dialog box, you can choose the *page orientation,* which determines how the worksheet data is printed on a page, vertically or horizontally. You can also adjust the *print scaling* (to reduce or enlarge the size of printed characters), change the *paper size* (to match the size of paper in your printer), and resize or realign the left, right, top, and bottom *margins* (the blank areas along each edge of the paper).

Change Page Orientation

1. Click the File menu, and then click Page Setup.

2. Click the Page tab.

3. Click the Portrait (8.5 x 11 inches) option button (the default) or click the Landscape (11 x 8.5 inches) option button to select page orientation.

4. Click OK.

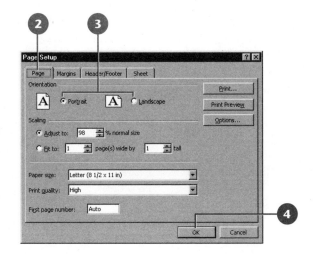

Change the Margin Settings

1. Click the File menu, and then click Page Setup.

2. Click the Margins tab.

   ◆ Click the Top, Bottom, Left, and Right up or down arrows to adjust the margins.

   ◆ Click to select the Center On Page check boxes to automatically center data relative to the left and right margins (horizontally) or the top and bottom margins (vertically).

3. Click OK.

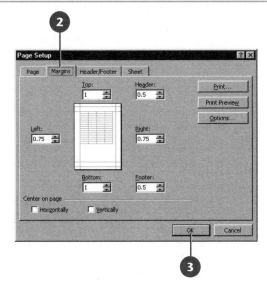

Adding a Header or Footer

Adding a header or footer to a workbook makes printouts easier for readers to reference. With the Page Setup command, you can add header and footer information, such as the page number, worksheet title, or current date, at the top and bottom of each page or section of a worksheet or workbook. Using the Custom Header and Custom Footer buttons, your pages can include your computer's system date and time, the page number, the name of the workbook and sheet, and other custom information.

TIP

Preview the header and footer. *Click the Print Preview button to make sure the header and footer add value to the worksheet and don't detract from it.*

Change a Header or Footer

1. Click the File menu, and then click Page Setup.

2. Click the Header/Footer tab.

3. If the Header box doesn't contain the information you want, click Custom Header.

4. Type the information in the left, middle, or right text boxes, or click a button to insert built-in header information.

   If you don't want a header to appear at all, delete the text and codes in the text boxes.

5. Select any text you want to format, and then click the Font button.

6. Click OK.

7. If the Footer box doesn't contain the information that you want, click Custom Footer.

8. Type the information in the left, middle, or right text boxes, or click a button icon to insert the built-in footer information.

9. Click OK.

10. Click OK.

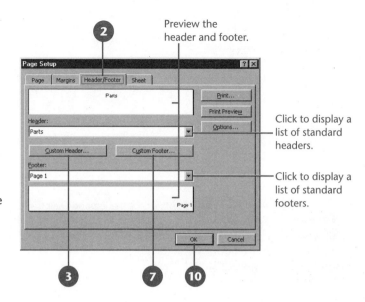

Preview the header and footer.

Click to display a list of standard headers.

Click to display a list of standard footers.

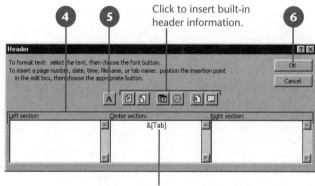

Click to insert built-in header information.

This symbol will insert the sheet name of the active sheet.

Customizing Worksheet Printing

At some point you'll want to print your work so you can distribute it to others or use it for other purposes. You can print all or part of any worksheet, and control the appearance of many features, such as whether gridlines are displayed, whether column letters and row numbers are displayed, and whether to include *print titles*, columns and rows that are repeated on each page.

TIP

If a print area has already been set, you do not need to select it. *If you have already set a print area, it will appear in the Print Area box on the Sheet tab of the Page Setup dialog box.*

SEE ALSO

See "Setting a Print Area" on page 80 for more information on selecting an area to print.

Print Part of a Worksheet

1. Click the File menu, and then click Page Setup.

2. Click the Sheet tab.

3. Click in the Print Area box, and then type the range you want to print. Or click the Collapse Dialog button, select the cells you want to print, and then click the Expand Dialog button to restore the dialog box.

4. Click OK.

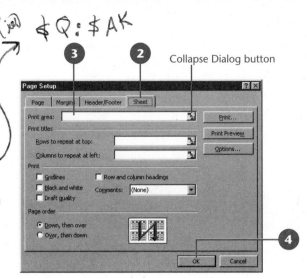

(i.e) $Q:$AK

Collapse Dialog button

Print Row and Column Titles on Each Page

1. Click the File menu, and then click Page Setup.

2. Click the Sheet tab.

3. Enter the number of the row or the letter of the column that contains the titles. Or click the appropriate Collapse Dialog button, select the row or column with the mouse, and then click the Expand Dialog box to restore the dialog box.

4. Click OK.

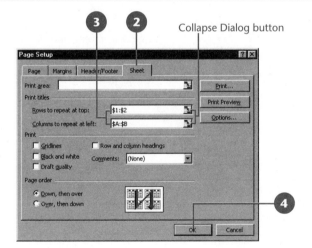

Collapse Dialog button

SEE ALSO

See "Selecting Cells" on page 27 for more information about selecting a range of cells.

TIP

Do not include columns or rows you want printed on every page when selecting the print area. *Doing so will cause that information to be printed twice on the first page. Instead, use the Print Titles option.*

TIP

Reduce or enlarge the size of printed characters. *Click the Adjust To up or down arrow to set the percentage size of the printed characters. Click the Fit To up or down arrow to specify the number of pages on which you want the worksheet to be printed; the size of the printed characters will adjust accordingly.*

TRY THIS

Print a large worksheet on a single page. *Large worksheets will always be printed on one page using the Fit To option.*

Print Gridlines, Column Letters, and Row Numbers

1. Click the File menu, and then click Page Setup.

2. Click the Sheet tab.

3. Click to select the Gridlines check box.

4. Click to select the Row And Column Headings check box.

5. Click OK.

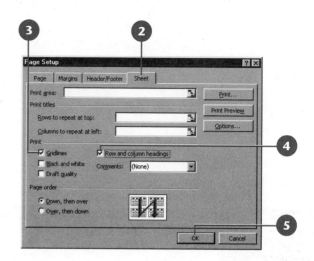

Fit Your Worksheet on a Specific Number of Pages

1. Click the File menu, and then click Page Setup.

2. Click the Page tab.

3. Select a scaling option.

   ◆ Click the Adjust To option button to scale the worksheet using a percentage.

   ◆ Click the Fit To option button to force a worksheet to be printed on a specific number of pages.

4. Click OK.

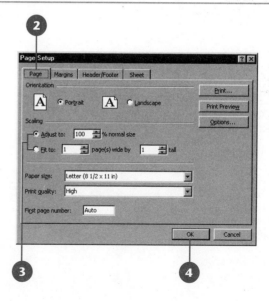

Setting a Print Area

A *print area* is that section of a worksheet that is printed when you use the Print command. You can set the print area when you customize worksheet printing or any time you are working on a worksheet. You might, for example, want to print a certain range within a worksheet for department managers. In order to use headers and footers, you must first establish, or *set*, the print area. Specific headers and footers can be designed for a specific print area. The print area can consist of a single cell or a contiguous or noncontiguous range.

Set the Print Area

1. Select the range of cells you want to print.

2. Click the File menu.

3. Point to Print Area, and then click Set Print Area.

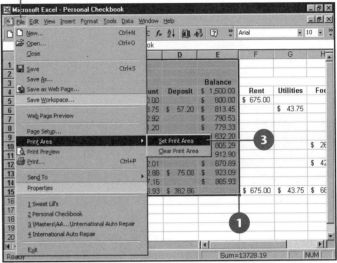

Clear the Print Area

1. Click the File menu.

2. Point to Print Area, and then click Clear Print Area.

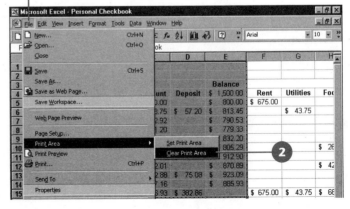

Formatting a Worksheet

IN THIS SECTION

Formatting Text and Numbers

Designing Conditional Formatting

Copying Cell Formats

Changing Fonts

Changing Data Alignment

Controlling Text Flow

Changing Data Color

Adding Color and Patterns to Cells

Adding Borders to Cells

Formatting Data with AutoFormat

Modifying an AutoFormat

Creating and Applying a Style

Modifying a Style

New2000 **Changing Languages**

Microsoft Excel 2000 offers several tools for making your worksheets look more attractive and professional. The look of a worksheet does not affect its functionality—as long as the values and formulas are correct, you'll get the results you need—but it can greatly enhance its effectiveness. If you want people to be able to easily read and interpret the information you have compiled, take the time to format your worksheet.

Formatting a Worksheet

Formatting a worksheet involves making cosmetic changes to cell contents and the worksheet grid. Without formatting, a worksheet can look like a sea of meaningless data. To make important information stand out, you can change the appearance of selected numbers and text by adding dollar signs, commas, and other numerical formats or by applying attributes such as boldface and italics. You can change font and font size, adjust the alignment of data in cells, and add colors, patterns, borders, and pictures. By using AutoFormats and styles to apply multiple changes, you can speed up the formatting process and ensure a greater degree of consistency among your worksheets. You can even add editing functionality for other languages to the Excel work environment.

Formatting Text and Numbers

You can change the appearance of the data in the cells of a worksheet without changing the actual value in the cell. You can format text and numbers with *font attributes*, such as bolding, italics, or underlining, to enhance this data to catch the reader's attention. You can also apply *numeric formats* to numbers to better reflect the type of information they represent—dollar amounts, dates, decimals, and so on. For example, you can format a number to display up to 15 decimal places or none at all.

SEE ALSO

See "Working with Menus and Toolbars" on page 14 for more information about personalizing toolbars.

Change the Appearance of Text

① Select a cell or range that contains the text you want to format.

② Click the More Buttons drop-down arrow to display formatting buttons, if necessary.

③ Click the formatting button you want to apply the attribute to the selected range. You can apply more than one attribute as long as the range is selected.

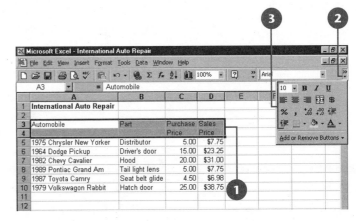

FORMATTING TOOLBAR BUTTONS

Button	Name	Example
B	Bold	**Excel**
I	Italic	*Excel*
U	Underline	<u>Excel</u>
$	Currency Style	$5,432.10
%	Percent Style	54.32%
,	Comma Style	5,432.10
.0 .00	Increase Decimal	5,432.10 becomes 5,432.100
.00 .0	Decrease Decimal	5,432.10 becomes 5,432.1

Remove a numeric format or font attribute quickly. *The buttons on the Formatting toolbar are toggle buttons, which means you simply click to turn them on and off. To remove a numeric format or a font attribute, select the cell, range, or text, and then click the appropriate button on the Formatting toolbar to turn the format or attribute off.*

Open the Format Cells dialog box quickly. *Right-click a selected cell or range, and then click Format Cells on the shortcut menu.*

Format numbers in international currencies. *In the Format Cells dialog box, click the Number tab, click Currency in the Category list, click the Symbol drop-down arrow, and then click an international currency symbol. Excel now supports the new Euro currency.*

See "Selecting Cells" on page 27 for more information about selecting cells and ranges.

Change the Appearance of a Number Quickly

1. Select a cell or range that contains the number(s) you want to format.

2. Click the More Buttons drop-down arrow to display numeric formatting buttons, if necessary.

3. Click a formatting button to apply the numeric attribute you want to the selected range.

Format a Number Using the Format Cells Dialog Box

1. Select a cell or range that contains the number(s) you want to format.

2. Click the Format menu, and then click Cells.

3. Click the Number tab.

4. Click to select a category.

5. Select the options you want to apply.

6. Preview your selections in the Sample box.

7. Click OK.

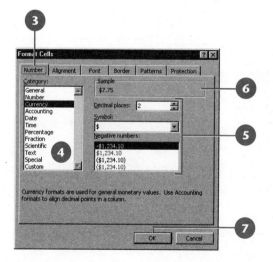

Designing Conditional Formatting

You can make your worksheets more powerful by setting up conditional formatting. *Conditional formatting* lets the value of a cell determine its formatting. For example, you might want this year's sales total to be displayed in red and italics if it's less than last year's total, but in green and bold if it's more.

Establish a Conditional Format

1. Select a cell or range you want to conditionally format.

2. Click the Format menu, and then click Conditional Formatting.

3. Select the operator and values you want for Condition 1.

4. Click the Format button, select the attributes you want applied, and then click OK.

5. Click Add to include additional conditions, and then repeat steps 3 and 4.

6. Click OK.

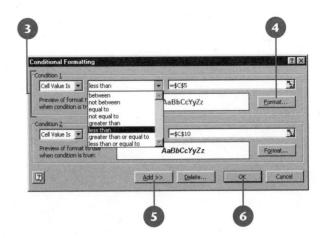

Delete a Conditional Format

1. Click the Format menu, and then click Conditional Formatting.

2. Click Delete.

3. Click to select the check box for the condition(s) to be deleted.

4. Click OK.

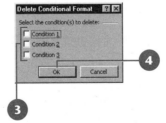

Copying Cell Formats

After formatting a cell on a worksheet, you might want to apply those same formatting changes to other cells on the worksheet. For example, you might want each subtotal on your worksheet to be formatted in italic, bold, 12-point Times New Roman, with a dollar sign, commas, and two decimal places. Rather than selecting each subtotal and applying the individual formatting to each cell, you can *paint* (that is, copy) the formatting from one cell to others.

TIP

Use the Esc key to cancel format painting. *If you change your mind about painting a format, cancel the marquee by pressing the Esc key.*

TRY THIS

Paint multiple attributes. *Apply several formats to a cell, and then use the Format Painter button to apply them to another cell or range.*

Copy a Cell Format

1. Select a cell or range containing the formatting you want to copy.

2. Click the Format Painter button on the Standard toolbar. If necessary, click the More Buttons drop-down arrow to display the button.

3. Drag to select the cell(s) you want to paint. When you release the mouse button, the cells appear with the new formatting.

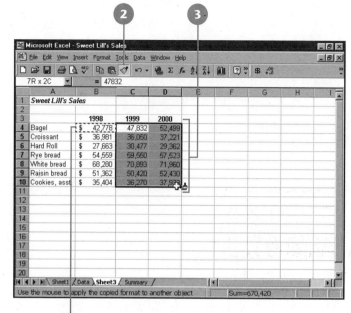

A marquee appears around the cell whose format you are copying.

Changing Fonts

A *font* is a collection of alphanumeric characters that share the same *typeface,* or design, and have similar characteristics. Most fonts are available in a number of styles (such as bold and italic) and sizes. The size of each font character is measured in points (a *point* is approximately 1/72 of an inch). You can use any font that is installed on your computer on a worksheet, but the default is 10-point Arial.

TIP

Each computer has different fonts installed.
Users with whom you share files may not have all the fonts you've used in a workbook installed on their computers.

Change Font and Font Size

1. Select a cell or range whose font and font size you want to change.

2. Click the Format menu, and then click Cells.

3. Click the Font tab.

4. Select a font name.

5. Select a font style.

6. Select a font size.

7. Select any additional formatting effects.

8. Preview the result of the selections you have made.

9. Click OK.

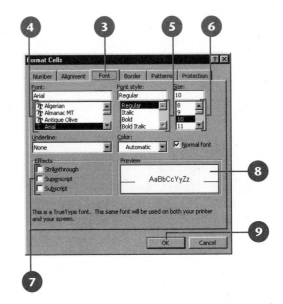

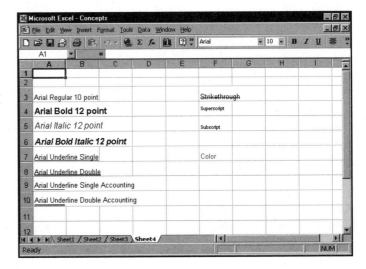

TIP

What is a TrueType font? *A TrueType font is a font that uses special software capabilities to print exactly what is seen on the screen.*

TIP

What is a printer font? *A printer font is a font that comes only in specified sizes. If you are creating a worksheet for publication, you need to use printer fonts.*

TIP

Display font names in their font. *Click the Tools menu, click Customize, click the Options tab, and then click to select the List Font Names In Their Font check box.*

SEE ALSO

See "Formatting Data with AutoFormat" on page 96 for more information about applying Excel's predesigned formats to worksheet cells.

Change Font and Font Size Using the Formatting Toolbar

1. Select a cell or range whose font and font size you want to change.

2. Click the Font drop-down arrow on the Formatting toolbar.

3. If necessary, scroll to find the font you want to use, and then click it.

4. Click the Font Size drop-down arrow on the Formatting toolbar. If necessary, click the More Buttons drop-down arrow to display the button.

5. If necessary, scroll to find the font size you want to use, and then click it.

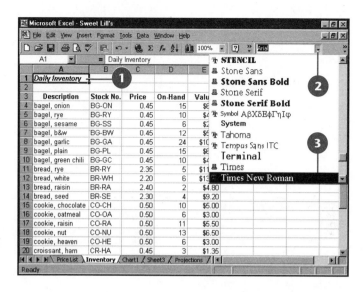

More Buttons drop-down arrow

Changing Data Alignment

When you enter data in a cell, Excel aligns labels on the left edge of the cell and aligns values and formulas on the right edge of the cell. *Horizontal alignment* is the way in which Excels aligns the contents of a cell relative to the left or right edge of the cell; *vertical alignment* is the way in which Excel aligns cell contents relative to the top and bottom of the cell. Excel also provides an option for changing the flow and angle of characters within a cell. The *orientation* of the contents of a cell is expressed in degrees. The default orientation is 0 degrees, in which characters are aligned horizontally within a cell.

SEE ALSO

See "Controlling Text Flow" on page 90 for information on using text control options.

Change Alignment Using the Format Cells Dialog Box

1. Select a cell or range whose alignment you want to change.

2. Click the Format menu, and then click Cells.

3. Click the Alignment tab.

4. Click the Horizontal drop-down arrow, and then select an alignment.

5. Click the Vertical drop-down arrow, and then select an alignment.

6. Select an orientation by clicking a point on the orientation map or by clicking the Degrees up or down arrow.

7. If you want, click to select one or more Text Control check boxes.

8. Click OK.

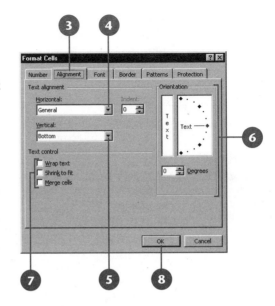

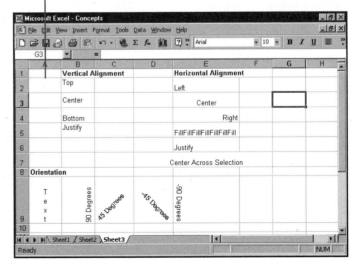

Sample data alignment

Change Alignment Using the Formatting Toolbar

1. Select a cell or range containing the data to be realigned.

2. Click the Align Left, Center, Align Right, or Merge And Center button on the Formatting toolbar.

   If necessary, click the More Buttons drop-down arrow to display the buttons.

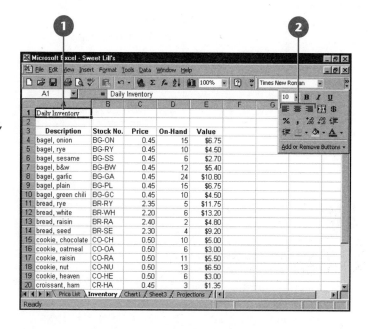

ALIGNMENT TOOLBAR BUTTONS		
Button	**Name**	**Description**
	Align Left	Aligns cell contents on the left edge of the cell
	Center	Centers cell contents in the middle of the cell
	Align Right	Aligns cell contents on the right edge of the cell
	Merge And Center	Centers cell contents across the columns of a selected range

6

Controlling Text Flow

The length of a label might not always fit within the width you've chosen for a column. If the cell to the right is empty, text spills over into it, but if that cell contains data, the text will be truncated (that is, cut off). A cell can be formatted so its text automatically wraps to multiple lines; that way, you don't have to widen the column to achieve an attractive effect. For example, you might want the label *2000 Division 1 Sales* to fit in a column that is only as wide as *Division*. Cell contents can also be modified to fit within the available space or can be combined with the contents of other cells.

TRY THIS

Use the Wrap Text feature.
Enter text that exceeds the width of a cell, and then use the Alignment tab of the Format Cells dialog box to wrap the text.

Control the Flow of Text in a Cell

1. Select a cell or range whose text flow you want to change.

2. Click the Format menu, and then click Cells.

3. Click the Alignment tab.

4. Click to select one or more Text Control check boxes.

   ◆ Wrap Text moves the text to multiple lines within a cell.

   ◆ Shrink To Fit reduces character size to fit within a cell.

   ◆ Merge Cells combines selected cells into a single cell.

5. Click OK.

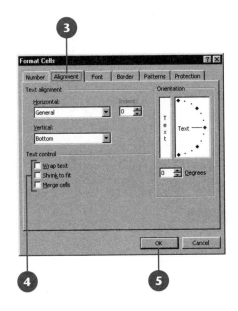

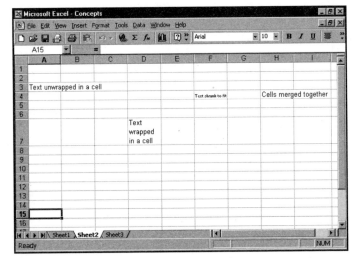

Changing Data Color

You can change the color of the numbers and text on a worksheet. Strategic use of *font color* can be an effective way of tying similar values together. For instance, on a sales worksheet you might want to display sales in green and returns in red.

Change Text Color Using the Format Cells Dialog Box

1. Select a cell or range that contains the text you want to change.

2. Click the Format menu, and then click Cells.

3. Click the Font tab.

4. Click the Color drop-down arrow, and then click a color.

5. Preview your selection in the Preview window.

6. Click OK.

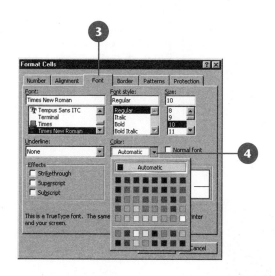

Change Font Color Using the Formatting Toolbar

1. Select a cell or range that contains the text you want to change.

2. Click the Font Color drop-down arrow on the Formatting toolbar. If necessary, click the More Buttons drop-down arrow to display the button.

3. Click a color.

More Buttons drop-down arrow

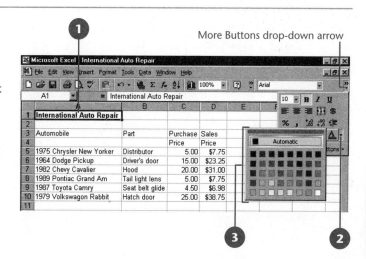

Adding Color and Patterns to Cells

You can *fill* the background of a cell with a color and a pattern to make its data stand out. Fill colors and patterns can also lend consistency to related information on a worksheet. On a sales worksheet, for example, formatting all fourth-quarter sales figures with a blue background and all second-quarter sales with a yellow background would make each group of figures easy to identify. You can use fill colors and patterns in conjunction with text attributes, fonts, and font colors to further enhance the appearance of your worksheet.

TIP

Painting formats. *When you paint a format using the Format Painter button on the Standard toolbar, the fill colors and patterns get copied too.*

Choose a Fill Color and Pattern Using the Format Cells Dialog Box

1. Select a cell or range you want to fill with a color or pattern.

2. Click the Format menu, and then click Cells.

3. Click the Patterns tab.

4. Click a color.

5. Click the Pattern drop-down arrow to display the available patterns, and then click a pattern.

6. Preview your selection.

7. Click OK.

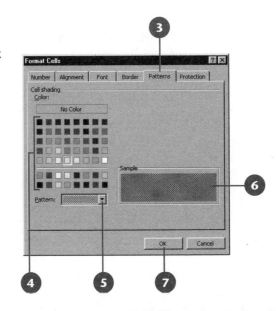

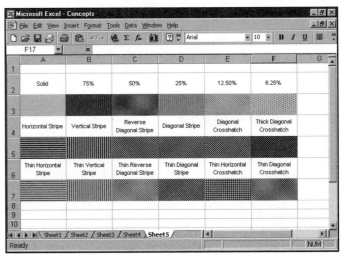

TIP

Use the Preview button on the Standard toolbar to save time. *Preview your worksheet before you print it, especially if you don't have a color printer. Some colors and patterns look great on screen but can make a worksheet difficult to read when printed in black and white.*

TRY THIS

Make a habit of previewing work before printing. *Using the Print Preview feature before printing any worksheet reduces paper waste.*

SEE ALSO

See "Copying Cell Formats" on page 85 for more information about painting a format to other cells.

Choose a Fill Color Using the Formatting Toolbar

1 Select a cell or range.

2 Click the Fill Color drop-down arrow on the Formatting toolbar.

If necessary, click the More Buttons drop-down arrow to display the button.

3 Click a color.

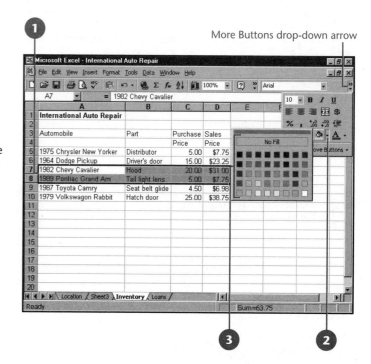

More Buttons drop-down arrow

Adding Borders to Cells

You've probably found that the light gray grid that is displayed on the worksheet screen helps your eyes flow from cell to cell. By default, Excel does not include this grid on printouts, but you can choose to print gridlines or improve on the grid pattern by adding different types of borders to a worksheet. You can add borders to some or all sides of a single cell or range. You can select borders of varying line widths and colors.

TRY THIS

Use a grid to improve readability. *Make it easier for readers to understand your worksheets by using gridlines, so they can easily match up labels with data across long rows or columns.*

Apply a Border Using the Format Cells Dialog Box

1. Select a cell or range to which you want to apply a border, or to select the entire worksheet, click the Select All button.

2. Click the Format menu, and then click Cells.

3. Click the Border tab.

4. Click to select a line type from the Style list.

5. Click the Color drop-down arrow, and then select a color for the border.

6. If you want a border on the outside of a cell or range, or lines inside a range of cells, click the Outline or Inside option. If you want to remove a border, click the None option.

7. To choose the other available border options, click in the Border box at the location where you want the border to appear, or click a Border button.

8. Click OK.

Select All button

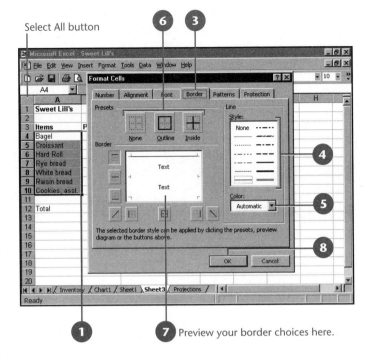

Preview your border choices here.

Use the Format Cells command to format a border. *To apply a border color other than the default (black), select the range that has an existing border or to which you want to apply a border. Right-click the range, click Format Cells on the shortcut menu, and then click the Border tab. Select the color you want for the border from the palette of available colors, and then click OK.*

See "Formatting Data with AutoFormat" on page 96 for information on predesigned formats that include borders and can be applied quickly.

Use the Select All button. *To place a border around the entire worksheet, click the Select All button, and then apply the border.*

See "Setting Up the Page" on page 76 for information about printing options.

Apply a Border Using the Formatting Toolbar

1. Select a cell or range to which you want to apply a border.

2. Click the Borders drop-down arrow on the Formatting toolbar or the Borders button to select the default border style. If necessary, click the More Buttons drop-down arrow to display the button.

3. Select a border from the palette of available borders. The previous border style you have chosen appears as the default Borders button on the Formatting toolbar.

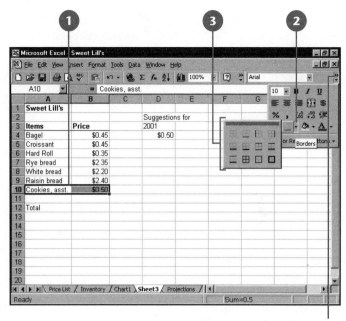

More Buttons drop-down arrow

Formatting Data with AutoFormat

Formatting worksheet data can be a lot of fun but also very time-consuming. To make formatting data more efficient, Excel includes 18 AutoFormats. An *AutoFormat* includes a combination of fill colors and patterns, numeric formats, font attributes, borders, and font colors, professionally designed to enhance your worksheets. And to make formatting even easier, Excel will "guess" which data should be formatted if you don't select any cells before choosing the AutoFormat command.

Apply an AutoFormat

1. Select a cell or range to which you want to apply an AutoFormat, or skip this step if you want Excel to "guess" which cells to format.

2. Click the Format menu, and then click AutoFormat.

3. Click an AutoFormat in the list. Refer to each sample to see the type of formatting that will be applied.

4. Click OK.

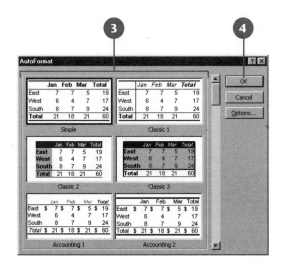

Modifying an AutoFormat

Excel AutoFormats give any worksheet a professional look, but you may need to modify an AutoFormat to better suit the needs of a particular project. For example, the AutoFormat you applied might be perfect except that the font used should be different—to match the font in the rest of your report. You can control individual elements in an AutoFormat so that not all are applied to the current worksheet. These changes are temporary; you can't permanently alter an AutoFormat.

Modify an AutoFormat

1. Select a cell or range whose AutoFormat you want to change, or skip this step if you want Excel to "guess" which cells to format.

2. Click the Format menu, and then click AutoFormat.

3. Click the AutoFormat you want to modify.

4. Click Options.

   Additional options appear at the bottom of the dialog box.

5. Click to select or clear one or more Formats To Apply check boxes to turn a feature on or off.

6. Click OK.

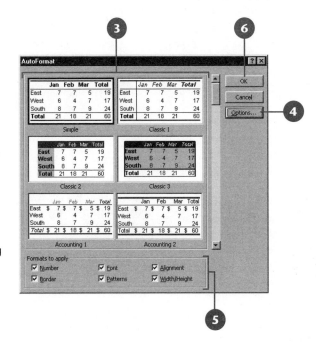

Creating and Applying a Style

A *style* is a defined collection of formats—font, font size, attributes, numeric formats, and so on—that you can store as a set and later apply to other cells. For example, if you always want sales figures to be displayed in blue 14-point Times New Roman, bold, italic, with 2 decimal places and commas, you can create a style that includes all these formats. Styles can also be copied from one workbook to another, so you can share styles among workbooks. Once you create a style, it is available to you no matter what workbook you open.

TIP

The Style dialog box check boxes reflect settings. *The check boxes in the Style dialog box correspond to the tabs in the Format Cells dialog box. The changes you make on the tabs are displayed to the right of the check box option.*

Create a New Style

1. Select a cell or range for which you want to create a style.

2. Click the Format menu, and then click Style.

3. Type the name of the new style in the Style Name box, for example, *Sales data*.

4. Click to clear the check boxes to turn off any option you do not want to include in the style.

5. Click Modify to make additional formatting changes to the style.

6. Make any necessary formatting changes; switch among the tabs of the Format Cells dialog box if necessary to complete this step.

7. Click OK.

8. Click OK.

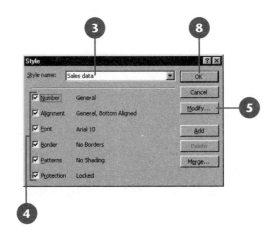

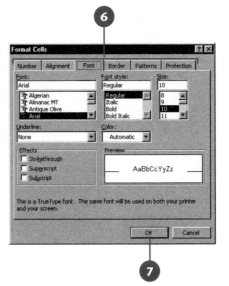

TIP

Apply styles before you enter data. *If you plan to enter repetitive information, such as a list of dollar amounts in a row or column, it's often easier to apply the desired style to the range before you enter the data. That way, you can simply enter each number, and Excel formats it as soon as you press Enter.*

SEE ALSO

See "Selecting Cells" on page 27 for information on selecting a range.

SEE ALSO

See "Modifying a Style" on page 100 for information on changing style settings.

TRY THIS

Create a unique style. *A style applied throughout a worksheet makes data visually identifiable. You might want to create such a style whenever you use the name of your company or department in a cell.*

Apply a Style

1. Select a cell or range to which you want to apply a style.

2. Click the Format menu, and then click Style.

3. Click the Style Name drop-down arrow, and then select the style you want to apply.

4. Click OK.

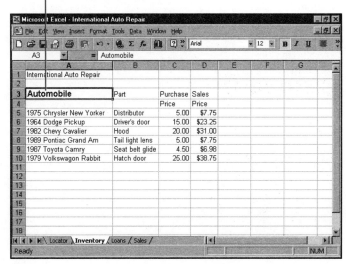

The Heading style is applied here.

Modifying a Style

Any style—whether it was supplied by Excel or created by you or someone else—can be modified. Suppose you created a style containing fonts and colors your company uses. If those specifications changed, you could modify the style to include the new attributes. If you want to use styles created or modified in another workbook, you can merge the styles into the open workbook. If you no longer use a style, you can delete it from the workbook.

SEE ALSO

See "Creating and Applying a Style" on page 98 for information on selecting style settings in the Style dialog box.

Modify a Style

1. Click the Format menu, and then click Style.

2. Click the Style Name drop-down arrow.

3. Click the style you want to modify.

4. Click Modify.

5. Make any changes you want in the Format Cells dialog box.

6. Click OK.

7. Click OK.

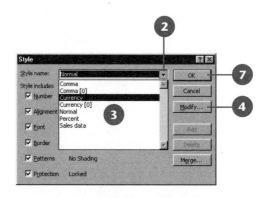

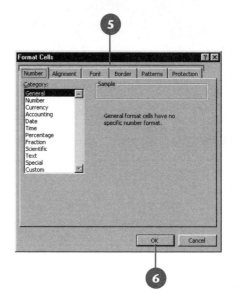

Merge Styles

1. Click the Format menu, and then click Style.

2. Click Merge.

3. Click the workbook that contains the styles you want to merge with the current workbook.

4. Click OK.

5. Click OK.

Delete a Style

1. Click the Format menu, and then click Style.

2. Click the Style Name drop-down arrow.

3. Click the style you want to delete.

4. Click Delete.

5. Click OK.

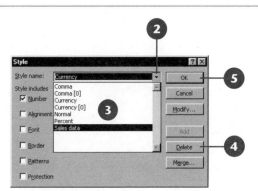

6

Changing Languages

International Microsoft Office users can change the language that appears on their screens by changing the default language settings. Users around the world can enter, display, and edit text in all support languages, including European languages, Japanese, Chinese, Korean, Hebrew, and Arabic to name a few. You'll probably be able to use Excel in your native language.

Change Languages

1 Click the Start button, point to Programs, point to Microsoft Office Tools, and then click Microsoft Office Language Settings.

2 Click to select the check box with the language you want enabled.

3 Click OK.

4 Click Yes to make the change or click No to cancel.

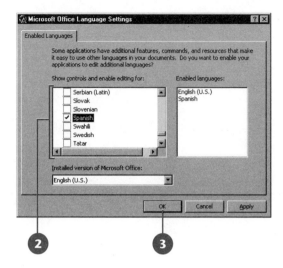

7

Inserting Graphics and Related Materials

IN THIS SECTION

Inserting Pictures

New2000 **Inserting Media Clips**

Stylizing Text with WordArt

Editing WordArt Text

Applying WordArt Text Effects

Inserting an Organization Chart

Modifying an Organization Chart

Creating and Reading a Cell Comment

Editing and Deleting a Cell Comment

Modifying Graphic Images

S pice up an otherwise drab worksheet using colorful graphic images that are included with Microsoft Excel 2000, purchased by you or your company, or created by you using a separate graphics program. Graphic images can serve to reinforce a corporate identity or illustrate subject matter in a worksheet. Used effectively, graphics add value by making your documents look more polished and professional.

You can add several different types of graphics, such as pictures, stylized text, or an organization chart, to your worksheet. From within Excel, you can access several Microsoft Office applications to create your own graphic elements. You can use the Clip Gallery to insert existing graphics, WordArt to design stylized text, and Organization Chart to build hierarchical charts. You can attach comments to cells—just as you might attach sticky notes to a piece of paper. These notes can include information you want to share with others who will be viewing or modifying your workbook online, or can serve as reminders to yourself. Once you have inserted a graphic image, you can modify the image to create the look you want. You can crop the image or change its color.

Inserting Pictures

You can add pictures to a worksheet. Your company might have a logo that it includes on all worksheets. Or you might want to use *clip art,* copyright-free graphics, on your worksheet for a special presentation. In Excel, a *picture* is any graphic object that you insert as a single unit. You can insert pictures that you've created in a drawing program or scanned in and saved as a file, or you can insert clip art provided with Microsoft Office or that you've acquired separately. After you insert a graphic object, you can easily delete it if it does not serve your purposes.

> **TIP**
>
> **Resize or move a picture if it's too big.** *To resize a picture so it does not obscure existing data, point to a handle and drag the handle to reduce or enlarge the picture. To move the picture, point to an edge but not to a handle, and then drag the picture to a new location.*

Insert Clip Art from the Clip Gallery

1. Select the cell or range where you want to insert a picture.

2. Click the Insert menu, point to Picture, and then click Clip Art.

3. Click the Pictures tab, if necessary.

4. Click a category in the list. Available pictures for the category you selected appear in the list.

5. Click a picture in the category. If necessary, scroll to see all the pictures available in the category.

6. Click the Insert Clip button.

   The picture is inserted at the cell or range you selected.

7. Click the Close button.

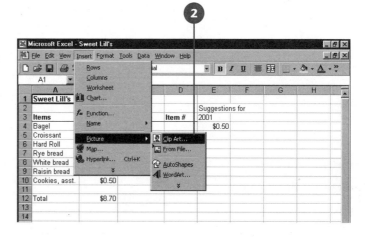

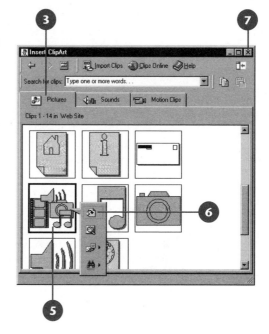

7

3 4

TIP

Display the Picture toolbar. *When you select a picture, the Picture toolbar will automatically appear.*

TIP

Add a border to a picture. *Select the image, click the Line Style button on the Picture toolbar, and then click the line style you want.*

SEE ALSO

See "Inserting Media Clips" on page 106 for information on inserting sounds and motion clips from the Clip Gallery and inserting an image from a scanner or digital camera.

SEE ALSO

See "Inserting AutoShapes from the Clip Gallery" on page 126 for information on searching for clip art from the Clip Gallery.

Insert a Picture from an Existing File

1. Click the cell or range where you want the picture to appear.

2. Click the Insert menu, point to Picture, and then click From File.

3. Click the Look In drop-down arrow, select the drive and folder with the picture, and then click the file you want to insert.

4. If you want, click the View button drop-down arrow, and then select Preview to view the picture.

5. Click Insert.

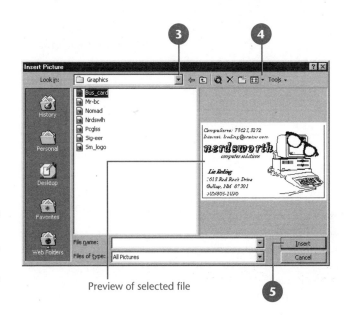

Preview of selected file

Delete a Picture

1. Click the object to display its handles.

   Selection handles are the little squares that appear on the edges of an object when it is selected.

2. Press the Delete key.

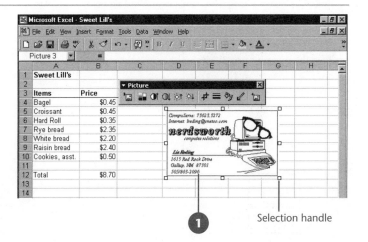

Selection handle

Inserting Media Clips

You can insert sounds or motion clips into a workbook by accessing them using the Clip Gallery. A *motion clip* is an animated picture—also known as an animated GIF—frequently used in Web pages. To play a motion clip, you need to view your workbook or worksheet as a Web page. When you insert a sound, a small icon appears representing the sound file. To play sounds other than your computer's internal sounds, you need a sound card and speakers. You can also insert images from a Twain-compatible scanner or digital camera. To insert an image, you need to connect the scanner or digital camera to your computer and install the Twain device software.

Insert a Clip Gallery Sound or Motion Clip

1. Click the Insert menu, point to Picture, and then click Clip Art.

2. Click the Sounds or Motion Clips tab.

3. Click the category you want.

4. Click the media you want to insert, and then click the Insert Clip button.

5. Click the Close button.

6. To play a sound, double-click the sound icon.

To play a motion clip, save your workbook or worksheet as a Web page, and then view it in a Web browser.

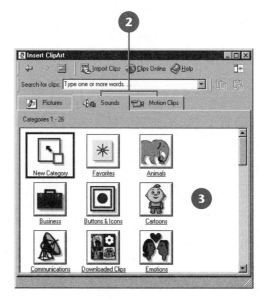

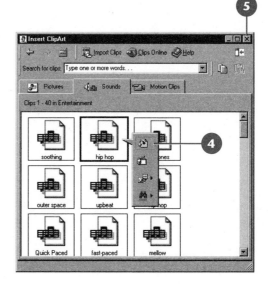

TIP

Preview a motion clip. *To see how a motion clip will appear, click the File menu, and then click Web Page Preview.*

TIP

Connect to the Web for access to additional clip art. *Click the Clips Online button to open your Web browser and connect to a clip art Web site to download files.*

SEE ALSO

See "Getting Data from the Web" on page 248 for information on getting clip art from the Web.

TIP

Display clip art categories. *Click the All Categories button on the Insert ClipArt toolbar.*

Insert an Image from a Scanner or Camera

1 Set up the image in the scanning device or digital camera.

2 Click the Insert menu, point to Picture, and then click From Scanner Or Camera.

3 Click the Device drop-down arrow, and then select the device you want to use.

4 Click the Resolution option button you want.

◆ Click Web Quality if you intend for your worksheet to be viewed on screen.

◆ Click Print Quality if you intend for your worksheet to be printed.

5 Click the insertion method you want.

◆ Click Insert if you're using a scanner and you want to use predefined settings to scan your picture.

◆ Click Custom Insert if you're using a scanner and you want to change image settings, or if you're using a camera.

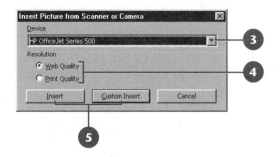

Stylizing Text with WordArt

WordArt is a Microsoft program you can use to stylize specific text on your worksheet. WordArt provides a wide variety of text styles predesigned with dynamic patterns and effects; all you have to do is choose a style and type in the text. For example, if you don't have a logo for your company, you can easily create one using WordArt. You can easily move or resize a WordArt object, even though it might contain many components.

Insert WordArt button

Create WordArt

1. Click the Insert menu, point to Picture, and then click WordArt.

2. Click a WordArt style.

3. Click OK.

4. Type the text you want in the Edit WordArt Text dialog box.

5. If you want, click the Font drop-down arrow, and then select a different font. Click the Size drop-down arrow, and then select a different size of the lettering.

6. If you want to add font attributes, click the Bold or Italic button or both.

7. Click OK.

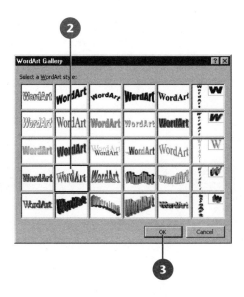

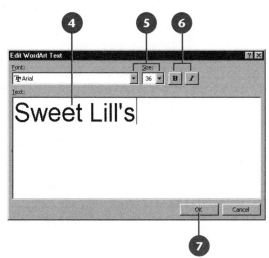

SEE ALSO

See "Editing WordArt Text" on page 110 for information about modifying WordArt text and using the WordArt toolbar.

SEE ALSO

See "Applying WordArt Text Effects" on page 112 for information on using WordArt effectively.

8 If you want, use the WordArt toolbar buttons to make additional modifications.

9 To deselect the WordArt, click anywhere on the worksheet, or press Esc.

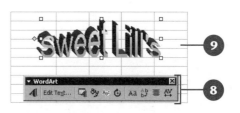

	USING WORDART TOOLBAR BUTTONS	
Button	**Name**	**Description**
	Word Art	Create new WordArt
Edit Text...	Edit Text	Edit the existing text in a WordArt object
	WordArt Gallery	Choose a new style for existing WordArt
	Format WordArt	Change the attributes of existing WordArt
	WordArt Shape	Modify the shape of an existing WordArt object
	Free Rotate	Rotate an existing object
	WordArt Same Letter Heights	Make uppercase and lower-case letters the same height
	WordArt Vertical	Change horizontal letters into a vertical formation
	WordArt Alignment	Modify the alignment of an existing object
	WordArt Character Spacing	Change the spacing between characters

Editing WordArt Text

With WordArt, in addition to applying one of the preformatted styles, you can create your own style. You can shape text into a variety of shapes, curves, styles, and color patterns. When you select a WordArt object to edit the text, the WordArt toolbar opens. This toolbar contains tools for coloring, rotating, and shaping your text. You can also format a WordArt object using the tools that are available in the Format dialog box, including positioning and sizing your WordArt.

TIP
Closing WordArt. *Once you are finished, either click anywhere on the worksheet or click the Close button to close the WordArt toolbar.*

Change the Shape of WordArt Text

1. Click the WordArt object.

2. Click the WordArt Shape button on the WordArt toolbar.

3. Click the shape you want to apply to the text.

4. Click a blank area of the worksheet to deselect the WordArt object.

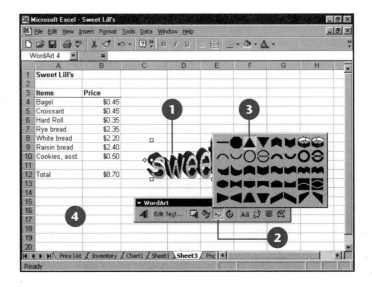

Rotate WordArt Text

1. Click the WordArt object.

2. Click the Free Rotate button on the WordArt toolbar.

3. Drag one of the rotate handles that appear in the four corners to rotate the object in any direction you want.

4. When you're done, click the Free Rotate button to deselect it.

5. Click a blank area of the worksheet to deselect the WordArt object.

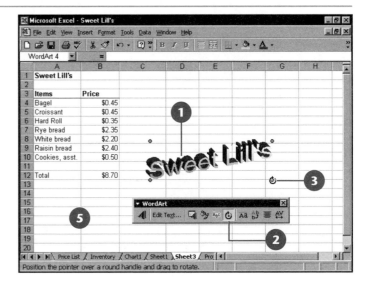

Format WordArt button

SEE ALSO

See "Applying WordArt Text Effects" on page 112 for information about enhancing WordArt text.

SEE ALSO

See "Stylizing Text with WordArt" on page 108 for information on using the Edit WordArt Text dialog box.

Edit Text...

SEE ALSO

See "Formatting Text and Numbers" on page 82 for more information about formatting text in cells using the Format Cells dialog box.

Color WordArt Text

1. Click the WordArt object.

2. Click the Format WordArt button on the WordArt toolbar.

3. Click the Colors And Lines tab.

4. Click the Fill Color drop-down arrow, and then select a color or fill effect.

5. Click OK.

6. Click a blank area of the worksheet to deselect the WordArt object.

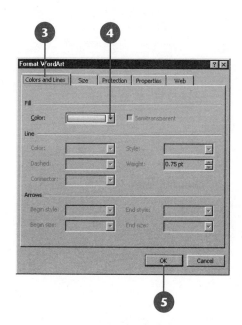

Edit or Format WordArt Text

1. Click the WordArt object.

2. Click the Edit Text button on the WordArt toolbar.

3. Click in the Text box to position the insertion point, and then edit or format the text.

4. Click OK.

5. Click a blank area of the worksheet to deselect the WordArt object.

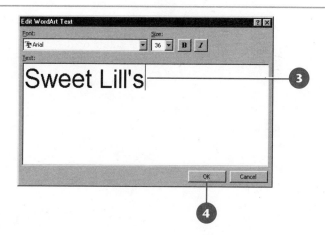

Applying WordArt Text Effects

You can apply a number of text effects to your WordArt objects to change letter heights, justification, and spacing. The effect of some of the adjustments you make will be more pronounced for certain WordArt styles than for others. Some of these effects will make the text unreadable for certain styles, so apply them carefully. Other effects—such as making uppercase and lowercase characters the same height—add an interesting dimension to the text.

WordArt Vertical Text button

Make All Letters the Same Height

1. Click the WordArt object.

2. Click the WordArt Same Letter Heights button on the WordArt toolbar.

3. Click a blank area of the worksheet to deselect the WordArt object.

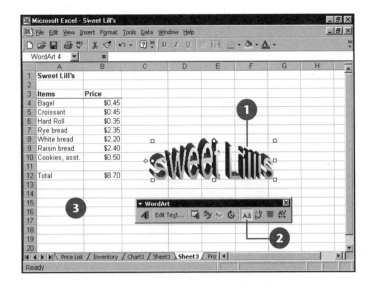

Format Text Vertically

1. Click the WordArt object.

2. Click the WordArt Vertical Text button on the WordArt toolbar.

3. Click a blank area of the worksheet to deselect the WordArt object.

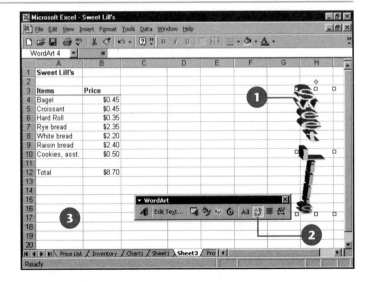

WordArt Character Spacing button

Align WordArt

1. Click the WordArt object.

2. Click the WordArt Alignment button on the WordArt toolbar.

3. Click an alignment button.

4. Click a blank area of the worksheet to deselect the WordArt object.

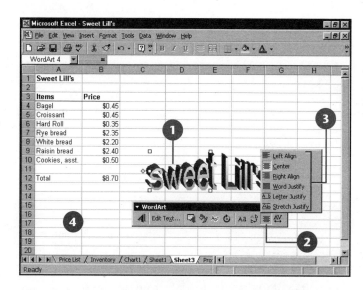

Adjust Character Spacing

1. Click the WordArt object.

2. Click the WordArt Character Spacing button on the WordArt toolbar.

3. Click a spacing setting button, or click the Custom button and type a custom percentage.

4. Click to select or clear the Kern Character Pairs option to adjust the space between characters.

5. Click a blank area of the worksheet to deselect the WordArt object.

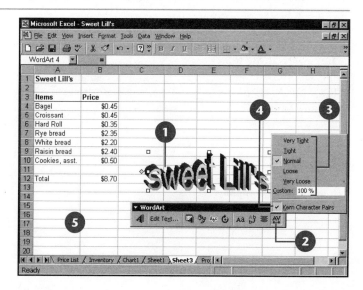

Inserting an Organization Chart

An *organization chart*, also known as an *org chart*, shows the personnel structure in an organization. You can include an organization chart on a worksheet using Microsoft Organization Chart. *Microsoft Organization Chart* provides chart structures; all you have to do is type names in the appropriate places. Each chart box is identified by its position in the chart. Managers, for example, are at the top, while subordinates are below, co-workers to the sides, and so on.

TRY THIS

Create an organizational chart for your company. *Experiment with various subordinate and co-worker positions in the hierarchy.*

Create an Organization Chart

1. Click the Insert menu, click Picture, and then click Organization Chart.

2. Click an org chart box, and then type replacement text.

3. To add subordinates or co-workers, click the appropriate toolbar button, and then click the box which contains the individual to whom the subordinate or co-worker reports.

4. To change groups of employees, click Styles, and then make a selection.

5. Click the File menu, and then click Exit And Return To [File Name] to return to your worksheet.

6. Click Yes to update the worksheet.

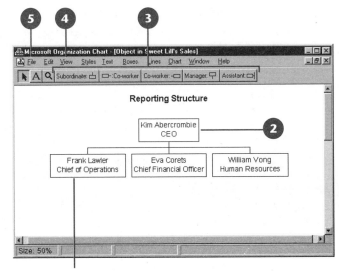

Each chart box represents one person or group in your company's structure. You can type up to four lines of information.

7

SEE ALSO

See "Modifying an Organization Chart" on page 116 for information about changing an organization chart.

TIP

Change presets for new charts. *Click the Edit menu, click Options, select the option you want for new charts, and then click OK.*

TIP

Get more help for Organization Chart. *Open or create an organization chart. Click the Help menu, and then click Index.*

Type Text in a Chart Box

1   Click a chart box in which you want to type text. (After you start Microsoft Organization Chart, the first chart box is selected for you, and you can just start typing.)

2   Type a person's name, and then press Enter.

3   Type a person's title, and then press Enter.

4   Type up to two lines of comments. If you don't want to include comments, leave the comment line placeholders blank.

5   When you are finished, click outside the chart box.

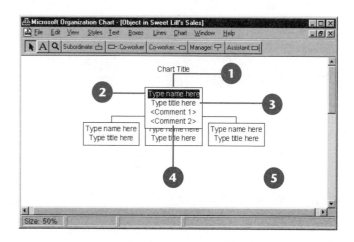

Add a Title

1   Select the sample title text *Chart Title* at the top of the organization chart.

2   Type a title you want for your org chart.

3   When you are finished, click outside the title area.

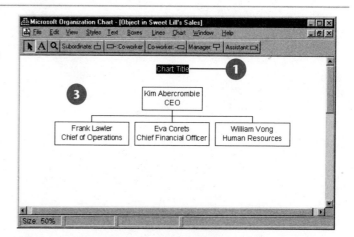

Modifying an Organization Chart

In most companies, personnel and corporate structures change often. You can modify an existing organization chart whenever changes occur at your company. These modifications are done in Microsoft Organization Chart. Chart boxes exist in relation to each other. For example, if you want to add a Subordinate chart box, you must select the chart box to which it will be attached. The buttons on the toolbar show the relationship between the different chart boxes you can add. When you add a Subordinate, it is automatically placed below the selected chart box. You can, however, display the chart box levels in a different structure, and you can customize the organization chart's appearance using the formatting options.

Add a Chart Box

1. Open Microsoft Organization Chart by double-clicking an existing organization chart.

2. On the Organizational Chart toolbar, click the chart box button that you want to add, such as Subordinate or Co-Worker.

3. Click the chart box to which you want to attach the new chart box.

4. Enter the information for the box you just added.

5. Click outside the box.

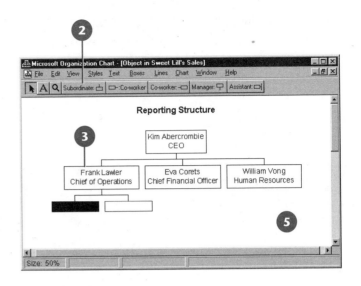

Change the Organization Chart Style

1. Select the chart box or chart boxes whose style you want to change.

2. Click the Styles menu.

3. Click the button with the organization chart style you want.

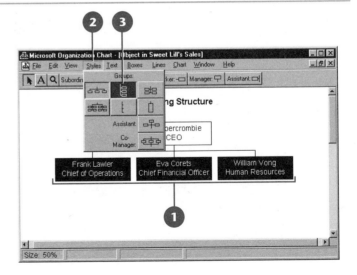

Change the hierarchical structure of an organizational chart. *Once an org chart is complete, move position boxes to best describe working relationships.*

Change chart line thickness, style, or color. *Select the chart line you want to change, click the Lines menu, point to Thickness or Style, and then click the line thickness or style you want, or click Color, click the color you want, and then click OK.*

Change chart box color, shadow, or border. *Select the chart box you want to change, click the Boxes menu, point to Shadow, Border Style, or Border Line Style, and then click the line shadow or style you want, or click Color or Border Color, click the color you want, and then click OK.*

Rearrange a Chart Box

1 Make sure the chart box you want to move is deselected.

2 Drag the chart box over an existing chart box. The pointer changes to a four-headed arrow.

3 Continue to drag the chart box in the direction you want, and notice that the pointer changes.

- ◆ A left arrow appears when you drag over the left side of a box.

- ◆ A right arrow appears when you drag over the right side of a box.

- ◆ A double-headed arrow and a small chart box appear when you drag over the bottom of a box.

4 Release the mouse button when the chart box is in the correct position.

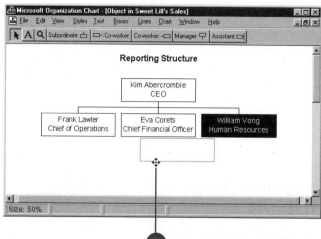

2 This pointer appears when you move the chart box below the selected chart box.

Creating and Reading a Cell Comment

Any cell on a worksheet can contain a *comment*—information you might want to share with co-workers or include as a reminder to yourself without making it a part of the worksheet. (Think of a comment as a nonprinting sticky note attached to an individual cell.) A cell containing a comment displays a red triangle in the upper-right corner of the cell. By default, comments are hidden and are displayed only when the mouse pointer is held over the red triangle.

TIP

Add and modify comments using the Reviewing toolbar. *Right-click any toolbar, and click Reviewing to display the toolbar. Position the mouse pointer over a button to display its function.*

Add a Comment

1. Click the cell to which you want to add a comment.

2. Click the Insert menu, and then click Comments.

3. Type the comment in the comment box.

4. Click outside the comment box when you are finished, or press Esc twice to close the comment box.

A red triangle indicates there's a comment in a cell.

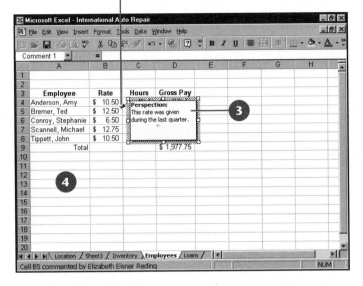

Read a Comment

1. Position the mouse pointer over a red triangle in a cell to read its comment.

2. Move the mouse pointer off the cell to hide the comment.

   To show all the comments on the worksheet, click the View menu, and then click Comments. The Reviewing toolbar appears with the Show All Comments button selected.

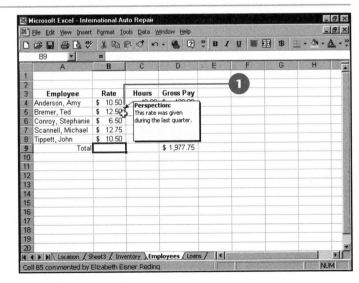

Editing and Deleting a Cell Comment

You can edit, delete, and even format cell comments just as you do other text on a worksheet. If you are working with others online, they may want to delete a comment after reading it. You might want to format certain comments to add emphasis.

Edit a Comment

1. Right-click the cell containing the comment.

2. Click Edit Comment on the shortcut menu.

3. Make your changes using common editing tools, such as the Backspace and Delete keys, as well as the Formatting toolbar buttons.

4. Press Esc twice to close the comment box.

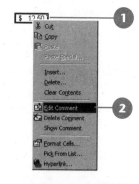

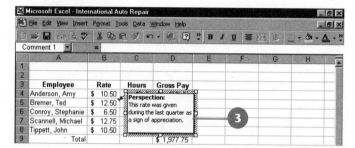

Delete a Comment

1. Right-click the cell containing the comment you want to delete.

2. Click Delete Comment.

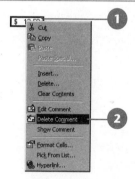

Modifying Graphic Images

If you have inserted a picture, you can crop or cut out portions of the image by using the Crop tool on the Picture toolbar. To further modify an image, you can change its color to default colors (automatic), grayscale, black and white, or watermark.

TIP

Change an image's brightness and contrast. *Select the image, and then click the More Brightness or Less Brightness button on the Picture toolbar, or click the More Contrast or Less Contrast button to achieve the desired effect.*

TIP

Set an image color to transparent. *Select the image, and click the Set Transparent Color button on the Picture toolbar.*

Crop an Image

1. Click the image you want to crop.

2. Click the Crop button on the Picture toolbar.

3. Drag the sizing handles until the borders surround the area you want to crop.

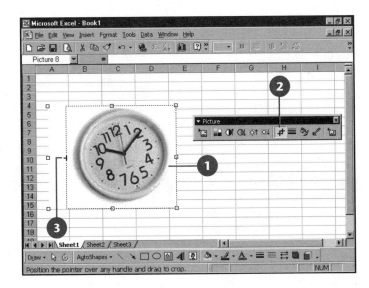

Choose a Color Type

1. Click the image whose color you want to change.

2. Click the Image Control button on the Picture toolbar.

3. Click one of the Image Control options.

   ◆ Automatic (default coloring)

   ◆ Grayscale (whites, blacks, and grays)

   ◆ Black & White

   ◆ Watermark (whites and very light colors)

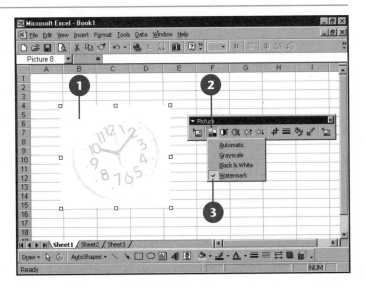

Drawing and Modifying Objects

IN THIS SECTION

Drawing Lines and Arrows

Drawing AutoShapes

New2000 **Inserting AutoShapes from the Clip Gallery**

Drawing a Freeform Object

Editing a Freeform Object

Moving and Resizing an Object

Rotating and Flipping an Object

Choosing Object Colors

Adding Object Shadows

Creating a 3-D Object

Aligning and Distributing Objects

Arranging and Grouping Objects

Changing Object View Settings

When you need to create your own pictures for a spreadsheet, Microsoft Excel 2000 is all you need to get the job done. You can choose from a set of predesigned shapes, or you can use tools that allow you to draw and edit your own shapes and forms. Excel's drawing tools help you control how objects are drawn and placed on your worksheet in relation to one another, so you can combine several simple drawings to create a sophisticated effect.

Drawing Objects

Drawing objects can be classified into three categories: lines, AutoShapes, and freeforms. *Lines* are simply the straight or curved lines (arcs) that connect two points. *AutoShapes* are preset objects, such as stars, circles, or ovals. A *freeform* is an irregular curve or polygon that you can create as a freehand drawing. To create a shape not included with the list of AutoShapes, you create it as a freeform.

Once you have created a drawing object, you can manipulate it in many ways, such as rotating it, coloring it, or changing its style. Excel also provides formatting commands that allow you more precise control over all aspects of your drawing object's appearance.

Drawing Lines and Arrows

The most basic drawing objects you create on your worksheets are lines and arrows. Excel includes several tools for this purpose. The Line tool creates line segments. The Drawing toolbar's Line Style and Dash Style tools let you determine the type of line used in any drawing object—solid, dashed, or a combination of solid and dashed lines. The Arrow tool lets you create arrows to emphasize key features of your worksheet.

TIP

Display the Drawing toolbar. *If the Drawing toolbar is not visible, click the View menu, point to Toolbars, and then click Drawing.*

SEE ALSO

See "Working with Menus and Toolbars" on page 14 for information on displaying and hiding a toolbar.

Draw a Straight Line

1. Click the Line button on the Drawing toolbar.

2. Drag the pointer to draw a line on your worksheet.

3. Release the mouse button when the line is the length you want.

The endpoints of the line are where you started and finished dragging.

Edit a Line

1. Click the line you want to edit.

2. Click the Line Style button on the Drawing toolbar to select a line thickness.

3. Click the Dash Style button on the Drawing toolbar to select a dash style.

4. Click the Line Color button on the Drawing toolbar to select a line color.

5. Drag the sizing handle at either end to a new location to change the size or angle of the line.

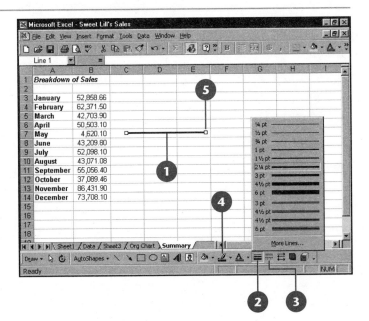

TIP

Use the keyboard as you draw your arrow. *Press and hold the Shift key as you drag the pointer to constrain the angle of the line to 15-degree increments. Press and hold the Ctrl key as you drag the pointer to draw the line from the center out, rather than from one endpoint to another.*

SEE ALSO

See "Drawing AutoShapes" on page 124 for information on using the AutoShape menu to create block arrows.

SEE ALSO

See "Customizing a Toolbar" on page 196 for information on adding and removing toolbar buttons.

Draw an Arrow

1. Click the Arrow button on the Drawing toolbar.

2. Drag the pointer from the base of the arrow to the arrow's point.

3. Release the mouse button when the arrow is the length and angle you want.

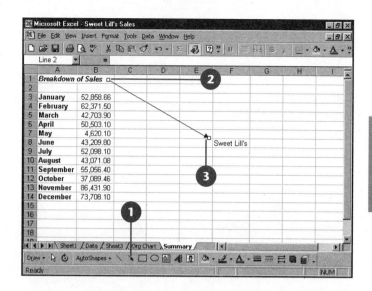

Edit an Arrow

1. Click the arrow you want to edit.

2. Click the Arrow Style button on the Drawing toolbar.

3. Click the arrow type you want to use, or click More Arrows.

4. If you clicked More Arrows, modify the arrow type in the Format AutoShape dialog box as necessary, and then click OK when you're done.

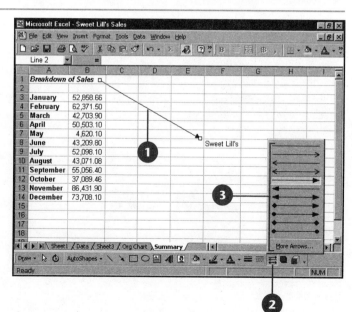

8

Drawing AutoShapes

You can choose from many different AutoShapes, ranging from hearts to lightening bolts, to draw on your worksheets. The two most common AutoShapes, the oval and the rectangle, are available directly on the Drawing toolbar. The rest of the AutoShapes are organized into categories that you can view and select from the AutoShapes menu on the Drawing toolbar. Once you have placed an AutoShape on a worksheet, you can resize it using the sizing handles (small white squares). Many AutoShapes have an *adjustment handle*, a small yellow diamond located near a resize handle, which you can drag to alter the shape of the AutoShape.

TIP

Draw a circle or square. *To draw a perfect circle or square, click the Oval or Rectangle button on the Drawing toolbar, and then press and hold the Shift key as you drag the shape.*

Draw an Oval or Rectangle

1. Click the Oval or Rectangle button on the Drawing toolbar.

2. Drag over the worksheet where you want to place the oval or rectangle.

3. Release the mouse button when the object is the shape you want.

    The shape you drew takes on the line color and fill color defined by the presentation's color scheme.

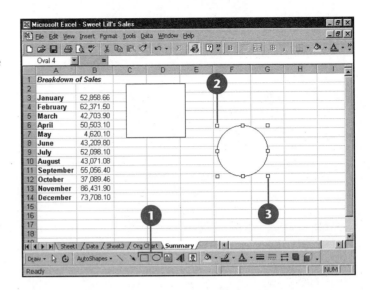

Draw an AutoShape

1. Click the AutoShapes menu on the Drawing toolbar, and then point to the AutoShape category you want to use.

2. Click the symbol you want.

3. Drag the pointer across the worksheet until the drawing object is the shape and size that you want.

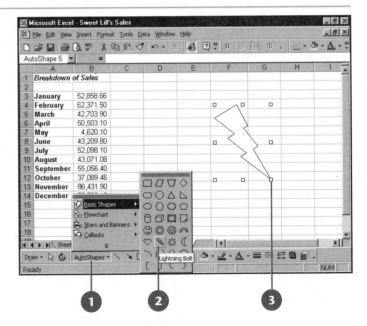

Adjust an AutoShape

1. Click the AutoShape you want to adjust.

2. Click one of the adjustment handles (yellow diamond), and then drag the handle to alter the form of the AutoShape.

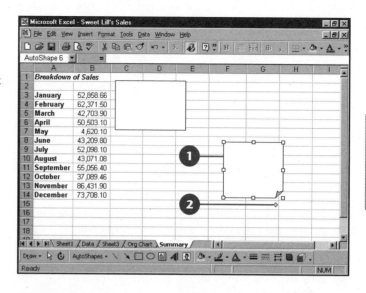

Resize an AutoShape

1. Click the AutoShape you want to resize.

2. Click one of the sizing handles (white square), and then drag the handle to change the size of the AutoShape.

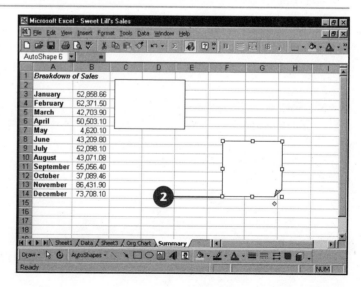

Inserting AutoShapes from the Clip Gallery

In addition to drawing AutoShapes, you can insert AutoShapes, such as computers and furniture, from the Clip Gallery. These AutoShapes are called *clips*. The Clip Gallery gives you a minature of each clip. You can drag the clip onto your worksheet or click the clip to select other options, such as previewing the clip or searching for similar clips.

Insert an AutoShape from the Clip Gallery

1. Click the AutoShapes menu on the Drawing toolbar, and then click More AutoShapes.

2. If necessary, click the down scroll arrow to display more AutoShapes.

3. Drag the shape you want onto your worksheet.

4. When you're done, click the Close button.

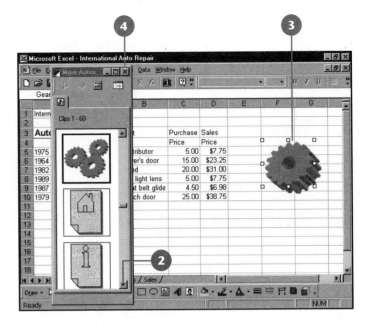

SEE ALSO

See "Inserting Pictures" on page 104 for information on inserting clip art from the Clip Gallery.

TIP

Import pictures into the Clip Gallery. *Click the Insert menu, point to Pictures, click Clip Art, click the Import Clips button on the toolbar, select the picture file you want to insert, select an import option, and then click Import.*

Find Similar AutoShapes in the Clip Gallery

1. Click the AutoShapes menu on the Drawing toolbar, and then click More AutoShapes.

2. Click the AutoShape similar to the one you want to find. Click the down scroll arrow to display more AutoShapes.

3. Click the Find Similar Clips button.

4. Click Artistic Style or Color & Shape.

5. Click one of the keywords to search for a similar clip.

   The Clip Gallery finds the clips you asked for.

6. If necessary, click the All Categories button to display all the clips in the Clip Gallery again.

7. When you're finished, click the Close button.

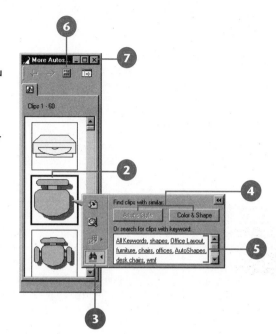

Drawing a Freeform Object

When you need to create a customized shape, you use the Freeform tools. They are all located in the Lines category in the list of AutoShapes. *Freeforms* are like the drawings you make yourself with a pen and paper, except that you have more control over the accuracy and length of the lines you draw. A freeform can either be an open curve or a closed curve. A freeform shape can be used to call attention to a specific area within a worksheet or can be used in a company logo or other unique graphic.

Freeform button

Draw an Irregular Polygon

1 Click the AutoShapes menu on the Drawing toolbar, and then point to Lines.

2 Click the Freeform button.

3 Click the location on the worksheet where you want to place the first vertex of the polygon.

4 Move the pointer to second point of your polygon, and then click the left mouse button. A line joins the two points.

5 Continue moving and clicking the mouse pointer to create additional sides of your polygon.

6 To close the polygon, click near the starting point.

Draw an Irregular Curve

1 Click the AutoShapes menu on the Drawing toolbar, and then point to Lines.

2 Click the Curve button.

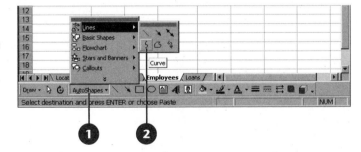

TIP

Switch between a closed curve and an open curve.

Right-click the freeform drawing. To switch from an open curve to a closed curve, click Close Curve on the shortcut menu, or to switch from a closed curve to an open curve, click Open Curve.

SEE ALSO

See "Editing a Freeform Object" on page 130 for information on vertices.

Scribble button

3 Click the location on the worksheet where you want to place the curve's starting point.

4 Move the pointer to the location where you want your irregular curve to bend and then click. Repeat this step as often as you need to create bends in your curve.

5 Finish the curve.

◆ For a closed curve, click near the starting point.

◆ For an open curve, double-click the last point in the curve.

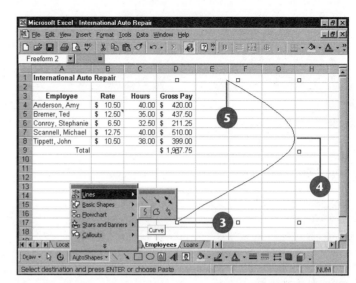

Scribble

1 Click the AutoShapes menu on the Drawing toolbar, and then point to Lines.

2 Click the Scribble button.

3 Drag the pointer across the screen to draw freehand.

4 Release the mouse button when you're done scribbling.

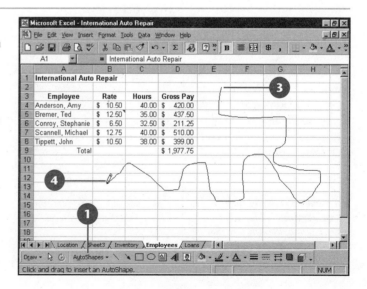

Editing a Freeform Object

Editing a freeform involves altering the vertices that create the shape using the Edit Points command. Each *vertex* (a corner in an irregular polygon or a bend in a curve) has two attributes: its position and the angle at which the curve enters and leaves it. You can move the position of each vertex and also control the corner or bend of a freeform shape. In addition, you can add or delete vertices. When you delete a vertex, Excel recalculates the freeform and smooths it among the remaining points. Similarly, if you add a new vertex, Excel adds a corner or bend in the freeform.

TIP

Edit vertices. *When you edit a freeform object, the selection handles change to small black squares.*

Move a Vertex in a Freeform

1. Click the freeform object.

2. Click the Draw menu on the Drawing toolbar, and then click Edit Points.

3. Drag one of the vertices to a new location.

4. Click outside the freeform when you are finished.

Insert a Freeform Vertex

1. Click the freeform object.

2. Click the Draw menu on the Drawing toolbar, and then click Edit Points.

3. Position the pointer on the curve or polygon border (not on a vertex), and then drag in the direction you want the new vertex.

4. Click outside the freeform to set the new shape.

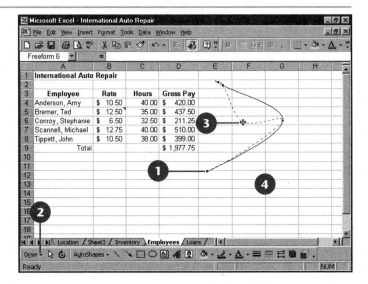

Delete a Freeform Vertex

1. Click the freeform object.

2. Click the Draw menu on the Drawing toolbar, and then click Edit Points.

3. Press the Ctrl key while clicking the vertex you want to delete.

4. Click outside the freeform to set the shape of the freeform.

Modify a Vertex Angle

1. Click the freeform object.

2. Click the Draw menu on the Drawing toolbar, and then click Edit Points.

3. Right-click a vertex, and then click Smooth Point, Straight Point, or Corner Point. Angle handles appear.

4. Drag one of the angle handles to modify the shape of the line segment going in and out of the vertex.

5. Click outside the freeform to set its shape.

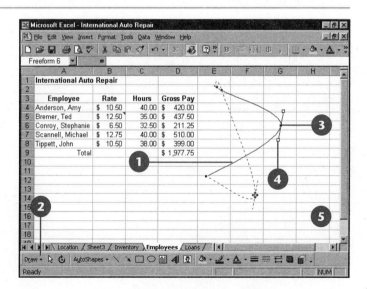

Moving and Resizing an Object

After you create a drawing object, you might need to change its size or move it to a different worksheet location. Although you can move and resize objects using the mouse, if you want more precise control over the object's size and position, use the AutoShape command on the Format menu to exactly specify the location and size of the drawing object. You can use the Nudge command to move drawing objects in tiny increments, up, down, left, or right.

Move an Object

1. Position the pointer over the object you want to move. (The pointer changes to a four-headed arrow.)

2. Drag the object to a new location on the worksheet. Make sure you aren't dragging a sizing handle or adjustment handle.

   If you are working with a freeform and you are in Edit Points mode, drag the interior of the object, not the border, or you will end up resizing or reshaping the object, not moving it.

Nudge an Object

1. Click the object you want to nudge.

2. Click the Draw menu on the Drawing toolbar, point to Nudge, and then click Up, Down, Left, or Right.

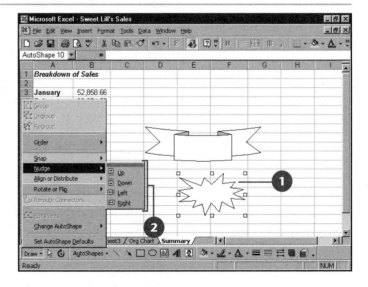

SEE ALSO

See "Moving and Resizing a Chart" on page 155 for more information on moving and resizing an object.

TIP

Display the Drawing toolbar. *If the Drawing toolbar is not visible, click the View menu, point to Toolbars, and then click Drawing.*

TIP

Retain the proportions of the object you're resizing. *Press and hold the Shift key as you drag the object to the new size.*

Resize a Drawing Object with the Mouse

1. Click the object to be resized.

2. Drag one of the sizing handles.

   ◆ To resize the object in the vertical or horizontal direction, drag a sizing handle on the side of the selection box.

   ◆ To resize the object in both the vertical and horizontal directions, drag a sizing handle on the corner of the selection box.

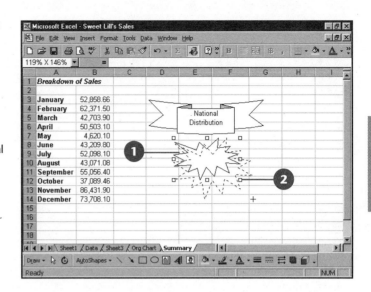

Resize an Object Precisely

1. Click the object to be resized.

2. Click the Format menu, and then click AutoShape.

3. Click the Scale Height and Width up or down arrows to resize the object.

4. Click OK.

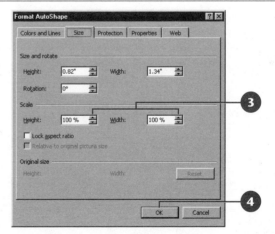

Rotating and Flipping an Object

You can change the orientation of a drawing object by rotating or flipping it. For example, if you want to create a mirror image of your object, you can flip it. To turn an object on its side, you can rotate it 90 degrees. Rotating and flipping tools work with drawing and text objects. You won't usually be able to rotate or flip objects such as charts and pictures.

TIP

Rotate an object 90 degrees. *To rotate an object 90 degrees to the left, click Rotate Left. To rotate an object 90 degrees to the right, click Rotate Right.*

TRY THIS

Fine-tune an object. *Once you've created an object, try rotating or flipping it to give it just the right look.*

Rotate an Object to Any Angle

1 Click the object you want to rotate.

2 Click the Free Rotate button on the Drawing toolbar.

3 Drag a rotation handle to rotate the object.

4 Click outside the object to set the rotation.

Rotate or Flip a Drawing Using Preset Increments

1 Click the object you want to rotate.

2 Click the Draw menu on the Drawing toolbar.

3 Point to Rotate Or Flip, and then click one of the Rotate or Flip commands.

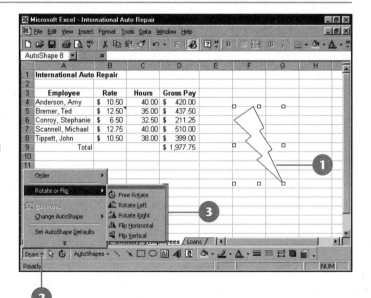

Constrain the rotation to 15 degree increments. *Press and hold the Shift key when rotating the object.*

Free Rotate button

Rotate a Drawing Object Around a Fixed Point

1. Click the object you want to rotate.

2. Click the Free Rotate button on the Drawing toolbar.

3. Click the rotate handle opposite the point you want to rotate, and then press and hold the Ctrl key as you rotate the object.

4. Click outside the object to set the rotation

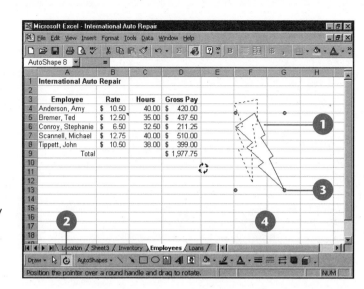

Rotate a Drawing Precisely

1. Click the object you want to rotate.

2. Click the Format menu, and then click AutoShape.

3. Click the Size tab.

4. Enter the angle of rotation.

5. Click OK.

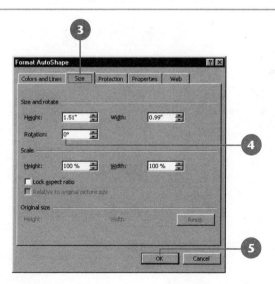

Choosing Object Colors

When you create a closed drawing object, you can choose the fill color and the line color. When you create a drawing object, it uses a default color. You can change the fill and line color settings for drawing objects using the same color tools you use to change a text color. You can use fill effects as well, including gradients, patterns, and even clip art pictures.

TIP

Set the color and line style for an object as the default for future drawing objects. *Right-click the object, and then click Set Object Defaults on the shortcut menu. Any new objects you create will use the same styles.*

Change a Drawing Object's Fill Color

1. Click the object whose fill color you want to change.

2. Click the Fill Color button drop-down arrow on the Drawing toolbar.

3. Select the fill color or fill effect you want.

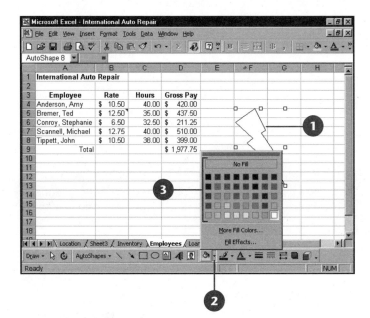

Change Colors and Lines in the Format AutoShape Dialog Box

1. Click the object you want to modify.

2. Click the Format menu, and then click AutoShape.

3. Click the Colors And Lines tab.

4. Set fill, line, and arrow format options.

5. Click OK.

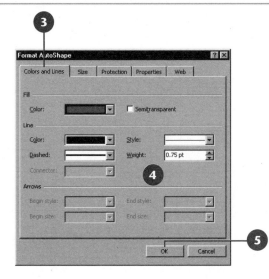

SEE ALSO

See "Changing Data Color" on page 91 for information on selecting colors.

SEE ALSO

See "Adding Color and Patterns to Cells" on page 92 for information on using fill colors and patterns.

TRY THIS

Create a logo using drawing tools. *Once the object is created, modify the fill color and line color, and you'll have a truly unique object.*

Create a Line Pattern

1 Click the object you want to modify.

2 Click the Format menu, and then click AutoShape.

3 Click the Color drop-down arrow, and then select Patterned Lines.

4 Click the Foreground drop-down arrow, and then select the color you want as a foreground.

5 Click the Background drop-down arrow, and then select the color you want as a background.

6 Click the pattern you want in the Pattern grid.

7 Click OK.

8 Click OK.

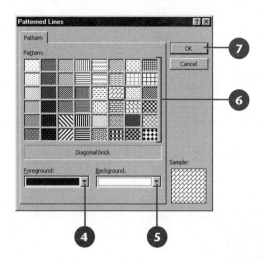

Adding Object Shadows

You can give objects on your worksheet the illusion of depth by adding shadows. Excel provides several preset shadowing options, or you can create your own by specifying the location and color of the shadow. If the shadow is falling on another object in your worksheet, you can create a semitransparent shadow that blends the color of the shadow with the color of the object underneath it.

Shadow button

TRY THIS

Change the mood of an object. *Once an object is formatted, you can give it a different character by adding a darker or lighter shadow.*

Use a Preset Shadow

1 Click the object to which you want to add a preset shadow.

2 Click the Shadow button on the Drawing toolbar.

3 Click one of the 20 preset shadow styles.

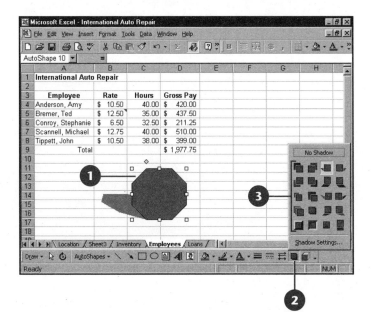

Change the Location of a Shadow

1 Click the object that has the shadow you want to change.

2 Click the Shadow button on the Drawing toolbar, and then click Shadow Settings.

3 Click an effects button on the Shadow Settings toolbar.

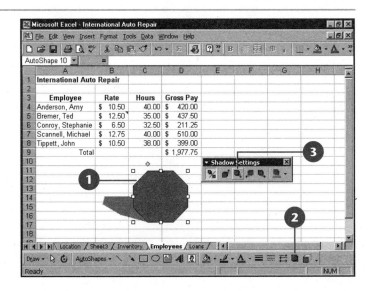

SEE ALSO

See "Adding Borders to Cells" on page 94 for information on adding and formatting borders to cells.

TIP

Nudge a shadow up, down, right, or left. *Click the Shadow button on the Drawing toolbar, and then click Shadow Settings. Click one of the Nudge buttons on the Shadow Settings toolbar.*

TIP

Turn a shadow on and off. *Click the Shadow button on the Drawing toolbar, and then click Shadow Settings. Click the Shadow On/Off button on the Shadow Settings toolbar.*

Change the Color of a Shadow

1. Click the object that has the shadow you want to change.

2. Click the Shadow button on the Drawing toolbar, and then click Shadow Settings.

3. Click the Shadow Color button drop-down arrow on the Shadow Settings toolbar, and then click a new color.

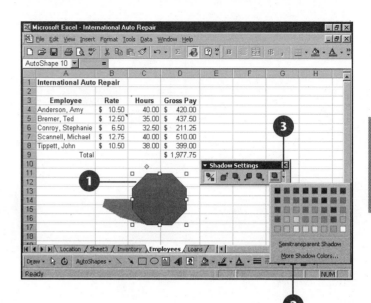

Creating a 3-D Object

You can add the illusion of depth to your worksheets by giving your drawings a three-dimensional appearance using the 3-D tool. Although not all objects can be turned into 3-D objects, most AutoShapes can. You can create a 3-D effect using one of the 20 preset 3-D styles, or you can use the 3-D tools to customize your own 3-D style. You can control several elements using the customization tools, including the angle at which the 3-D object is tilted and rotated, the depth of the object, and the direction of light falling upon the object.

3-D Button

Apply a Preset 3-D Style

1. Click the object you want to apply a preset 3-D style.

2. Click the 3-D button on the Drawing toolbar.

3. Click one of the 20 preset 3-D styles.

Spin a 3-D Object

1. Click the 3-D object you want to spin.

2. Click the 3-D button on the Drawing toolbar, and then click 3-D Settings.

3. Click the spin setting you want.

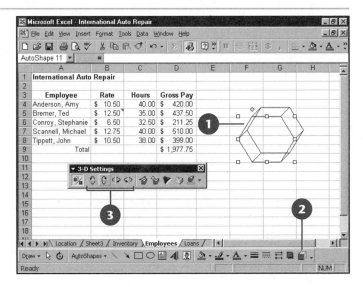

TIP

There are restrictions on use of shadows and 3-D effects. *You cannot use both drop shadows and 3-D effects on the same object.*

TIP

Set surface for a 3-D object. *On the 3-D Settings toolbar, click the Surface button, and then click the surface (Wire Frame, Matte, Plastic, or Metal) you want.*

TIP

Set direction for a 3-D object. *On the 3-D Settings toolbar, click the Directions button, and then click the direction you want. You can also change the direction to show the object with a perspective or parallel point of view.*

Set Lighting for a 3-D Object

1. Click the 3-D object.

2. Click the 3-D button on the Drawing toolbar, and then click 3-D Settings.

3. Click the Lighting button.

4. Click the spotlight that creates the effect you want.

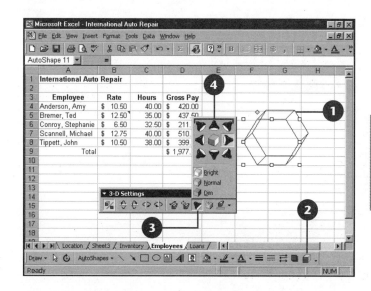

Set Depth for a 3-D Object

1. Click the 3-D object.

2. Click the 3-D button on the Drawing toolbar, and then click 3-D Settings.

3. Click the Depth button.

4. Click the size of the depth in points, or enter the exact number of points you want in the Custom box.

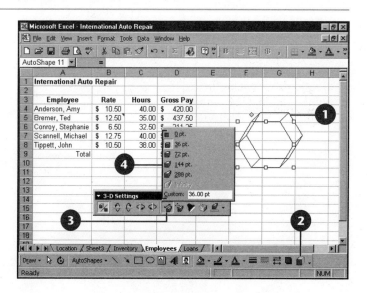

8

Aligning and Distributing Objects

Often when you work with three similar or identical objects, they look best when aligned in relation to each other. For example, you can align three objects so the tops of all three objects match along an invisible line. Sometimes your task will not be alignment but distributing objects evenly across a space. Excel includes commands to distribute your items horizontally and vertically. You can specify whether you want the distribution to occur in the currently occupied space or across the entire worksheet.

TIP

Open the Drawing toolbar.
If the Drawing toolbar is not open, click the View menu, point to Toolbars, and then click Drawing.

Align Objects

1. Press Shift while you click to select the objects that you want to align.

2. Click the Draw menu on the Drawing toolbar, and then point to Align Or Distribute.

3. Click the alignment option you want.

   ◆ Align Left lines up the left edges of the selected objects.

   ◆ Align Center lines up the centers of the selected objects.

   ◆ Align Right lines up the right edges of the selected objects.

   ◆ Align Top lines up the top edges of the selected objects.

   ◆ Align Middle lines up horizontally the middles of the selected objects.

   ◆ Align Bottom lines up the bottom edges of the selected objects.

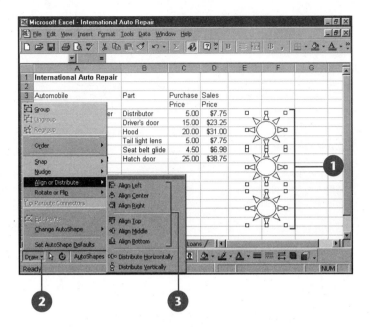

SEE ALSO

See "Moving and Resizing an Object" on page 132 for information on moving and resizing distributed objects.

TRY THIS

Line up multiple objects. *Without alignment, objects look haphazard and sloppy. It's almost impossible to visibly align multiple objects with any accuracy, so make use of this feature. See how easy it is to align multiple objects in a variety of ways.*

TIP

Snap an object to a shape or grid. *When you drag an object, you can have Excel snap the object you're dragging to another object or an invisible grid on the worksheet. Click the Draw menu on the Drawing toolbar, point to Snap, and then click To Grid or To Shape.*

Distribute Objects

1 Press Shift while you click to select the objects that you want to distribute.

2 Click the Draw menu on the Drawing toolbar, and then point to Align Or Distribute.

3 Click the distribution option you want.

◆ Distribute Horizontally distributes the objects evenly horizontally.

◆ Distribute Vertically distributes the objects evenly vertically.

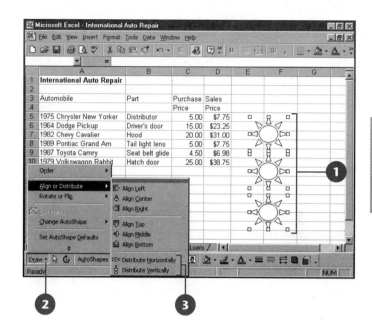

Arranging and Grouping Objects

When a worksheet contains multiple objects, you might need to consider how they interact with each other. If the objects overlap, the most recently created drawing will be placed on top of older drawings, but you can change how the stack of objects is ordered. If you have created a collection of objects that work together, you might want to group them to create a new drawing object that you can move, resize, or copy as a single unit.

TRY THIS

Arrange and group objects. *Create multiple objects using drawing tools. Several objects—such as shapes used to create a logo—can be moved or manipulated more easily if they are grouped. Once the objects are created, change their order and grouping.*

Arrange a Stack of Objects

1. Click the drawing object you want to place.

2. Click the Draw menu on the Drawing toolbar, and then point to Order.

3. Click the stacking option you want.

   ◆ Click Bring To Front or Send To Back to move the drawing to the top or bottom of the stack.

   ◆ Click Bring Forward or Bring Backward to move a drawing up or back one location in the stack.

Group Objects Together

1. Press Shift while you click to select the drawing objects you want to group together.

2. Click the Draw menu on the Drawing toolbar.

3. Click Group.

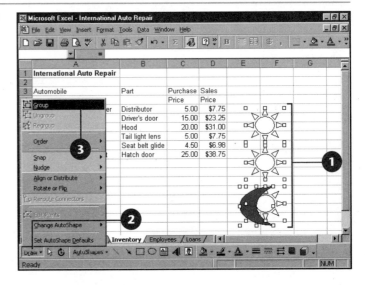

SEE ALSO

See "Moving and Resizing an Object" on page 132 for information on moving and resizing grouped objects.

TIP

Align objects before grouping them. *Align objects before you group them for the best visual effect.*

SEE ALSO

See "Aligning and Distributing Objects" on page 142 for more information on aligning objects.

Ungroup a Drawing

1. Select the object you want to ungroup.

2. Click the Draw menu on the Drawing toolbar.

3. Click Ungroup.

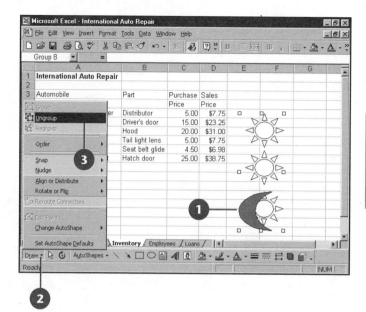

Regroup a Drawing

1. Click one or more of the objects in the original group.

2. Click the Draw menu on the Drawing toolbar.

3. Click Regroup.

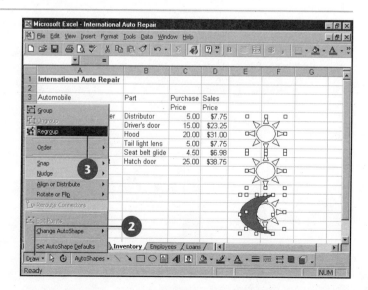

Changing Object View Settings

After drawing or inserting different types of objects on your worksheet, you might find it difficult to work with the information on the worksheet. You can change view settings in Excel to show or hide objects on your worksheets. You can also show objects as placeholders. A *placeholder* is an empty box that takes the place of the object.

SEE ALSO

See "Customizing Your Excel Environment" on page 190 for information on changing other Excel options.

Change View Settings for Objects

1 Click the Tools menu, and then click Options.

2 Click the View tab.

3 In the Objects area, click the view setting options you want.

4 Click OK.

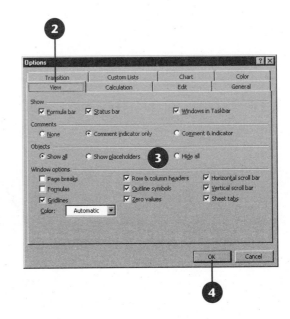

Creating Charts and Maps

IN THIS SECTION

Understanding Chart Terminology

Choosing the Right Type of Chart

New2000 **Creating a Chart**

Editing a Chart

Selecting a Chart

Changing a Chart Type

Moving and Resizing a Chart

Pulling Out a Pie Slice

Adding and Deleting a Data Series

Enhancing a Data Series

Enhancing a Chart

Drawing on a Chart

Formatting Chart Elements

Creating a Map

Modifying a Map

When you're ready to share data with others, a worksheet might not be the most effective way to present the information. A page full of numbers, even if formatted attractively, can be hard to understand and perhaps a little boring. To help you present information more effectively, Microsoft Excel 2000 makes it easy to create and modify charts and maps based on worksheet data.

Creating Charts and Maps

A *chart*, also called a graph, is a visual representation of selected data in your worksheet. A well-designed chart draws the reader's attention to important data by illustrating trends and highlighting significant relationships between numbers. Excel generates charts based on data you select, and the Chart Wizard makes it easy to select the best chart type, design elements, and formatting enhancements for any type of information.

In Excel, a *map* displays data—such as population values in the United States—within a geographic area. A variety of maps are included with Excel's Microsoft Map component. This program includes the United States and other countries, so you can create maps that cover any states or countries you need.

Understanding Chart Terminology

Handles
Small black boxes that appear around the perimeter of a selected object, indicating that you can move, resize, copy, or delete the object

Title
Optional text that identifies the purpose of a chart

Data marker
A chart object, such as a circle, dot, or square, that denotes a data point

Gridlines
Vertical and horizontal guidelines that appear behind a chart to make the chart easier to read

Y-axis
The vertical axis of a chart— by default, a value axis

Legend
A key that explains the colors, patterns, or symbols in a chart

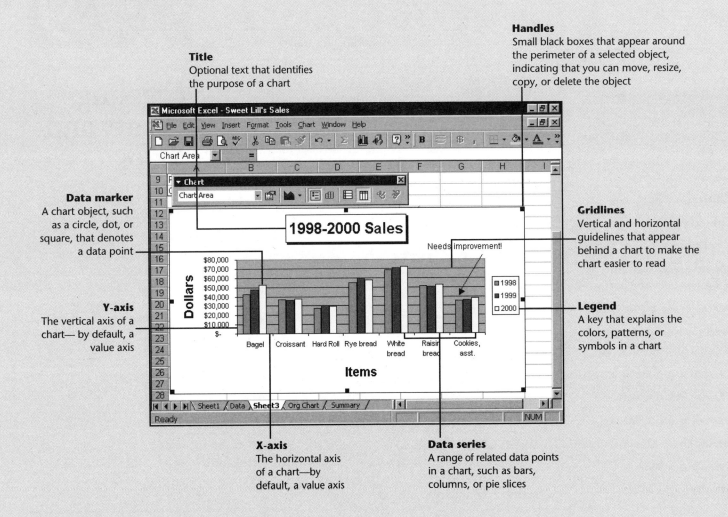

X-axis
The horizontal axis of a chart—by default, a value axis

Data series
A range of related data points in a chart, such as bars, columns, or pie slices

Choosing the Right Type of Chart

When you create a chart in Excel, you can choose from a variety of chart types. Each type interprets data in a slightly different way. For example, a pie chart is great for comparing parts of a whole, such as regional percentages of a sales total, while a column chart is better for showing how different sales regions performed throughout a year. Although there is some overlap, each chart type is best suited for conveying a different type of information.

When you generate a chart, you need to evaluate whether the chart type suits the data being plotted, and whether the formatting choices clarify or overshadow the information. Sometimes a colorful 3-D chart is just what you need to draw attention to an important shift; other times, special visual effects might be a distraction.

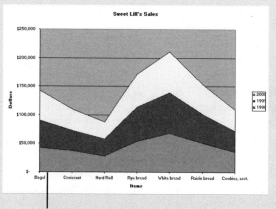

An **area chart** shows how volume changes over time.

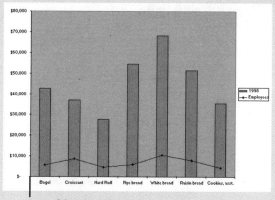

A **combination chart** contains data having different scales.

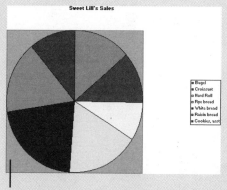

A **pie chart** compares elements of a whole unit.

Creating a Chart

You have many decisions to make when you create a chart, from choosing the chart type you want to use to choosing the objects you want to include and the formatting you want to apply. Excel simplifies the process with a feature called the Chart Wizard. The *Chart Wizard* is a series of dialog boxes that lead you through all the steps necessary to create an effective, eye-catching chart. In Excel 2000, the Chart Wizard includes additional step and 3-D combination charts and options to format data, multilevel axes, and time-scale labels. Once the chart is created, you can always go back later and make changes to it.

> **TIP**
>
> **Change your mind while working in the Chart Wizard.** *Click the Back button to move to previous dialog boxes and the Forward button to move forward again.*

Create a Chart Using the Chart Wizard

1 Select the data range you want to chart. Include the column and row labels in the data range.

The labels will be added to the chart automatically.

2 Click the Chart Wizard button on the Standard toolbar.

3 Click a chart type.

4 Click a chart sub-type.

5 If you want, click the Click And Hold To View Sample button to preview your chart as you build it.

6 Click Next to continue.

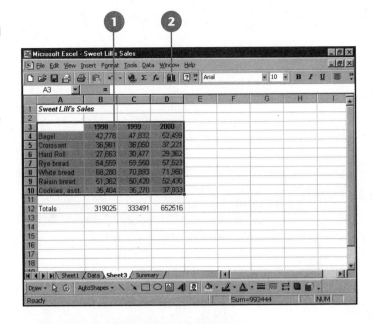

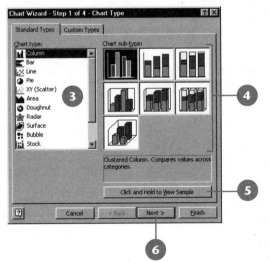

Choosing a chart type.
Learn to think like your audience. When viewing a new chart, imagine that you're seeing it for the first time. Would you grasp the important information? If not, how can you improve it?

What's an embedded chart? *If you choose to place the chart on an existing sheet rather than on a new sheet, the chart is called an* embedded object. *You can then resize or move it just as you would any graphic object.*

See "Linking and Embedding Files" on page 230 for more information on embedding a chart.

See "Moving and Resizing a Chart" on page 155 for more information on changing the location or size of a chart.

7. Make sure the correct data range is selected.

8. Select the appropriate option button to plot the data series in rows or in columns.

9. Click Next to continue.

10. Type titles in the appropriate text boxes to identify each category of data.

If you want, click any of the other tabs to make other chart option changes.

11. Click Next to continue.

12. Click an option to choose whether to place the chart on a new worksheet or on an existing worksheet.

13. Click Finish.

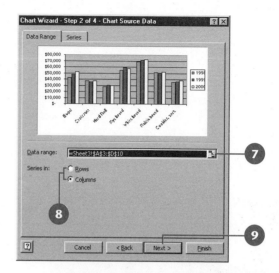

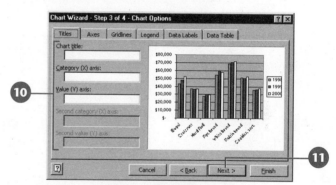

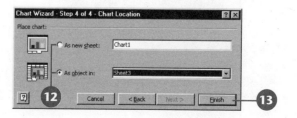

Editing a Chart

Editing a chart means altering any of its features, from data selection to formatting elements. You might want to use more effective colors or patterns in a data series, for example. To change a chart's type or any element within it, you must select the chart or element. When a chart is selected, handles are displayed around the window's perimeter, and the Chart toolbar is displayed: all buttons on this toolbar function when the chart is selected. As the figure below illustrates, you can point to any object or area on a chart to see what it is called. When you select an object, its name appears in the Chart Objects list box on the Chart toolbar, and you can then edit it.

Editing a chart has no effect on the data used to create it. You don't need to worry about updating a chart if you change worksheet data because Excel automatically does it for you. The only chart element you might need to edit is a data range. If you decide you want to plot more or less data in a range, you can select the data series on the worksheet, as shown in the figure below, and drag the outline to include the range you want in the chart.

Point to any chart object to see what type of object it is.

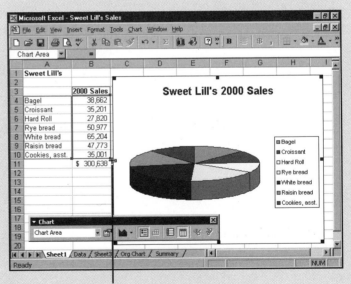

Change the plotted data by dragging the outline.

Selecting a Chart

You need to select a chart object before you can move, resize, or make formatting changes to it. When an object is selected, it is surrounded by small black squares called *handles*. You can also see which object is currently selected by clicking the Chart Objects drop-down arrow on the Chart toolbar.

TIP

Use ScreenTips to find out about an object. *If you can't remember the name of the chart object you want to format, position the mouse pointer over the object, and a ScreenTip will be displayed beneath the pointer.*

TRY THIS

Become familiar with chart objects. *Click objects within a chart to familiarize yourself with them. Read their descriptions, or click the Chart Objects drop-down arrow.*

Select and deselect a Chart Object

1 Select a chart.

The Chart toolbar appears when you select a chart.

2 Position the mouse pointer over a chart object, and then click to select it, or click the Chart Objects drop-down arrow on the Chart toolbar, and then click the name of the object you want to select.

3 Click another area of the chart or press the Esc key to deselect a chart object.

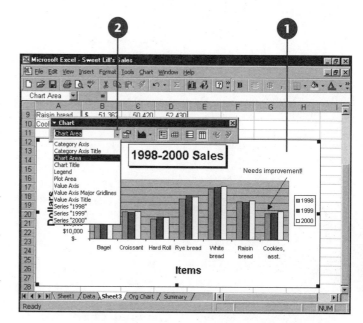

Changing a Chart Type

Excel's default chart type is the column chart, although there are many other types from which to choose. A column chart might adequately display your data, but you should experiment with a variety of chart types to find the one that shows the data in the most effective way.

Change a Chart Type Quickly

1 Select a chart whose chart type you want to change.

2 Click the Chart Type drop-down arrow on the Chart toolbar.

3 Select a chart type.

Excel automatically changes the chart type when you release the mouse button.

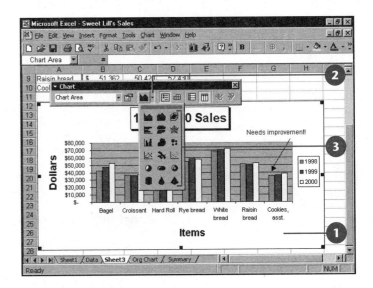

Use the Chart Wizard to change a chart type. *If you finish creating a chart and don't like the result, simply click the chart to select it, click the Chart Wizard button on the Standard toolbar, and then choose a different chart type.*

Experiment with chart types. *Once a chart is created, change its type and determine which type is the most effective.*

Change a Chart Type Using the Chart Dialog Box

1 Select a chart whose chart type you want to change.

2 Click the Chart menu, and then click Chart Type.

3 Click a new chart type.

4 Click a new chart sub-type.

5 Click the Click And Hold To View Sample button to preview your chart in its new layout.

6 Click OK.

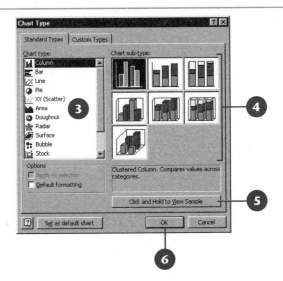

Moving and Resizing a Chart

You can move or resize an embedded chart after you select it. If you've created a chart as a new sheet instead of an embedded object on an existing worksheet, the chart's size and location are fixed by the sheet's margins. You can change the margins to resize or reposition the chart.

TIP

Avoid clicking a chart's handle. *Clicking and dragging a chart's handle resizes the chart. If you accidentally resize a chart, press Ctrl+Z to undo the change.*

SEE ALSO

See "Setting Up the Page" on page 76 for more information on adjusting margins.

Move an Embedded Chart

1 Select a chart you want to move.

2 Position the mouse pointer over a blank area of the chart, and then drag the pointer to move the outline of the chart to a new location.

3 Release the mouse button.

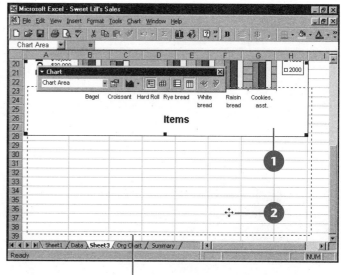

Outline indicates new position

Resize an Embedded Chart

1 Select a chart you want to resize.

2 Position the mouse pointer over one of the handles.

3 Drag the handle to the new chart size.

4 Release the mouse button.

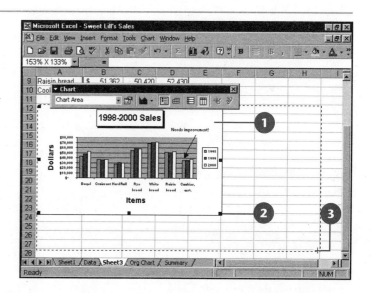

Pulling Out a Pie Slice

A pie chart is an effective and easily understood chart type for comparing parts that make up a whole entity, such as departmental percentages of a company budget. You can call attention to individual pie slices that are particularly significant by moving them away from the other pieces, or *exploding* the pie.

TIP

Select a pie slice. *Because a pie chart has only one data series, clicking any slice selects the entire data series. Click a second time to select a specific slice.*

TRY THIS

Explode a pie slice. *Create a pie chart and then pull out one or more slices. Determine whether this adds to or detracts from the chart's effectiveness.*

Explode a Single Pie Slice

1 Select a pie chart.

2 Click to select the pie slice you want to explode.

3 Drag the slice away from the pie.

4 Release the mouse button.

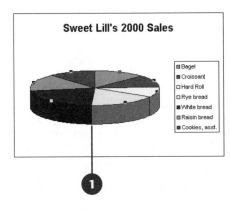

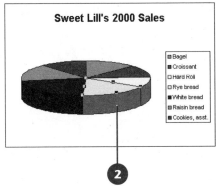

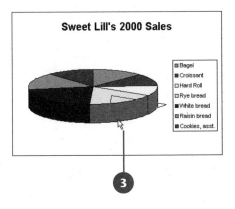

Explode an Entire Pie

1. Select a pie chart.

2. Drag a pie slice away from the center of the pie.

3. Release the mouse button.

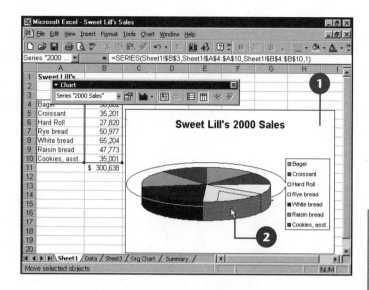

Undo a Pie Explosion

1. Select a pie chart.

2. Drag a slice towards the center of the pie.

3. Release the mouse button.

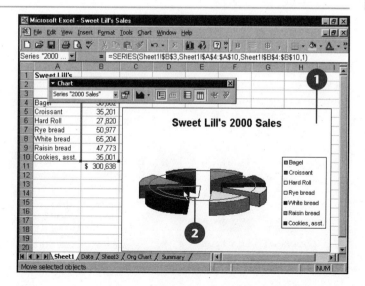

Adding and Deleting a Data Series

Many components make up a chart. Each range of data that comprises a bar, column, or pie slice is called a *data series;* each value in a data series is called a *data point.* The data series is defined when you select a range on a worksheet and then open the Chart Wizard. But what if you want to add a data series once a chart is complete? Using Excel, you can add a data series by using the mouse, the Chart menu, or the Chart Wizard. As you create and modify more charts, you might also find it necessary to delete or change the order of one or more data series. You can delete a data series without re-creating the chart.

SEE ALSO

See "Creating a Chart" on page 150 for information about using the Chart Wizard.

Add a Data Series to a Chart Quickly

1. Select the range that contains the data series you want to add to your chart.

2. Drag the range into the existing chart.

3. Release the mouse button.

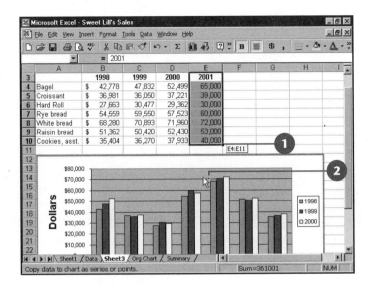

Add a Data Series Using the Add Data Dialog Box

1. Select the chart to which you want to add a data series.

2. Click the Chart menu, and then click Add Data.

3. Type the range in the Range box, or click the Collapse Dialog button and then drag the pointer over the new range you want to add. When you release the mouse button, the Add Data dialog box reappears.

4. Click OK.

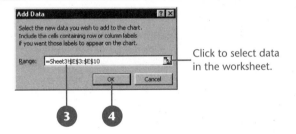

Click to select data in the worksheet.

Delete one data point in a chart. *To delete one data point but keep the rest of the series in the chart, click the data point twice so that it is the only point selected, and then press the Delete key.*

Use the Undo button to reverse a deletion. *Click the Undo button on the Standard toolbar to restore the deleted data series or data point in the chart.*

Use the Chart toolbar to select chart elements. *Select a chart element by clicking the Chart Objects drop-down arrow. Once an element is selected, double-click it to open a corresponding Format dialog box.*

Delete a Data Series

1. Select the chart that contains the data series you want to delete.

2. Click any data point in the data series.

3. Press Delete.

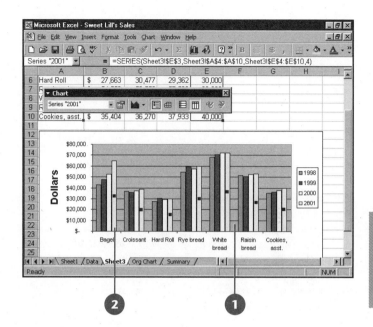

9

Change Data Series Order

1. Select the chart that contains the data series you want to delete.

2. Double-click any data point in the data series.

3. Click the Series Order tab.

4. Click the series you want to change.

5. Click Move Up or Move Down.

6. Click OK.

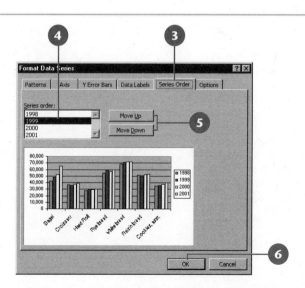

Enhancing a Data Series

When you initially use the Chart Wizard, Excel automatically decides which colors should be used to represent each data series. Sometimes these colors are not to your liking. Perhaps you want more dynamic colors—adding patterns and texture to further enhance a data series—or maybe you'll be printing your charts in black and white and you want to control the appearance of each data series. You can also insert a picture in a chart so that its image occupies a bar or column.

TIP

Format a chart object quickly. *Double-clicking an object opens a corresponding Format dialog box, which you can use to change the object's attributes. Depending on which objects are selected, your formatting options will vary.*

Change a Data Series Color or Pattern

1. Click any data point in a data series to select it.

2. Double-click a data point in the selected data series.

3. Click the Patterns tab.

4. Click a color in the Area palette. The selected color is displayed in the Sample box.

5. If you want to add effects, such as textures, patterns, gradients, or pictures, click Fill Effects.

6. Click the Gradient, Texture, or Pattern tab to change the qualities of the data series color.

7. When you're done, click OK.

8. Click OK if you're satisfied with the results shown in the Sample box.

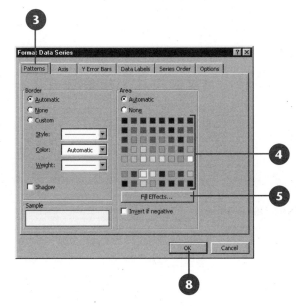

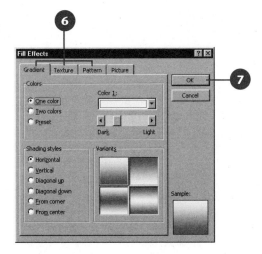

SEE ALSO

See "Editing a Chart" on page 152 for more information on modifying a chart.

SEE ALSO

See "Inserting Pictures" on page 104 for more information on inserting pictures and clip art.

TRY THIS

Incorporate a logo into a data series. *Insert a picture file of your corporate logo in a data series.*

SEE ALSO

See "Adding and Deleting a Data Series" on page 158 for more information on using data series.

Add a Picture to a Data Series

1. Select a data series.

2. Double-click a data point in the selected series.

3. Click Fill Effects.

4. Click the Picture tab.

5. Click Select Picture.

6. Locate and select the graphics file.

7. Click OK.

8. If you want the data point to contain one copy of the image stretched to fill it, click the Stretch option button; or if you want the data point to contain many copies of the image, click the Stack option button.

9. Click OK.

10. Click OK.

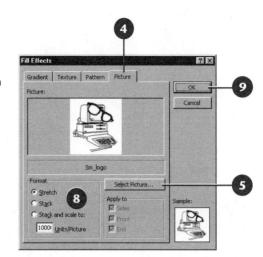

Enhancing
a Chart

Add *chart objects,* such as titles, legends, and text annotations, and *chart options* such as gridlines to a chart to enhance the appearance of the chart and increase its overall effectiveness. A *chart title* identifies the primary purpose of the chart; a title for each axis further clarifies the data that is plotted. Titles can be more than one line and can be formatted just like other worksheet text. You can also add a *text annotation,* additional text not attached to a specific axis or data point, to call attention to a trend or some other area of interest. A *legend* helps the reader connect the colors and patterns in a chart with the data they represent. *Gridlines* are horizontal and vertical lines you can add to help the reader determine data point values in a chart.

Add a Title

1. Select a chart to which you want to add a title or titles.

2. Click the Chart menu, and then click Chart Options.

3. Click the Titles tab.

4. Type the text you want for the title of the chart.

5. To add a title for the x-axis, press Tab and type the text.

6. To add a title for the y-axis, press Tab and type the text.

7. If you want a second line for the x- or y-axis, press Tab to move to the Second Category or Second Value box, and then type the title text (if available).

8. Preview the title(s) you are adding.

9. Click OK.

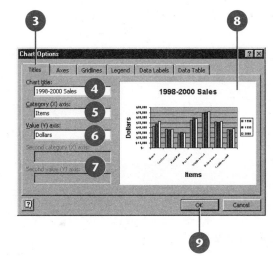

Add or Delete a Legend

1. Select the chart to which you want to add or delete a legend.

2. Click the Legend button on the Chart toolbar. You can drag the legend to move it to a new location.

Resize the text box to create a multiple-line title. *Type the title text, and then resize the text box.*

Major guidelines vs. minor gridlines. Major gridlines *occur at each value on an axis; minor gridlines occur between values on an axis. Use gridlines sparingly and only when they improve the readability of a chart.*

Add gridlines to a chart. *Experiment adding major and minor gridlines and determine which looks better and adds value to your chart. You might find minor gridlines more helpful when charting data that spans large distributions.*

Add a Text Annotation

1. Select a chart to which you want to add a text annotation.

2. Type the text for the annotation, and then press Enter. A text box containing your text appears within the chart area.

3. Position the mouse pointer over the text box until the pointer changes shape.

4. Drag the selected text box to a new location.

5. Press Esc to deselect the text box.

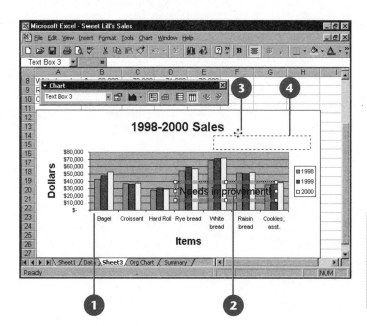

Add Gridlines

1. Select a chart to which you want to add gridlines.

2. Click the Chart menu, and then click Chart Options.

3. Click the Gridlines tab.

4. Select the type of gridlines you want for the x-axis (vertical) and y-axis (horizontal).

5. Click OK.

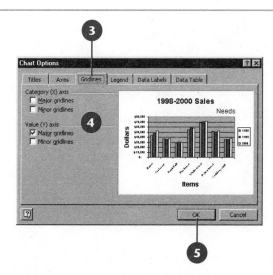

9

Drawing on a Chart

Once titles and text have been added and the chart fine-tuned, you might want to accentuate information in a chart using tools on the Drawing toolbar. For example, a drop shadow adds dimension to a chart's title; an arrow shows a connection between annotated text and specific data in your chart.

TIP

Use the Drawing toolbar to draw objects on a chart. *Click the Drawing button on the Standard toolbar to display or hide the toolbar.*

SEE ALSO

See "Drawing AutoShapes" on page 124 for more information on drawing other objects in a chart.

Add a Drop Shadow to a Text Annotation

1. Select a chart that contains a text annotation you want to enhance.

2. Select the text annotation in the chart.

3. Click the Drawing button on the Chart toolbar.

4. Click the Shadow button on the Drawing toolbar.

5. Select a shadow based on the effect you want. Experiment until you find the one you want.

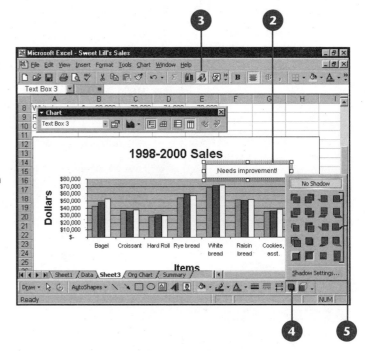

Add a Drop Shadow to a Chart Title

1. Select the chart.

2. Double-click the title.

3. Click the Patterns tab, if necessary.

4. Click to select the Shadow check box.

5. Click OK.

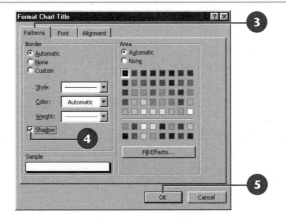

TIP

Use the Shift key to draw straight lines. *Press and hold the Shift key while you drag the pointer to create a vertical, horizontal, or diagonal arrow.*

TIP

Use the Drawing toolbar to modify the arrow object. *Click the Line Style, Dash Style, or Arrow Style button on the Drawing toolbar to modify the arrow object.*

SEE ALSO

See "Moving and Resizing a Chart" on page 155 for more information changing the location and size of a chart.

TIP

Arrow-drawing techniques. *When you draw an arrow, the arrowhead appears at the conclusion (or end) of the line.*

Draw an Arrow on a Chart

1 Select the chart.

2 If necessary, click the Drawing button on the Standard toolbar to display the Drawing toolbar.

3 Click the Arrow button on the Drawing toolbar.

4 Position the mouse pointer near the object that you want as the starting point, or base, of the arrow.

5 Click and drag the pointer from the base object to another object. The arrowhead appears at the point of the second object.

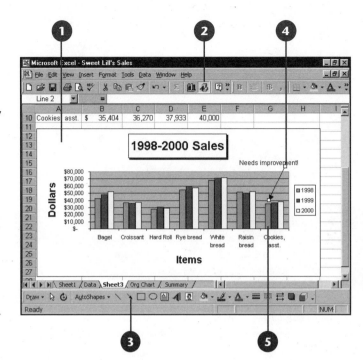

Formatting Chart Elements

Objects such as annotated text, data labels, and titles contain *chart text*. To make chart text more readable, you can change the text font, style, and size. You can also change the format of a *chart axis*. For example, if axis labels or scale are too long and unreadable, you might want to reduce the font size or change the scale to make the labels fit better in a small space.

TIP

Change chart text alignment. *Double-click the text you want to change, click the Alignment tab, change the orientation, and then click OK.*

TIP

Change chart axis patterns. *Double-click the axis you want to change, click the Patterns tab, change the line style, major or minor tick mark type, and labels, and then click OK.*

Format Chart Text

1. Select the chart that contains the text you want to change.
2. Double-click the object that contains the text. A Format dialog box opens.
3. Click the Font tab.
4. Select a font, font style, and size you want.
5. Select any combination of the Underline, Color, Background, and Effects options.
6. Click OK.

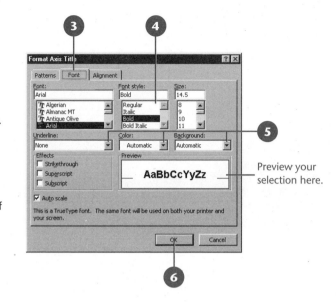

Preview your selection here.

Format a Chart Axis

1. Select the chart that contains the axis you want to change.
2. Double-click the axis you want to format. A Format dialog box opens.
3. Click the Scale tab.
4. Select the scale and display units you want.
5. To change the number format, click the Number tab, and then select the number format you want.
6. Click OK.

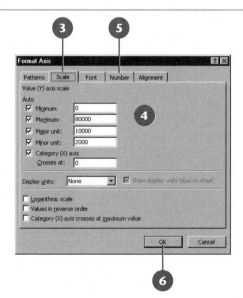

Creating a Map

Data for geographic locations can be charted using any existing chart type, but you can add real impact by using Excel's special mapping feature, *Microsoft Map*. This mapping feature analyzes and charts your data in an actual geographic map containing countries or states and helps readers understand the relationship of geographic data when viewed within a map. For example, seeing population data displayed within a map of the United States would probably have more meaning for you than to see the same information displayed in a column chart.

TIP

Install Map on the fly. *If Microsoft Map is not installed, you can install it without closing Excel. Follow the steps to create a map, and then insert the Microsoft Excel 2000 or Office 2000 CD when requested.*

Create a Geographic Map

1. Select a range that contains the geographic data you want to map.

2. Click the Insert menu, click Object, click Microsoft Map, and then click OK.

   If you have Microsoft MapPoint 2000 installed on your computer, you can click Microsoft MapPoint.

3. Click the map you want to use.

4. Click OK.

5. Press Esc to deselect the map.

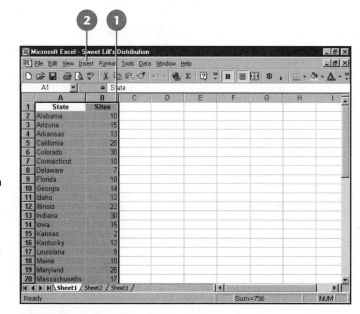

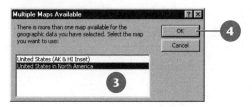

Modifying a Map

An existing geographic map can be modified to reflect updated data. You must update the geographic map when you change the data. In addition, you can change the colors and patterns used to display the data within the map.

TIP

Always refresh a map after changing worksheet data. *Unlike chart data, Excel does not automatically update map data whenever the worksheet data changes.*

SEE ALSO

See "Moving and Resizing an Object" on page 132 for more information changing the location and size of an object.

SEE ALSO

See "Creating a Map" on page 167 for information on using Microsoft Map.

Modify a Geographic Map

1. Make the necessary changes to the worksheet data that is used in your geographic map.

2. Double-click the map.

3. If necessary, click the Map Refresh button on the Microsoft Map toolbar.

4. Change data and the way it is displayed in the map using buttons on the Microsoft Map Control dialog box.

5. Press Esc to deselect the map.

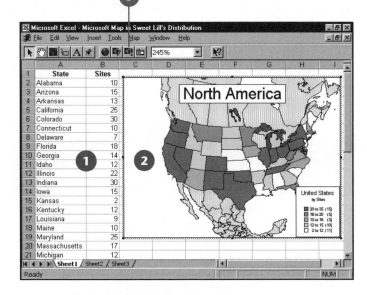

10

Analyzing Worksheet Data

IN THIS SECTION

Understanding List Terminology

Creating a List

Understanding a Data Form

Adding and Managing Records Using a Data Form

Sorting Data in a List

Displaying Parts of a List with AutoFilter

Creating Complex Searches

Entering Data in a List

Adding Data Validation to a Worksheet

New2000 **Analyzing Data Using a PivotTable**

Updating a PivotTable

New2000 **Modifying a PivotTable and PivotChart**

New2000 **Charting a PivotTable**

Auditing a Worksheet

In addition to using a worksheet to calculate values, you can also use it to manage and analyze a list of information, sometimes called a *database*. You can use a Microsoft Excel 2000 worksheet to keep an inventory list, a school grade book, or a customer database. Excel provides a variety of tools that make it easy to keep lists up to date and analyze them to get the information you want quickly. For example, you can use these tools to find out how many inventory items are out of stock or who your best customers are.

Analyzing Worksheet Data

Excel's data analysis tools includes alphanumeric organizing (called *sorting*), displaying information that meets specific criteria (called *filtering*), and summarizing data within a table (called a *PivotTable*). You can analyze data directly in a worksheet, or use a feature called a *Data Form*, an on-screen data entry tool, which looks similar to a paper form. A Data Form lets you easily enter data by filling in blank text boxes, and then it adds the information to the bottom of the list. You can, for example, determine not only sales in a given time frame, but also the departments in which they occurred, as well as the top sales people.

Understanding List Terminology

A database is a collection of related records. Examples of databases are an address book, a customer list, product inventory, and a telephone directory. In Excel, a database is referred to as *list*.

Field name
The title given to a field. In an Excel list, the first row contains the names of each field. Each field name's maximum length is 255 characters, including upper- and lowercase letters and spaces.

List range
The block of cells that contains the list or part of the list you want to analyze. A list range can occupy no more than one worksheet.

Record
One set of related fields, such as all the fields pertaining to one customer or one product. On a worksheet, each row represents one record.

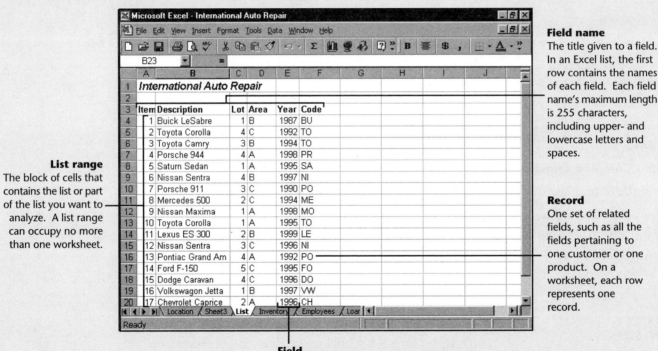

Field
One piece of information, such as a customer's last name or an item's code number. On a worksheet, each column represents a field.

Creating a List

To create a list in Excel, you enter data in worksheet cells, just as you do when creating any other worksheet. However, there are a few rules you need to follow:

- ◆ Enter field names as the first, single row in a list.

- ◆ Enter each record in a single row, with each field in the column corresponding to the correct field name.

- ◆ Do not include any blank rows within the list range.

- ◆ Do not use more than one worksheet for a single list range.

You can enter records in any order and then sort them after.

SEE ALSO

See "Sorting Data in a List" on page 176 for information on sorting data in a list.

Create a List

1. Open a blank worksheet, or use a worksheet that has enough empty columns and rows for the list.

2. Enter a name for each field in adjacent columns across the first row of the list.

3. Enter the field information for each record in a separate row, starting with the row directly beneath the field names.

Take advantage of features such as AutoComplete and AutoFill, which make data entry easier.

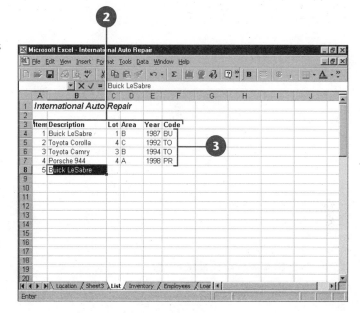

Understanding a Data Form

If you prefer entering information in a predesigned form to typing and tabbing on a worksheet, you'll appreciate the Data Form feature. A Data Form is a dialog box that contains field names from your list range and text boxes you fill in to enter the data. Excel automatically generates a Data Form based on the field names you assign when you create a list.

Data Form

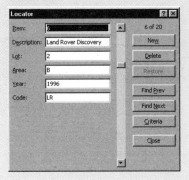

You can use the Data Form to enter repetitive information one record at a time. You can also use the Data Form to move around in a list and to search for specific data.

When you select a list range and open the Data Form, the form displays a field name and text boxes for all fields in the list. Data for the currently selected record appears in the text boxes (if the list already contains data). In a Data Form, you can enter new data in text boxes of a blank record, edit data in existing records (although you cannot change field names), navigate to different records, and search for selected records.

- ◆ Click the New button to enter a new record.

- ◆ Click the Delete button to remove an existing record.

- ◆ Click the Restore button to undo the previous action.

- ◆ Click the Find Prev button to locate the closest previous record matching the criteria.

- ◆ Click the Find Next button to locate the closest record matching the criteria.

- ◆ Click the Criteria button to display the Data Form with all fields blank. Enter the field items you want to find.

- ◆ Click the Close button to close the Data Form and return to the worksheet.

Adding Records Using a Data Form

A Data Form provides an optional method of entering information in a list. Once field names are entered, you access a Data Form using the Data menu. You don't even need to select the list range first; as long as the active cell is somewhere within the list range when the Data Form is opened, Excel will automatically locate the list. As you add new records to the form, the list range is constantly updated with the new rows, and Excel automatically enlarges the list range to include them.

SEE ALSO

See "Entering Data in a List" on page 180 for information on using AutoComplete and PickList.

Add Records Using a Data Form

1. Click any cell within the list range. If you have not entered any records for the list yet, click one of the field names.

2. Click the Data menu, and then click Form.

3. Click New.

4. Type each field entry in the appropriate text box.

   Click in each field or press the Tab key to move from field to field.

5. Click Close.

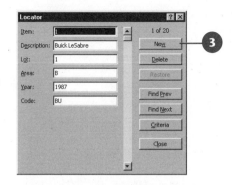

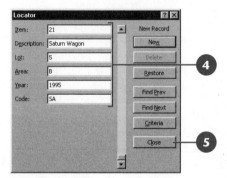

Managing Records Using a Data Form

You can use a Data Form to display, edit, or delete selected records in a list. To display only selected records in the Data Form, you specify the search *criteria*— the information a record must contain—in the Data Form, and Excel uses that criteria to find and display matching records. Although the Data Form shows only the records that match your criteria, the other records still exist in the list. If more than one record matches your criteria, you can use the Data Form buttons to move through the records, editing or deleting them.

TIP

Return to the complete list of records. *Return to the initial Data Form by clicking the Form button.*

Display Selected Records

1. Click anywhere within the list range.

2. Click the Data menu, and then click Form.

3. Click Criteria.

4. Type the information you want matching records to contain. You can fill in one or more fields.

5. Click Find Prev or Find Next to advance to a matching record.

6. Repeat step 5 until Excel beeps or enough records have been viewed.

7. Click Close.

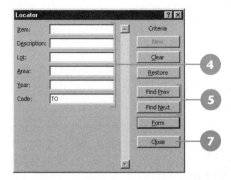

Edit a Record

1. Click anywhere within the list range.

2. Click the Data menu, and then click Form.

3. Find a record that requires modification.

4. Click to position the insertion point in the field you want to edit, and then use the Backspace and Delete keys to modify the text.

5. Click Close.

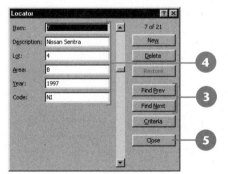

Delete a Record

1. Click anywhere within the list range.

2. Click the Data menu, and then click Form.

3. Click Criteria.

4. Type the information you want matching records to contain. You can fill in one or more fields.

5. Click Find Prev or Find Next to advance to a matching record.

6. Click Delete.

7. Click OK in the warning dialog box.

8. Click Close.

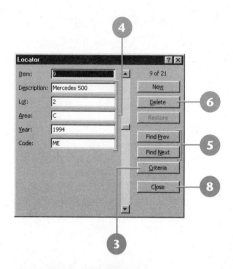

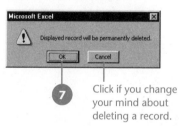

Click if you change your mind about deleting a record.

Sorting Data in a List

Once you enter records in a list, you can reorganize the information by *sorting* the records. You can sort a list alphabetically or numerically (in ascending or descending order) using one or more fields as the basis for the sort. You can quickly perform a simple sort (sorting a list on one field) using the Standard toolbar, or do a complex sort (sorting on multiple fields) using the Data menu. Organizing a list of first names, last names, and telephone numbers alphabetically by last name is an example of a simple sort. Sorting by last name and by first name (so people with the same last name can be alphabetized by first name as well by last name) is an example of a complex sort.

Sort Data Quickly

1. Click a field name you want to sort on.

2. Click the Sort Ascending or the Sort Descending button on the Standard toolbar.

In a list sorted in ascending order, records beginning with a number in the sort field are listed before records beginning with a letter (0-9, A-Z).

In a list sorted in descending order, records beginning with a letter in the sort field are listed first (Z-A, 9-0).

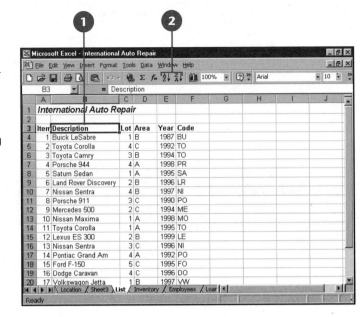

Sort data in rows. *If the data you want to sort is listed across a row instead of down a column, click the Options button in the Sort dialog box, and then click the Sort Left To Right option button in the Sort Options dialog box.*

Protect your original list order with an index field. *Before sorting a list for the first time, add an* index *field, a field that contains an ascending consecutive number (1, 2, 3, etc.) for each record. That way, you'll always be able to restore the original order of the list by sorting on this field.*

Sort on multiple fields. *Use the Data menu to create a multiple-field sort. Try sorting the list using different fields. See how this impacts the list.*

Sort a List Using More Than One Field

1 Click anywhere within the list range.

2 Click the Data menu, and then click Sort.

3 Click the Sort By drop-down arrow, and then select the field on which the sort will be based (the *primary sort field*).

4 Click the Ascending or Descending option button.

5 Click the first Then By drop-down arrow, and then click the Ascending or Descending option button.

6 If necessary, click the second Then By drop-down arrow, and then select the Ascending or Descending option button.

7 Click the Header Row option button to *exclude* the field names (in the first row) from the sort, or click the No Header Row option button to *include* the field names (in the first row) in the sort.

8 Click OK.

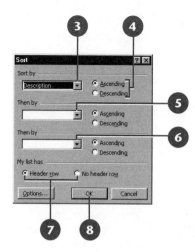

10

Displaying Parts of a List with AutoFilter

Working with a list that contains numerous records can be difficult—unless you can narrow your view of the list when necessary. For example, rather than looking through an entire inventory list, you might want to see records that come from one distributor. The *AutoFilter* feature creates a list of the items found in each field. You select the items that you want to display in the column (that is, the records that meet certain criteria). Then you can work with a limited number of records.

TIP

Speed up your work with the Top 10 list. *The AutoFilter offers a Top 10 command in the drop-down list of every field. Click this command to quickly create a filter for the top or bottom 10 items in a list.*

Display Specific Records Using AutoFilter

1. Click anywhere within the list range.

2. Click the Data menu, point to Filter, and then click AutoFilter.

3. Click the drop-down arrow of the field for which you want to specify search criteria.

4. Select the item that records must match in order to be included in the list.

5. Repeat steps 3 and 4, as necessary, to filter out more records using additional fields.

6. Click the Data menu, point to Filter, and then click AutoFilter to turn off AutoFilter and redisplay all records in the list.

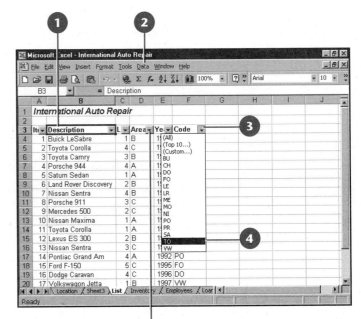

A drop-down arrow appears to the right of the field name when you turn on AutoFilter.

Creating Complex Searches

There are many times you'll want to search for records that meet multiple criteria. For example, you might want to see out-of-stock records of those orders purchased from a particular distributor. Using the AutoFilter feature and the Custom command, you can create complex searches. You use *logical operators* to measure whether an item in a record qualifies as a match with the selected criteria. You can also use the *logical conditions* AND and OR to join multiple criteria within a single search. The result of any search is either true or false; if a field matches the criteria, the result is *true*. The *OR* condition requires that only one criterion be true in order for a record to qualify. The *AND* condition, on the other hand, requires that both criteria in the statement be true in order for the record to qualify.

Create a Complex Search Using AutoFilter

1. Click anywhere within the list range.

2. Click the Data menu, point to Filter, and then click AutoFilter.

3. Click the drop-down arrow next to the first field you want to include in the search.

4. Click Custom.

5. Click the Code drop-down arrow (on the left), and then select a logical operator.

6. Click the drop-down arrow (on the right), and then select a field choice.

7. Click the And or the Or option button.

8. Click the drop-down arrow (on the left), and then select a logical operator.

9. Click the drop-down arrow (on the right), and then select a field choice.

10. Click OK.

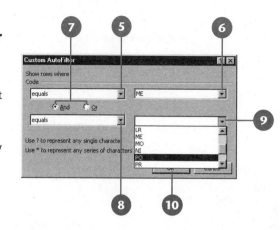

LOGICAL OPERATORS			
Symbol	Operator	Symbol	Operator
=	Equal to	<>	Not equal to
>	Greater than	<	Less than
>=	Greater than or equal to	<=	Less than or equal to

10

Entering Data in a List

Entering data in a list—whether you use the Data Form or the worksheet—can be tedious and repetitive. You can enter data using the PickList or List AutoFill feature to make the job easier. PickList is activated once you have entered at least one record in the list; it uses your previous entries to save you the trouble of typing repetitive information. *PickList* displays previous entries made in the current field in a list format. *List AutoFill* automatically extends the list's formatting and formulas to adjacent cells. As data is added to a list, AutoFill looks at the preceding cells to determine what formatting and formulas should be extended.

SEE ALSO

See "Entering Labels on a Worksheet" on page 28 for information on entering labels using AutoComplete.

Enter Data in a List Using PickList

① Right-click the cell in which you want to use PickList, and then click Pick From List on the shortcut menu.

② Click a selection in the list.

③ Press Enter or Tab to accept the entry, or press Esc to cancel the entry.

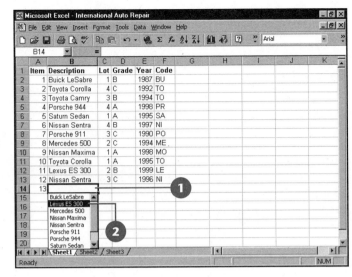

Copy Data Formats and Formulas in a List Using List AutoFill

① Format the data in a list the way you want.

② Select the next cell in the list.

③ Type the data label.

④ Click the Enter button on the formula bar, or press Enter.

The data is automatically formatted.

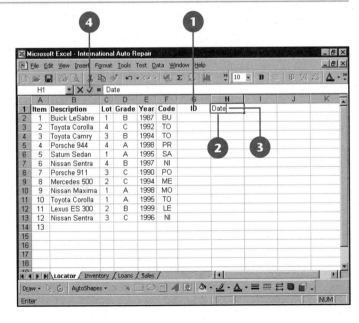

Adding Data Validation to a Worksheet

Worksheet cells can be adjusted so that only certain values can be entered. Controlling how data is entered decreases errors and makes a worksheet more reliable. You might, for example, want it to be possible to enter only specific dates in a range of cells. You can use logical operators (such as equal, not equal to, less than, or greater than to) to set validation rules. When invalid entries are made, a message— written by you—appears indicating that the entry is in violation of validation rules.

Create Validation Rules

1. Select the range you want covered in the validation rules.

2. Click the Data menu, and then click Validation.

3. Click the Settings tab.

4. Click the Allow drop-down arrow, and then select a value type.

5. Click the Data drop-down arrow, then select a logical operator.

6. Enter values or use the Collapse Dialog button to select a range for the minimum and maximum criteria.

7. Click the Input Message tab.

8. Type a title and the input message that should be displayed when invalid entries are made.

9. Click OK.

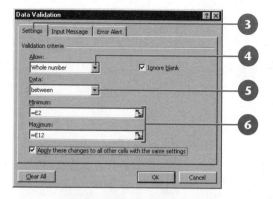

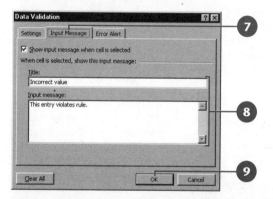

10

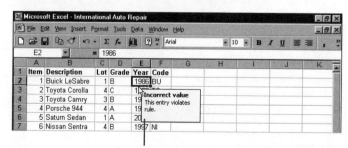

A warning appears when an invalid entry is made.

Analyzing Data Using a PivotTable

When you want to summarize information in a lengthy list using complex criteria, use the PivotTable to simplify your task. Without the PivotTable, you would have to manually count or create a formula to calculate which records met certain criteria, and then create a table to display that information for a report or presentation. Once you determine what fields and criteria you want to use to summarize the data and how you want the resulting table to look, the PivotTable and PivotChart Wizard does the rest.

Create a PivotTable Report

1. Click any cell within the list range.

2. Click the Data menu, and then click PivotTable And PivotChart Report.

3. If using the list range, click the Microsoft Excel List Or Database option button.

4. Click the PivotTable option button.

5. Click Next to continue.

6. If the range you want is "Database" (the active list range), skip to step 9.

7. If the range does not include the correct data, click the Collapse Dialog button. Drag the pointer over the list range, including the field names, to select a new range, and then click the Expand Dialog button.

8. Click Next to continue.

9. Drag field name(s) to the ROW and COLUMN and DATA areas.

10. Click OK.

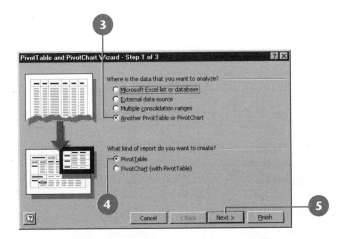

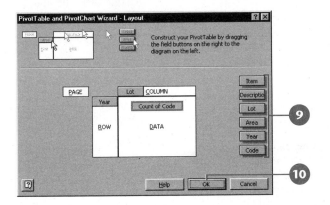

SEE ALSO

See "Generating Multiple-Page Reports" on page 208 for information on creating customized reports using the Report Manager.

SEE ALSO

See "Creating a Web Page" on page 242 for information on displaying interactive PivotTable reports on the Web.

TIP

Change data or fields included in the source range for a PivotTable or PivotChart. *Click any field in the PivotTable, click PivotTable Wizard on the PivotTable toolbar, click Back, select the new source data range, and then click Finish.*

Create a PivotTable Report from an Existing PivotTable or PivotChart

1 Open the worksheet containing the PivotTable.

2 Click the Data menu, and then click PivotTable And PivotChart Report.

3 Click the Another PivotTable Or PivotChart option button.

4 Click the PivotTable option button.

5 Click Next to continue.

6 Click the name of the report associated with the PivotChart.

7 Click Next to continue.

8 Click a location option for the new PivotTable.

9 If you want, click Layout or Options to change the way the PivotTable looks or functions, and then click OK.

10 Click Finish.

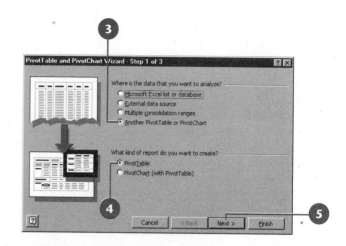

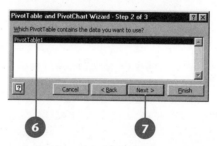

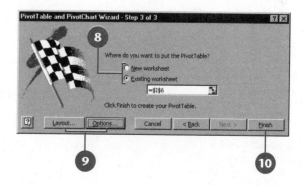

Updating a PivotTable

You can quickly update a PivotTable report using the PivotTable toolbar, which appears whenever a PivotTable is active. This saves you from having to re-create a PivotTable every time you add new data to a list. When you do want to add new data, Excel makes it easy by allowing you to drag data fields to and from a PivotTable or PivotChart.

TIP

Hide and display fields on the PivotTable toolbar. *Click the Hide Fields button on the PivotTable toolbar. Click the button again to display the PivotTable fields.*

TIP

Change the layout of a PivotTable. *Click a field in the PivotTable, click the PivotTable Wizard button on the PivotTable toolbar, click Layout, make the changes you want, click OK, and then click Finish.*

Update a PivotTable Report

1. Make any necessary change(s) in the list range data.

2. Click any cell in the PivotTable Report.

3. Click the Refresh Data button on the PivotTable toolbar, or click the PivotTable drop-down arrow on the PivotTable toolbar, and then click Refresh Data.

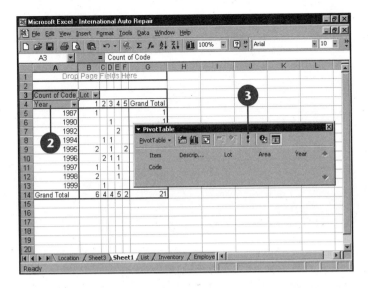

Add or Remove a Field in a PivotTable or PivotChart Report

1. Position the pointer over the field on the PivotTable toolbar that you want to add to or remove from the PivotTable.

2. Drag the field on the PivotTable to add the field or off the PivotTable to remove the field.

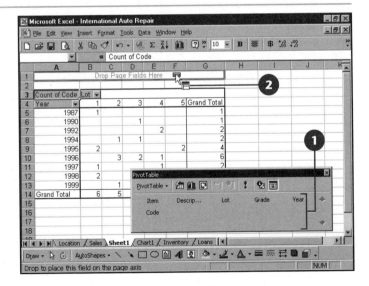

Modifying a PivotTable and PivotChart

You can modify PivotTable or PivotChart reports. With Excel's AutoFormat feature, you can quickly format a PivotTable to create professional-looking reports. You can also change field settings to format a number or show the data in a different form.

TIP

Display a list of formulas in a PivotTable or PivotChart report. *Click the PivotTable or PivotChart drop-down arrow on the PivotTable toolbar, point to Formula, and then click List Formulas.*

SEE ALSO

See "Analyzing Data Using a PivotTable" on page 182 and "Charting a PivotTable" on page 186 for information on PivotTables and PivotCharts.

AutoFormat a PivotTable Report

1. Click any field in the PivotTable report.

2. Click the Format Report button on the PivotTable toolbar.

3. Click the AutoFormat style you want.

4. Click OK.

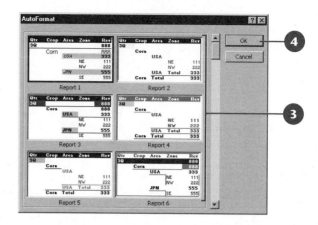

Change Field Settings in a PivotTable or PivotChart Report

1. Select the field you want to change.

2. Click the Field Settings button on the PivotTable toolbar.

3. To change the number format, click Number, select a format, and then click OK.

4. To show the data in a different form, click the Show Data As drop-down arrow, and select a form.

5. Click OK.

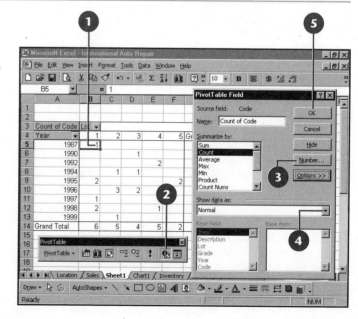

10

Charting a PivotTable

Data summarized in a PivotTable is an ideal candidate for a chart, since the table itself represents an overwhelming amount of difficult-to-read data. A chart of a PivotTable is called a *PivotChart*. Once you select data within the PivotTable, you can chart it like any other worksheet data using the Chart Wizard. If you don't have a PivotTable, you can create a PivotChart and a PivotTable at the same time.

SEE ALSO

See "Creating a Chart" on page 150 and "Formatting Chart Elements" on page 166 for more information on using the Chart Wizard and formatting a chart.

TIP

Hide and display PivotChart field buttons. *Click the PivotChart drop-down arrow on the PivotTable toolbar, and then click Hide PivotChart Field Buttons. Click Hide PivotChart Field Buttons again to display the field buttons.*

Create a PivotChart Report from a PivotTable Report

1 Click any data field in the PivotTable.

2 Click the Chart Wizard button on the PivotTable or Standard toolbar.

The PivotChart is created on a new worksheet.

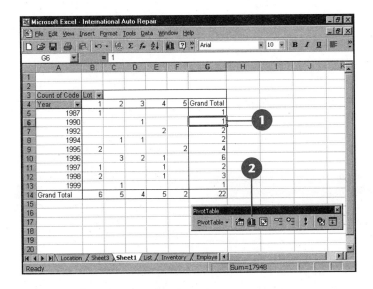

Modify a PivotChart Report

1 Click the worksheet tab with the PivotChart you want to modify.

2 Click the Chart Wizard button on the Standard or PivotTable toolbar.

3 Make selections from each of the four Chart Wizard dialog boxes.

4 Click Finish.

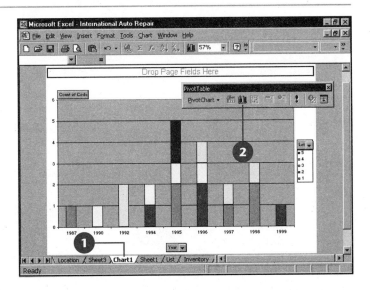

Create a non-pivoting chart from PivotTable data. *Select the PivotTable data, click the Copy button on the Standard toolbar, click the top-left cell where you want the chart data, click the Edit menu, click Paste Special, click the Values option button, click OK, click the Chart Wizard button on the Standard toolbar, and then follow the Chart Wizard steps.*

Use static data when creating a non-pivoting chart from a PivotTable. *In order to create a non-pivoting chart from a PivotTable, the data must not be in a PivotTable.*

See "Analyzing Data Using a PivotTable" on page 182 for information on creating PivotTables using the PivotTable And PivotChart Report Wizard.

Create a PivotChart Report with a PivotTable Report

1. Click any cell within the list range.

2. Click the Data menu, and then click PivotTable And PivotChart Report.

3. If using the list range, click the Microsoft Excel List Or Database option button.

4. Click the PivotChart (With PivotTable) option button.

5. Click Next to continue.

6. If the range does not include the correct data, click the Collapse Dialog button, drag the pointer over the list range, including the field names, to select a new range, and then click the Expand Dialog button.

7. Click Next to continue.

8. Click the desired location of the new PivotTable.

9. Click Finish.

10. Drag the data and fields you want from the PivotTable toolbar to the different area of the PivotChart.

The PivotTable is created as you create the PivotChart.

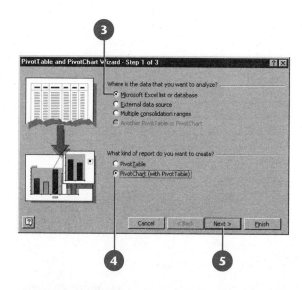

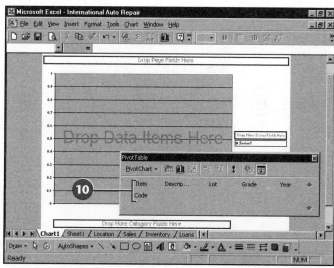

Auditing a Worksheet

In a complex worksheet, it can be difficult to understand the relationships between cells and formulas. Auditing tools enable you to clearly determine these relationships. When the *Auditing feature* is turned on, it uses a series of arrows to show you which cells are part of which formulas. When you use the auditing tools, *tracer arrows* point out cells that provide data to formulas and the cells that contain formulas that contain formulas that refer to the cells. A box is drawn around the range of cells that provide data to formulas.

TIP

Circle invalid data. *To circle invalid data in a formula, click the Circle Invalid button on the Auditing toolbar. Click the Clear Validation Circles button to clear the circles.*

Trace Worksheet Relationships

1 Click the Tools menu, point to Auditing, and then click Show Auditing Toolbar.

2 To find cells that provide data to a formula, select the cell that contains the formula, and then click the Track Precedents button.

3 To find out which formulas refer to a cell, select the cell, and then click the Track Dependents button.

4 If a formula displays an error value, such as #DIV/0!, click the cell, and then click the Trace Error button to locate the problem.

5 To remove arrows, click the Remove Precedent Arrows, Remove Dependent Arrows, or Remove All Arrows button.

6 Click the Close button on the Auditing toolbar.

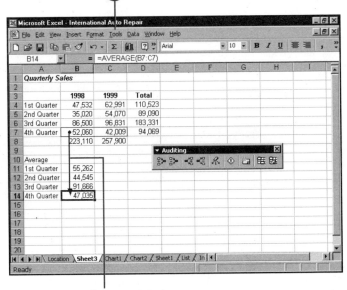

Trace precedents

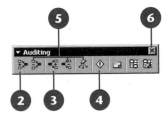

Tools for Working More Efficiently

IN THIS SECTION

Customizing Your Excel Work Environment

Viewing Multiple Workbooks

Changing Your Worksheet View

Creating a Toolbar

Customizing a Toolbar

New 2000 **Adding Menus and Menu Items**

New 2000 **Creating Groups and Outlines**

Saving Time with Templates

Creating a Template

Working with Templates

Tracking Changes

Protecting Your Data

You might be surprised by all the tools Microsoft Excel 2000 offers for saving time and effort while you work. These tools enable you to see more of the worksheet you're working on, to use and create customized worksheets, and to change your Excel work environment. By taking advantage of any or all of these tools, you can create a working environment that suits your personal preferences. Your productivity can only improve when you work more efficiently.

Working More Efficiently

You can increase your efficiency by customizing the look of the Excel window, the way you execute commands, and even the way you create a worksheet. Excel lets you arrange your worksheet windows in a variety of ways. You can see as much of your work area as possible, so you spend less time scrolling through a sheet and switching from sheet to sheet, and more time working with data. You can work more efficiently by creating templates— worksheets that contain formatting and formulas. If you share your worksheets with others, you can password protect your files to prevent unauthorized users from gaining access. You can also monitor and control the changes that are made to your worksheets.

Customizing Your Excel Work Environment

You can customize several settings in the Excel work environment to suit the way you like to work. If you always save workbooks in a specific folder, you can change the default location where workbooks are saved. You can make general changes, including the default font and the number of sheets in a new workbook. If your workbooks usually contain five sheets, you could make five the work-book default. You can also change editing options, such as whether the active cell moves after you enter data, and whether to allow drag-and-drop moving. Taking a few minutes to change Excel's default setting saves time in the long run.

Change General Options

1. Click the Tools menu, and then click Options.

2. Click the General tab.

3. To turn on a setting in Excel, click to select the check box for the option you want.

4. To change the number of recently used files listed at the bottom of the File menu, click the up or down arrow to set the number of files you want.

5. To change the default number of sheets in a new workbook, click the up or down arrow to set a number.

6. To change the default font, click the Standard Font drop-down arrow, and then select a new font.

7. To change the default font size, click the Size drop-down arrow, and then select a new font size.

8. To specify where Excel should automatically look for existing files or newly saved files, enter the location of your default folder.

9. Click the User Name box, and edit its contents.

10. Click OK.

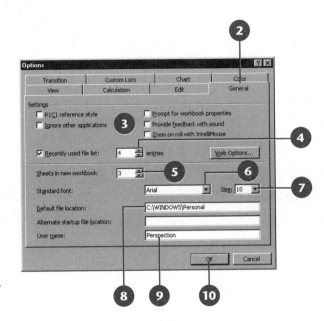

TIP

Edit directly in a cell.
Turning on the Edit Directly In A Cell option allows you to make changes in a cell by double-clicking it.

TIP

Alert before overwriting cells. *Turning off the Alert Before Overwriting Cells option can save you time, but you might accidentally lose data.*

TRY THIS

Make your environment more efficient. *Experiment with all of the features that can be changed in the Options dialog box. You can always change back if the new environment doesn't improve your efficiency.*

SEE ALSO

See "Changing Your Worksheet View" on page 193 for more information on customizing Excel.

Change Edit Options

1. Click the Tools menu, and then click Options.

2. Click the Edit tab.

3. Click to select or clear any of the check boxes to change the editing options you want.

   ◆ Make edits directly in a cell.

   ◆ Use drag-and-drop to copy cells.

   ◆ Determine the direction the active cell takes once you press Enter.

   ◆ Determine the number of decimals to the right of the decimal point if using a fixed number format.

   ◆ Choose to cut, copy, and sort objects with cells.

   ◆ Have Excel ask whether links should be updated.

   ◆ Have Excel provide animated feedback.

   ◆ Enable the AutoComplete feature to make data entry easier and more accurate.

4. Click OK.

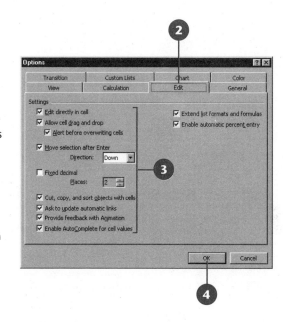

Viewing Multiple Workbooks

As you use many worksheets, it's quite possible that you'll want to work with more than one workbook at a time. You can arrange multiple workbooks on your desktop in a variety of ways. For example, when working with workbooks from more than one fiscal year, it might be helpful to be able to view workbooks from each year side-by-side.

TIP

Find out which workbooks are open. *The bottom of the Window menu lists all open files.*

TIP

Arrange multiple views of one workbook. *To view different parts of the active workbook in multiple windows, select the Windows Of Active Workbook check box in the Arrange Windows dialog box.*

View Multiple Workbooks

1. Open all the workbooks you want to work with.

2. Click the Window menu, and then click Arrange.

3. Click the arrangement you want for viewing your multiple workbooks.

   ◆ The Tiled option arranges the workbook windows clockwise starting in the top-left position.

   ◆ The Horizontal option arranges the workbook windows one beneath another.

   ◆ The Vertical option arranges the workbook windows side-by-side.

   ◆ The Cascade option arranges the workbook windows one under another.

4. Click OK.

5. To move from workbook to workbook, click the workbook, or click the workbook button on the taskbar to make it active.

6. To return to a single workbook view, click the workbook Maximize button.

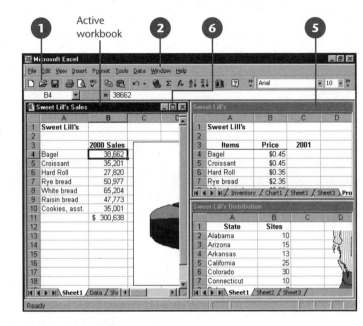

Active workbook

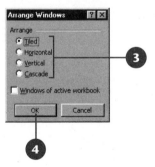

Changing Your Worksheet View

You can print a single worksheet in a variety of ways depending on who will be reading it. Perhaps your department heads need a detailed worksheet printed in landscape orientation with headers and footers providing information about the file and revision date; your sales staff needs the same worksheet printed in portrait orientation with only a few columns displayed and no headers and footers. Rather than having to change the print settings for each occasion, Excel lets you save each set of settings as a *custom view*. Each view contains print settings, as well as hidden columns and rows that you can access easily at any time.

SEE ALSO

See "Setting Up the Page" on page 76 for information on changing print settings.

Create a Custom View

1. Specify the print settings you want for a worksheet.

2. If necessary, hide any columns and rows.

3. Click the View menu, and then click Custom Views.

4. Click Add.

5. Type a name of the view.

6. If necessary, click to select the Print Settings check box and the Hidden Rows, Columns And Filter Settings check box to include them in the view.

7. Click OK.

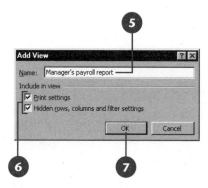

Display a Custom View

1. Click the View menu, and then click Custom Views.

2. Click the name of the view you want to use.

3. Click Show.

The print settings you set in this view are in effect when you print.

11

Creating a Toolbar

If none of the existing Excel toolbars fits your needs or if you just want a toolbar to call your own, you can create a new toolbar. You might use the Page Break command very often. Wouldn't it be easier if you had that button on your own toolbar? Perhaps your workbooks require a lot of formatting. Wouldn't it be more convenient if you had a special toolbar containing a variety of formatting buttons? Creating a toolbar that contains the buttons necessary for your most common tasks can dramatically increase your efficiency. Besides creating toolbars, you can change toolbar and menu options to best meet your working habits.

Create a Toolbar

1. Click the View menu, point to Toolbars, and then click Customize.

2. Click New.

3. Type a name for the new toolbar.

4. Click OK.

   The new toolbar appears on your screen. The toolbar name may not fit in the title bar until the toolbar is long enough.

5. Click the Commands tab.

6. Click a category that contains the command(s) you want to add.

7. Click a command you want to add to the toolbar.

8. Drag the button to the new toolbar.

9. Repeat steps 6 through 8 until all buttons you want are added.

10. Click Close.

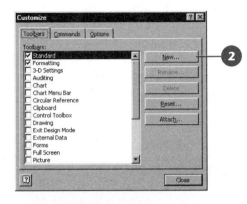

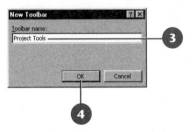

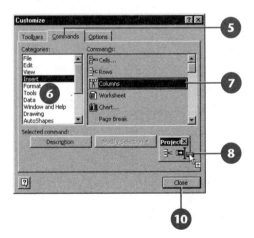

SEE ALSO

See "Understanding How Macros Automate Your Work" on page 214 and "Recording a Macro" on page 215 for more information on macros and how to record them.

SEE ALSO

See "Working with Menus and Toolbars" on page 14 for more information on using toolbars, and see "Customizing a Toolbar" on page 196 for information on modifying a toolbar.

SEE ALSO

See "Adding Menus and Menu Items" on page 198 for more information on creating your own menus or modifying existing ones.

Change Toolbars and Menus Options

1. Click the View menu, point to Toolbars, and then click Customize.

2. Click the Options tab.

3. To share one toolbar row, click to select the Standard And Formatting Toolbars Share One Row check box.

4. To personalize your menus, click to select the Menus Show Recently Used Commands First check box.

5. To reset your toolbars and menus, click Reset My Usage Data.

6. To animate your menus, click the Menu Animations drop-down arrow, and then select an animation.

7. Click Close.

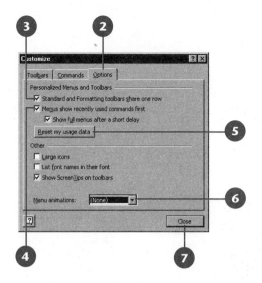

Customizing a Toolbar

Excel contains predesigned toolbars; by default, the Standard and Formatting toolbars appear on the screen at all times. These two toolbars contain buttons for commonly used Excel commands. However, since everyone works differently, you may find that these toolbars display some buttons you never use, while they do not display others you want available on your screen. The More Buttons menu makes these toolbars inherently customizable by displaying buttons you select from the drop-down menu. You can also customize the toolbar display by displaying different Excel toolbars and by adding or deleting different buttons on any toolbar.

SEE ALSO

See "Working with Menus and Toolbars" on page 14 for information on displaying and hiding a toolbar.

Personalize a Toolbar Quickly

1. Click the More Buttons drop-down arrow on a toolbar.

2. To move a button from More Buttons to the toolbar, click the toolbar button you want.

   The toolbar button is displayed on the toolbar.

3. To quickly add or remove a button from a toolbar, point to Add Or Remove Buttons, and then click the button you want to add or remove.

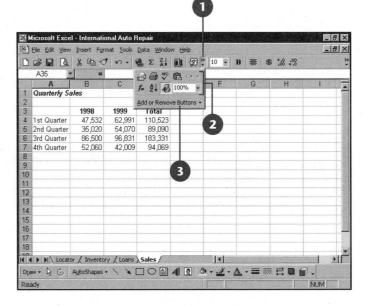

Delete a Button from a Toolbar

1. Click the View menu, point to Toolbars, and then click Customize.

2. Click the Toolbars tab.

3. Make sure the toolbar you want to change is selected.

4. Drag the button you want to delete off the toolbar.

5. Click Close.

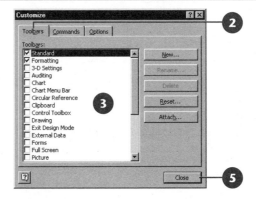

Add a Button to a Toolbar

1. Click the View menu, point to Toolbars, and then click Customize.

2. Make sure the toolbar you want to change is selected.

3. Click the Commands tab.

4. Click the category that contains the command you want to add.

5. Click the command you want to add.

6. Drag the button you want to add to any location on the selected toolbar.

7. Repeat steps 4 through 6 until all the buttons you want are added.

8. Click Close.

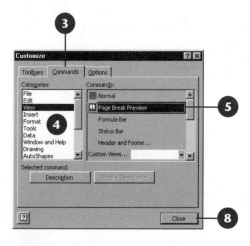

Adding Menus and Menu Items

Just as you can add toolbar buttons to toolbars, you can add commands to any existing menus. You can even create your own menu and add just the commands you want. If, for example, you design a specific worksheet that will be used by others, you can create a specific menu just for their use. This menu can contain the commands they'll need while using your worksheet.

TIP

A custom menu can increase a user's comfort level. *Inexperienced Excel users may feel more comfortable finding all the commands they need on a single menu.*

SEE ALSO

See "Working with Menus and Toolbars" on page 14 for information on choosing menu options.

Add a Menu Item

1. Click the Tools menu, click Customize, and then click the Commands tab.

2. Click the category that contains command(s) you want to add to the menu.

3. Click the command you want.

4. Drag the command to the desired location on the menu.

5. Click Close.

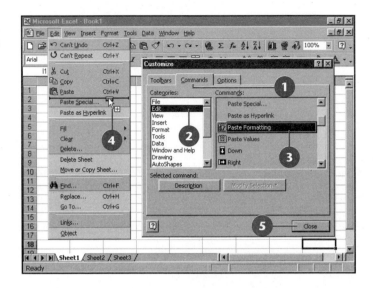

Create a New Menu

1. Click the Tools menu, click Customize, and then click the Commands tab.

2. Click the New Menu category, and then drag New Menu to the desired location on the menu bar.

3. Right-click the new menu on the menu bar.

4. Type a name for the menu, and then press Enter.

5. Click a category, and then drag the commands you want to the new menu.

6. Click Close.

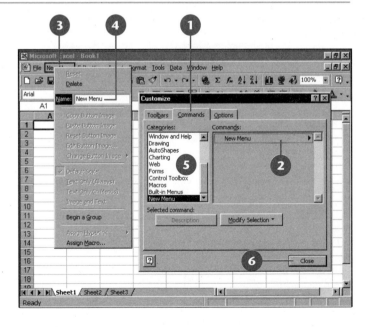

Creating Groups and Outlines

A sales report with daily, weekly, and monthly totals displayed in a hierarchical format, such as an outline, helps the reader to sift through and interpret the pertinent information. In *outline format*, a single item can have several topics or levels of information within it. An outline in Excel indicates multiple layers of content by displaying a plus sign (+) on its left side. A minus sign (-) indicates that the item has no contents, is fully expanded, or both.

TIP

Clear an outline. *Select the outline, click the Data menu, point to Group And Outline, and then click Clear Outline.*

TIP

Ungroup outline data. *Select the data group, click the Data menu, point to Group And Outline, click Ungroup, click the Rows or Columns option button, and then click OK.*

Create an Outline or Group

1. Organize summary rows below detail rows and summary columns to the right of detail columns.

2. Select the data you want outlined.

3. To create an outline, click the Data menu, point to Group And Outline, and then click Auto Outline.

   To create a group, click the Data menu, point to Group And Outline, click Group, click the Rows or Columns option button, and then click OK.

Collapse and Expand an Outline or Group

1. Click a plus sign (+) to expand an outline level; click a minus sign (-) to collapse an outline level.

   To display levels, you can also click 1, 2, etc.

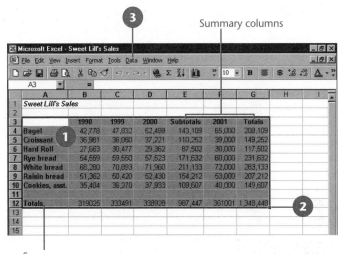

Summary columns

Summary row

Click to display levels.

A plus sign (+) indicates additional levels exist and the level is currently collapsed.

Sublevels are indented and no longer display a plus sign.

Saving Time with Templates

Many of the worksheets you create may be very similar to those other users create. Perhaps you use Excel to generate client invoices. Each time you need to bill a client, you spend time creating an invoice. Wouldn't it be easier if you could open a new workbook that already contained the necessary information so that all you had to do was fill in the new data as if you were filling in a form? Excel templates make this possible. A *template* is a workbook that can contain formulas, labels, graphics, and formatting. When you start a new workbook based on a template, your new workbook contains all the information from the template; all you have to is fill in the blanks. Excel contains several built-in templates designed to adapt to almost any business situation.

Create and Save a Workbook Using a Template

1. Click the File menu, and then click New.

2. Click the Spreadsheet Solutions tab.

3. Click the name of the template you want to use.

4. Click OK.

5. Fill in the form with your own information.

6. Click Save.

The Save As dialog box opens so that you can save the file as a workbook (not a new template).

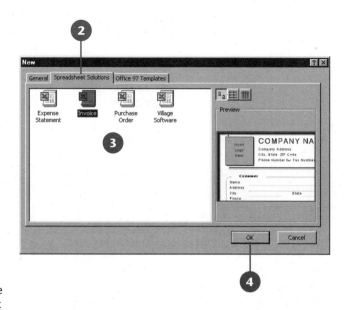

TEMPLATE	DESCRIPTION
Expense Statement	Creates a form for submitting business expenses
Invoice	Creates a form containing customer and product information with unit and extended prices
Purchase Order	Creates a purchase order form; similar to Invoice template
Village Software	Contains a complex form that lets a user visit a Web site, see software products, and view customer specials

Creating a Template

You can create your own template as easily as you create a worksheet. Like those that come with Excel, custom templates can save you time. Perhaps each month you create an inventory worksheet in which you enter repetitive information; all that changes is the actual data. By creating your own template, you have a custom form that is ready for completion each time you take inventory.

Create a Template

1. Enter all the necessary information in a new workbook—including formulas, labels, graphics, and formatting.

2. Click the File menu, and then click Save As.

3. Click the Save In drop-down arrow, and then select a location for the template.

    To have your new template appear in the Spreadsheet Solutions tab of the New dialog box, select the location C:/Program Files/ Microsoft Office/Templates/Spreadsheet Solutions.

4. Type a filename that will clearly identify the purpose of the template.

5. Click the Save As Type drop-down arrow.

6. Click Template.

7. Click Save.

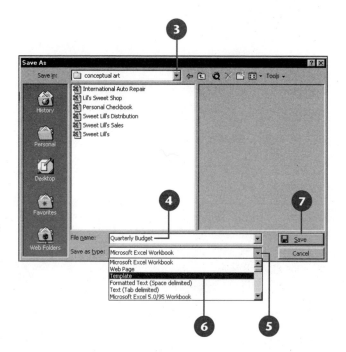

Working with Templates

You may not realize it, but every workbook you create is based on a template. When you start a new workbook without specifying a template, Excel creates a new workbook based on the *default template*, which includes three worksheets and no special formulas, labels, or formatting. When you specify a particular template in the New dialog box, whether it's one supplied by Excel or one you created yourself, Excel starts a new workbook that contains the formulas, labels, graphics, and formatting contained in that template. The template itself does not change when you enter data in the new workbook, because you are working on a new file, not with the template file.

Open a Template

1. Click the Open button on the Standard toolbar.

2. Click the Look In drop-down arrow, and then select the drive and folder that contain the template you want to open.

3. Click the Files Of Type drop-down arrow.

4. Click Templates.

5. Click the filename of the template you want open.

6. Click Open.

Change an Excel Template

1. Click the Open button on the Standard toolbar.

2. Click the Look In drop-down arrow, and change the location to C:/Program Files/Microsoft Office/Templates/Spreadsheet Solutions.

3. Click the template you want to modify.

4. Click Open.

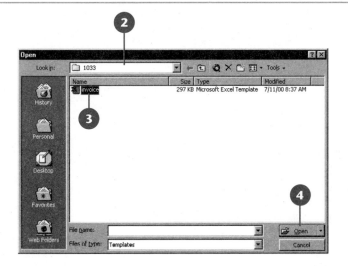

TIP

Use the New button to open a default workbook. *Clicking the New button on the Standard toolbar opens a new workbook based on the default template.*

TIP

Changing the default template affects all new workbooks you create. *Be careful if you decide to make any changes to this template.*

TIP

Modify a template. *If you want to make changes to an existing template so that all new workbooks incorporate the change, open the actual template—not a copy—and make and save your changes.*

SEE ALSO

See "Understanding Excel Program Add-Ins" on page 220 for information on Excel's Template Wizard and other template utilities.

⑤ Make the changes you want. Remember that these changes will affect all new workbooks you create using this template.

⑥ Click the Save button on the Standard toolbar.

⑦ Close the template before using it to create a new workbook.

Customize an Excel Template

① Open the Excel template you want to customize. Excel templates are located in the Program Files/ Microsoft Office/Templates/Spreadsheet Solutions folder.

② Click the Customize Your [Template Name] tab.

③ Point to cell notes for comments that help you customize the template.

④ Replace the placeholder text with your own information.

⑤ Click the Save button on the Standard toolbar.

⑥ Close the template before using it to create a new workbook.

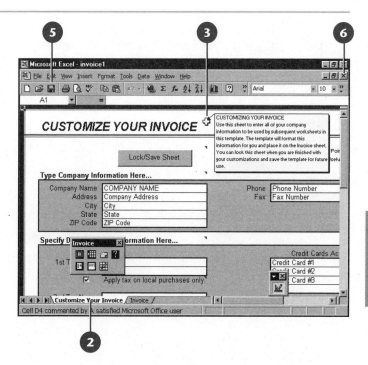

Tracking Changes

As you build and fine-tune a workbook—particularly if you are sharing workbooks with co-workers—you can keep track of all the changes that are made at each stage in the process. The *Track Changes* feature makes it easy to see who made what changes and when, and to accept or reject each change. To take full advantage of this feature, turn it on the first time you or a co-worker edits a workbook. Then, when it's time to review the workbook, all the changes will be recorded. You can review tracked changes in a workbook at any point. Cells containing changes are surrounded by a blue border, and the changes made can be viewed instantly by moving your mouse pointer over any outlined cell. When you're ready to finalize the workbook, you can review each change and either accept or reject it.

Turn On the Track Changes Feature

1. Click the Tools menu, point to Track Changes, and then click Highlight Changes.

2. Click to select the Track Changes While Editing check box.

3. Click to select the When, Who, or Where check box. Click an associated drop-down arrow, and then select the option you want.

4. Click OK.

5. Make changes in worksheet cells.

Column and row indicators for changed cells appear in red. The cell containing the changes has a blue outline.

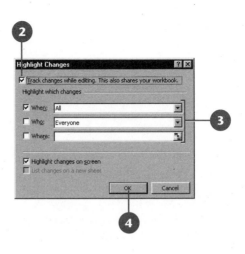

View Tracked Changes

1. Position the mouse pointer over an edited cell.

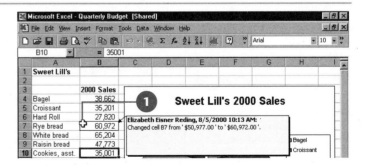

Title bar changes to alert you of shared status. *When you or another user applies the Track Changes command to a workbook, the message "[Shared]" appears in the title bar of the workbook to alert you that this feature is active.*

Keep track of revisions by tracking changes. *Use the Track Changes feature to follow important changes in data, even if you are the only user of a worksheet.*

See "Editing Cell Contents" on page 33 for more information about editing cells.

See "Customizing Your Excel Work Environment" on page 190 for more information about changing the user name that is displayed when you track your changes.

See "Auditing a Worksheet" on page 188 for more information about tracking relationships between cells.

Accept or Reject Tracked Changes

1 Click the Tools menu, point to Track Changes, and then click Accept Or Reject Changes. If necessary, click OK in the message box.

2 Click OK to begin reviewing changes.

3 If necessary, scroll to review all the changes, and then click one of the following buttons.

- ◆ Click Accept to make the selected change to the worksheet.

- ◆ Click Reject to remove the selected change from the worksheet.

- ◆ Click Accept All to make all of the changes to the worksheet after you have reviewed them.

- ◆ Click Reject All to remove all of the changes to the worksheet after you have reviewed them.

4 Click Close.

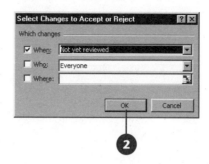

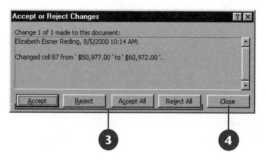

Protecting Your Data

To preserve all your hard work—particularly if others use your files—you can protect it with a password. You can protect a sheet or an entire workbook. In each case, you'll be asked to supply a password, and then enter it again when you want to work on the file.

TIP

Protect your password.
Keep your password in a safe place. Avoid obvious passwords like your name, your company, or your favorite pet.

TIP

You need your password to unprotect a worksheet.
Turn off protection by clicking the Tools menu, pointing to Protection, and then clicking Unprotect Sheet. Enter the password, and then click OK.

TIP

Protect a workbook. *To protect a workbook, follow the same steps, but choose Protect Workbook on the Tools menu.*

Protect a Worksheet

1. Click the Tools menu, point to Protection, and then click Protect Sheet.

2. Click to select the check boxes for the options you want protected in the sheet.

3. Type a password.

4. Click OK.

5. Retype the password.

6. Click OK.

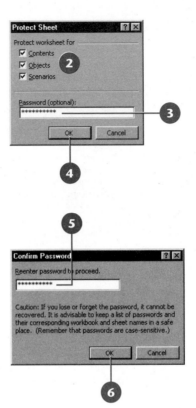

Building More Powerful Worksheets

IN THIS SECTION

Generating Multiple-Page Reports

Creating Scenarios

Looking at Alternatives with Data Tables

Asking "What If" with Goal Seek

Understanding How Macros Automate Your Work

Recording a Macro

Running a Macro

Understanding Macro Code

Debugging a Macro Using Step Mode

Editing a Macro

Understanding Excel Program Add-Ins

If your worksheet or workbook needs to go beyond simple calculations, Microsoft Excel 2000 offers several tools to help you create more specialized projects. With Excel, you can create custom reports and perform "what if" analyses using several different methods to get the results you want.

Automating Your Work

You can customize Excel by automating frequently performed tasks and keystrokes using macros. A macro records a series of tasks and keystrokes so you don't have to repeat them each time. Once a macro is recorded, you can run it, make modifications to it, add comments so other users will understand its purpose, and test it to make sure it runs correctly. Excel also includes a variety of add-ins—programs that provide added functionality—to increase your efficiency. Some of these supplemental programs, such as AutoSave, are useful to almost anyone using Excel. Others, such as the Analysis ToolPak, add customized features, functions, or commands specific to use in financial, statistical, and other highly specialized fields. The purpose of each of these customization features is the same—to make Excel even easier to use and to enable you to accomplish more with less effort.

Generating Multiple-Page Reports

The sheets, custom views, and scenarios that you create in a workbook combine to produce powerful individual worksheets. Because a workbook contains sheets with related data, you might want to generate reports that contain any combination of the data from your worksheets. Using Excel's *Report Manager,* an add-in program, you can create reports that contain numerous workbook sheets and incorporate custom views and scenarios. Report Manager lets you name and save your reports so you can use them in the future.

SEE ALSO

See "Understanding Excel Program Add-Ins" on page 220 for information on other available add-ins.

Create a Report

1. Open the workbook you want to use to create the report.

2. Create the custom views you want.

3. Create the scenarios you want.

4. Click the View menu, and then click Report Manager.

5. Click Add.

6. Type a name for the report.

7. Click the Sheet drop-down arrow, and then select a sheet to add to the report.

8. If you want, click to select the View or Scenario check box, and then click the associated drop-down arrow and select the view or scenario you want.

9. Click Add.

10. Repeat steps 7 through 9 until all the necessary sheets have been added.

11. Click to select the Use Continuous Page Numbers check box to add consecutive numbering to the report.

12. Click OK.

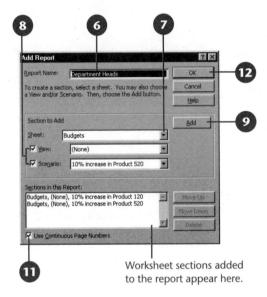

Worksheet sections added to the report appear here.

SEE ALSO

See "Creating Scenarios" on page 210 for information on creating scenarios.

SEE ALSO

See "Changing Your Worksheet View" on page 193 for information on creating custom views.

Change the Order of Report Sections

① Click the View menu, and then click Report Manager.

② Select the scenario you want to change, and then click Edit.

③ Click the section you want to move.

④ Click the Move Up or Move Down button to change the order of the section.

⑤ Click Delete to remove the selected section from the report.

⑥ Click OK.

⑦ Click Close.

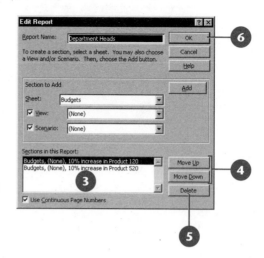

Creating Scenarios

Because some worksheet data is constantly evolving, the ability to create multiple scenarios lets you speculate on a variety of outcomes. For example, the marketing department might want to see how its budget would be affected if sales decreased by 25 percent. Although it's easy enough to plug in different numbers in formulas, Excel allows you to save these values and then recall them at a later time. The ability to create, save, and modify scenarios means a business will be better prepared for different outcomes to avoid economic surprises.

SEE ALSO

See "Asking 'What If' with Goal Seek" on page 213 for more information about creating multiple data solutions.

Create a Scenario

1. Click the Tools menu, and then click Scenarios.

2. Click Add.

3. Type a name that identifies the scenario.

4. Type the cells you want to modify in the scenario, or click the Collapse Dialog button, use your mouse to select the cells, and then click the Expand Dialog button.

5. If you want, type a comment.

6. Click OK.

7. Type values for each of the displayed changing cells.

8. Click OK.

9. Click Close.

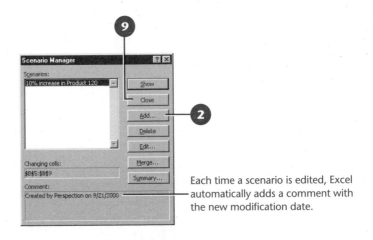

Each time a scenario is edited, Excel automatically adds a comment with the new modification date.

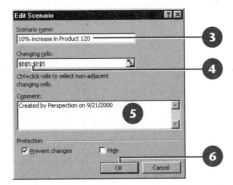

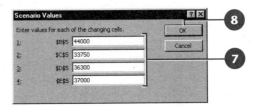

Show a Scenario

1. Click the Tools menu, and then click Scenarios.

2. Select the scenario you want to see.

3. Click Show.

4. Click Close.

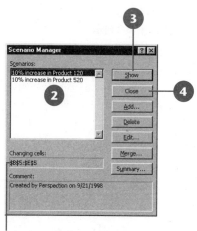

Cells that will change appear here.

Cells B5 through E5 change to reflect the scenario selected in the Scenario Manager dialog box.

Looking at Alternatives with Data Tables

You can look to see a range of possible values for your formulas. Data tables provide a shortcut by calculating all of the values in one operation. A *data table* is a range of cells that shows the results of substituting different values in one or more formulas. For example, you can compare loan payments for different interest rates. There are two types of data tables: one-input and two-input. With a *one-input table*, you enter different values for one variable and see the effect on one or more formulas. With a *two-input table*, you enter values for two variables and see the effect on one formula.

TIP

Delete a data table. *Select the cells of the data table, click the Edit menu, point to Clear, and then click Contents.*

Create a One-Input Data Table

1. Enter the formula you want to use.

   If the input values are listed down a column, specify the new formula in a blank cell to the right of an existing formula in the top row of the table. If the input values are listed across a row, enter the new formula in a blank cell below an existing formula in the first column of the table.

2. Select the data table, including the column or row that contains the new formula.

3. Click the Data menu, and then click Table.

4. Enter the input cell.

   If the input values are in a column, enter the reference for the input cell in the Column Input Cell box. If the input values are in a row, enter the reference for the input cell in the Row Input Cell box.

5. Click OK.

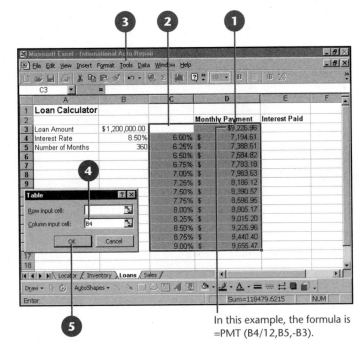

In this example, the formula is =PMT (B4/12,B5,-B3).

Asking "What If" with Goal Seek

Excel's powerful functions make it easy to create powerful formulas, such as calculating payments over time. Sometimes, however, being able to make these calculations is only half the battle. Your formula might tell you that a monthly payment amount is $2,000, while you might only be able to manage a $1,750 payment. *Goal Seek* enables you to work backwards to a desired result, or goal, by adjusting the input values.

TRY THIS

Adjust a payment amount. *Create a formula using the PMT function, and then adjust the monthly amount by changing the interest rate.*

SEE ALSO

See "Looking at Alternatives with Data Tables" on page 212 for information on another method for working with data.

Create a "What-If" Scenario with Goal Seek

① Click any cell within the list range.

② Click the Tools menu, and then click Goal Seek.

③ Click the Set Cell box, and then type the cell address you want to change.

You can also click the Collapse Dialog button, use your mouse to select the cells, and then click the Expand Dialog button.

④ Click the To Value box, and then type the result value.

⑤ Click the By Changing Cell box, and then type the cell address you want Excel to change.

You can also click the Collapse Dialog button, use your mouse to select the cells, and then click the Expand Dialog button.

⑥ Click OK.

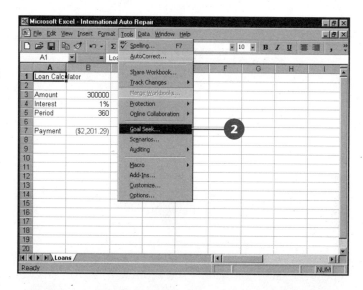

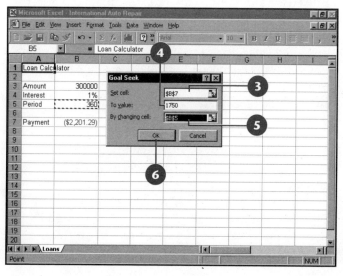

Understanding How Macros Automate Your Work

To complete many tasks in Excel, you need to execute a series of commands and actions. To print two copies of a selected range of Sheet2 of a worksheet, for example, you need to open the workbook, switch to Sheet2, select the print area, open the Print dialog box, and specify that you want to print two copies. If you often need to complete the same task, you'll find yourself repeatedly taking the same series of steps. It can be tiresome to continually repeat the same commands and actions when you can easily create a mini-program, or *macro*, that accomplishes all of them with a single command.

Creating a macro is easy and requires no programming knowledge on your part. Excel simply records the steps you want included in the macro while you use the keyboard and mouse. When you record a macro, Excel stores the list of commands with any name you choose. You can store your macros in the current workbook, in a new workbook, or in Excel's Personal Macro workbook. Storing your macros in the Personal Macro workbook makes the macros available to you from any location in Excel, even when no workbook is open.

Once a macro is created, you can make modifications to it, add comments so other users will understand its purpose, and test it to make sure it runs correctly.

You can run a macro by choosing the Macro command on the Tools menu, or by using a shortcut key or clicking a toolbar button you've assigned to it. When you click the Tools menu, point to Macro, and then click Macros, the Macro dialog box opens. From this dialog box, you can run, edit, test, or delete any Excel macro on your system, or create a new one.

If you have problems with a macro, you can step through the macro one command at a time, known as *debugging*. Once you identify any errors in the macro, you can edit it.

Indicates the workbook(s) from which you can access the highlighted macro

When you create a macro, you can add a description of what the macro does.

Recording a Macro

Recording a macro is almost as easy as recording your favorite CD or TV show. Once you turn on the macro recorder, Excel records every mouse click and keystroke action you execute until you turn off the recorder. Then you can "play," or run, the macro whenever you want to repeat that series of actions—but Excel will execute them at a much faster rate. You don't even need to press a rewind button when you want to run it again!

TIP

Make macros available to all worksheets. *To make a macro available to all worksheets, save it in the Personal Macro workbook.*

SEE ALSO

See "Understanding How Macros Automate Your Work" on page 214 for more information on where to save a macro.

Record a Macro

1. Click the Tools menu, point to Macro, and then click Record New Macro.

2. Type a name for the macro.

3. Assign a shortcut key to use a keystroke combination instead of a menu selection to run the macro.

4. Click the Store Macro In drop-down arrow, and then select a location.

5. Type a description, if you want. The description appears at the bottom of the Macro dialog box.

6. Click OK.

7. Execute each command or action you need to complete the macro's task. Take the time to complete each action correctly, since the macro will repeat all moves you make.

8. Click the Stop Recording button.

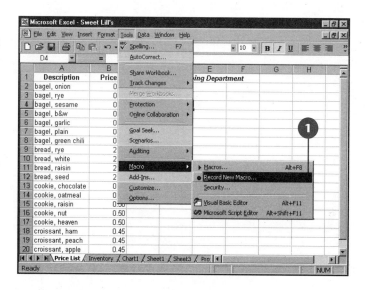

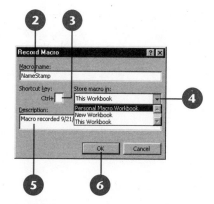

Running a Macro

Running a macro is similar to choosing a command in Excel. When you record or edit the macro, you have the choice of making it available through a menu command, a keyboard combination, or even a toolbar button. As with other options in Excel, your choice depends on your personal preferences—and you can choose to make more than one option available. Where you store a macro when you save it determines its availability later. Macros stored in the Personal Macro workbook are always available, and macros stored in any other workbooks are only available when the workbook is open.

SEE ALSO

See "Customizing a Toolbar" on page 196 for information on adding a macro to a toolbar.

Run a Macro Using a Menu Command

1. Click the Tools menu, point to Macro, and then click Macros.

2. If necessary, click the Macros In drop-down arrow, and then select the workbook that contains the macro you want to run.

3. Click the name of the macro you want to run.

4. Click Run.

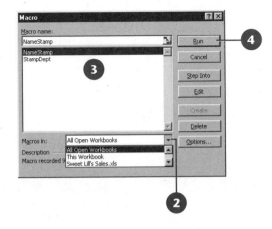

Run a Macro Using a Toolbar or Shortcut Key

1. Click the button assigned to the macro, or press the shortcut key combination you assigned to the macro.

Understanding Macro Code

Macro codes may look cryptic and confusing, but they are the actual commands used within Excel. Back before tools such as the macro recorder existed, you'd create a macro by typing all the command code necessary to perform each action in the macro.

Each action listed in a macro either performs a step or states what attributes are turned on (true) or off (false). Quotation marks are used to indicate typed text, and the terms *Sub* and *End Sub* are used to indicate the beginning and ending of subroutines, respectively.

Because not everyone wants to read through codes to figure out what a macro does, comments are often included within the code. The comments don't affect the macro; they simply clarify its purpose or actions for a person viewing the code. Comments can be used to help you remember why you took the steps you did or to help co-workers understand what is going on in the macro and how the macro should be used. A comment always begins with an apostrophe to distinguish it from command code.

To learn more about working with macro code, check out Visual Basic titles on the Microsoft Press Web site at *http://www.mspress.microsoft.com.*

These comments tell the name the macro was assigned when it was created and its function.

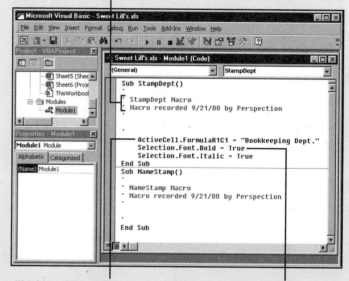

This line indicates what to enter in the active cell.

This line means that the Bold attribute is turned on, or true.

12

Debugging a Macro Using Step Mode

If a macro doesn't work exactly the way you want it to, you can fix the problem without re-creating the macro. Instead of recording the macro over again, Excel allows you to *debug*, or repair, an existing macro, so that you change only the actions that aren't working correctly. Excel's *step mode* shows you each action in a macro, such as a particular menu command, being executed one step at a time, and it also shows you the programming code corresponding to the action in a separate window called a Module sheet. Using step mode, you can determine which actions need modification, and then you make the necessary changes.

SEE ALSO

See "Editing a Macro" on page 219 for information on the Module sheet.

Debug a Macro Using Step Mode

1 Click the Tools menu, point to Macro, and then click Macros.

2 Click the name of the macro you want to debug.

3 Click Step Into.

4 Click the Debug menu, and then click Step Into to proceed through each action.

5 When you're done, click the File menu, and then click Close And Return To Microsoft Excel.

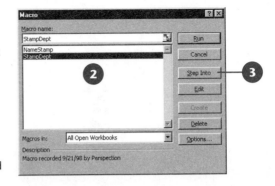

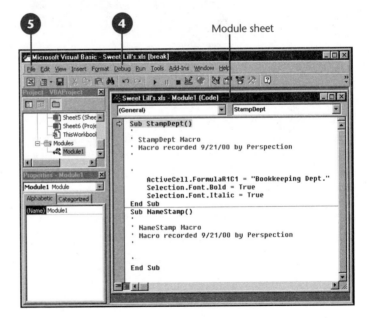

Module sheet

Editing a Macro

Even if a macro works correctly, you may sometimes find that you want to change the way it runs or the steps it contains. To do so, you can edit the existing code—the list of instructions Excel recorded when you turned on the macro recorder. As you recorded the macro steps, Excel kept track of each action in a separate location called a *Module sheet*. You can edit macro code by opening its Module sheet and using the keyboard to make changes just as you would to a word processing document. You can use the Delete and Backspace keys to remove characters and then type the corrections.

SEE ALSO

See "Recording a Macro" on page 215 for information on creating a macro.

Edit a Macro

1 Click the Tools menu, point to Macro, and then click Macros.

2 Click the macro you want to edit.

3 Click Edit.

4 Select the text to be edited, and then make the necessary corrections.

5 When you're done, click the File menu, and then click Close And Return To Microsoft Excel.

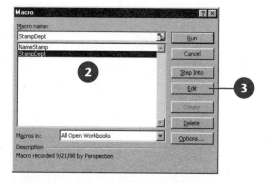

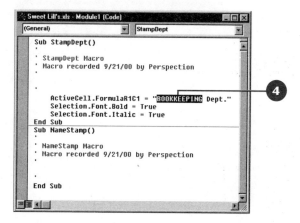

12

Understanding Excel Program Add-Ins

To increase your efficiency, Excel includes a variety of *add-ins*—programs that are included with Excel but not essential to its functionality. Some of these supplemental programs, such as AutoSave, are useful to almost anyone using Excel. Others, such as the Analysis ToolPak, add customized features, functions, or commands for use in financial, statistical, engineering or other highly special-ized fields.

You might have installed one or more add-ins when you installed Excel. To see what add-ins are installed on your system, open the Add-Ins dialog box by clicking the Tools menu and then clicking Add-Ins.

In the interest of conserving memory, Excel does not activate installed add-ins when you start the program, so you need to activate each one before you use it using the Add-Ins command on the Tools menu. Then the add-in will be available either as a menu command or an option within a dialog box.

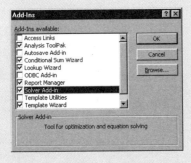

COMMONLY USED EXCEL ADD-INS		
Add-In	**What the Program Does**	**Location of Active Feature**
Access Links	Provides Microsoft Access forms and reports in Excel data tables	Data menu
MS Query	Helps retrieve data stored in external databases	Data menu
AutoSave	Saves an open workbook at timed intervals as you work	Automatic feature
Conditional Sum Wizard	Creates a formula that totals list data based on your criteria	Tools menu
Lookup Wizard	Helps create formulas to find data in lists	Tools menu
Report Manager	Creates multipage reports using sheets within a workbook and which can include views and scenarios	View menu
Solver	Calculates solutions to what-if scenarios	Tools menu
Template Utilities	Provides useful utilities used in Excel's built-in templates	Data menu
Template Wizard	Creates form templates with data tracking	Data menu

Tools for Working Together

IN THIS SECTION

Sharing Workbooks

Merging Workbooks

Sharing Information Among Documents

New2000 **Exporting and Importing Data**

Linking and Embedding Files

Linking Data

Consolidating Data

New2000 **Getting Data from Queries**

Getting Data from Another Program

Converting Excel Data into Access Data

Creating successful workbooks is not always a solitary venture: you may need to share a workbook with others or get data from other programs before a project is complete. In Microsoft Excel 2000, you have several choices for combining your efforts. In many offices, co-workers and their computers across the country are joined through networks that permit users to share information by opening each other's files and simultaneously making modifications. In addition to sharing workbooks, you can merge information from different workbooks into a single document, and you can link data between or consolidate data from different worksheets and workbooks.

Working Together

The beauty of teamwork is that people can combine their efforts to create a product that no one could accomplish alone, at least not in as short an amount of time or with the same perspective. In a shared environment, however, users have to be more conscious of who controls the file, the version being used, and what parts of the file can be updated. Using a variety of techniques, data can be linked, embedded, hyperlinked, exported, or converted to create one seamless document that reflects the efforts of many people.

Sharing Workbooks

When you're working with others in a networked environment, you may want to share workbooks you created. You may also want to share the responsibilities of entering and maintaining data. *Sharing* means users can add columns and rows, enter data, and change formatting, while allowing you to review their changes. This type of work arrangement is particularly effective in team situations in which multiple users have joint responsibility for data within a single workbook. In cases in which multiple users modify the same cells, Excel can keep track of changes, and you can accept or reject them at a later date.

SEE ALSO

See "Tracking Changes" on page 204 for information about identifying modifications made in a workbook by other users.

Enable Workbook Sharing

1. Open the workbook you want to share.

2. Click the Tools menu, and then click Share Workbook.

3. Click the Editing tab.

4. Click to select the Allow Changes By More Than One User At The Same Time check box.

5. Click OK, and then click OK again to save your workbook.

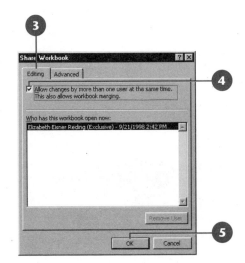

Change Sharing Options

1. Open the workbook you want to share.

2. Click the Tools menu, and then click Share Workbook.

Indicates that the workbook is shared

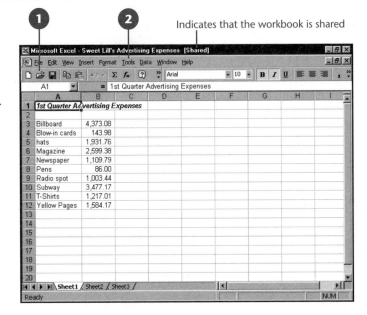

13

Excel alerts you if you are working in a shared file. *When sharing is enabled, "[Shared]" appears in the title bar of the shared workbook.*

See "Working with the Excel Window" on page 8 for information about arranging worksheets.

See "Customizing Your Excel Work Environment" on page 190 for information about seeing more worksheet data on the screen.

Make changes to another user's workbook. *Take turns making changes in a workbook created by someone else. Try accepting or rejecting the other user's modifications.*

3 Click the Advanced tab.

4 To indicate how long to keep changes, select one of the Track Changes options, and if necessary, set the number of days.

5 To indicate when changes should be saved, select one of the Update Changes options, and if necessary, set a time internal.

6 To resolve conflicting changes, select one of the Conflicting Changes Between Users options.

7 Click to select one or both of the Include In Personal View check boxes.

8 Click OK.

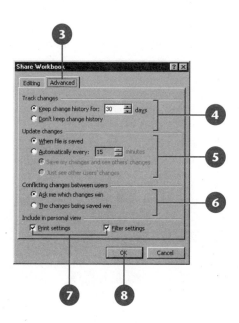

Merging Workbooks

Excel automates the process of merging workbook data with the Template Wizard. The *Template Wizard* takes data from a list template within a worksheet and consolidates the data in a list. The Template Wizard lets you make individual entries on a worksheet that is actually compiled in a database. For example, if you are a manager at a local trucking company that requires each driver to file a daily run report, each entry would be added to a central database that contains all the reports. The template created by the wizard ensures that each driver supplies the same information; the template is actually linked to the database.

SEE ALSO

See "Understanding Excel Program Add-Ins" on page 220 for information on commonly used Microsoft Excel Add-Ins, such as the Template Wizard.

Merge Workbook Data with the Template Wizard

1. Open the workbook that you want to use as the template.

2. Click the Data menu, and then click Template Wizard.

3. If the name of the workbook that you want to use as the template does not appear in the text box, click the drop-down arrow and select it.

4. If you are not satisfied with the template name and storage location assigned by Excel, enter a different name and location.

5. Click Next to continue.

6. Click Next to accept the type of database as an Excel workbook and the default location of the database.

7. Click in the Cell 1 box, click a cell, and then press Tab.

8. Repeat step 7 until all cells are identified.

9. Click Next to continue.

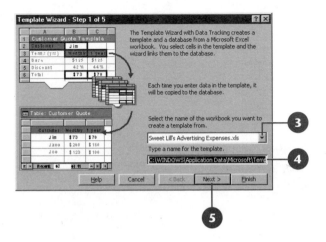

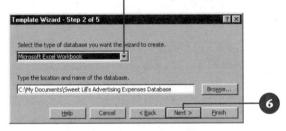

Click to change the type of database.

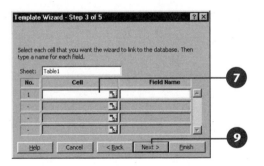

⑩ Click the Yes, Include option button if you want to add information from existing workbooks, or click the No, Skip It option button if you don't want to add any data.

⑪ Click Next to continue.

⑫ If you chose the Yes, Include option button in step 10, click Select to add any files whose data will be added.

⑬ Click Next to continue.

⑭ Click Finish.

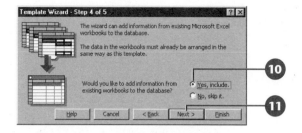

Sharing Information Among Documents

One of the great recent advances in personal computing is the technology that lets you insert an object created in one program into a document created in another program. This technology is known as *Object Linking and Embedding (OLE)*. OLE allows you to move text or data between programs in much the same way as you move them within a program. The familar cut-and-paste and drag-and-drop methods work between programs and documents just as they do within a document. In addition, Excel and all Office programs have special ways to move information from one program to another, including exporting and importing, embedding, linking, and hyperlinking.

Terms that you'll find useful when sharing objects among documents include:

TERM	DEFINITION
Source program	The program that created the original object
Source file	The file that contains the original object
Destination program	The program that created the document into which you are inserting the object
Destination file	The file into which you are inserting the object

For example, if you place an Excel chart into a PowerPoint presentation, Excel is the source program, and PowerPoint is the destination program. The chart is the source file; the presentation is the destination file.

Pasting

You can cut or copy information from one document and then paste it into another using the Cut, Copy, and Paste buttons on the source and destination program toolbars. You can also drag selected information from one section of a document to another.

Exporting and Importing

Importing and exporting information are two sides of the same coin. *Exporting* converts a copy of your open file into the file type of another program. *Importing* copies a file created with the same or another program into your open file. The information becomes part of your open file, just as if you created it in that format, although formatting and program-specific information can be lost. In other words, importing brings information into your open document, while exporting moves information from your open document into another program file.

Embedding

When you *embed* an object, you place a copy of the object in the destination file, and when you select the object, the tools from the source program become available on your worksheet. For example, if you insert an Excel chart into a PowerPoint presentation, the Excel menus and toolbars become available, replacing the PowerPoint menus and toolbars, so you can edit the chart if necessary. With embedding, any changes you make to the chart in the presentation do not affect the original file.

Linking

When you *link* an object, you insert a representation of the object itself into the destination file. The tools of the source program are available, and when you use them to edit the object you've inserted, you are actually editing the source file. Moreover, any changes you make to the source file are reflected in the destination file.

Hyperlinking

The newest way to share information between programs—hyperlinking—comes from World Wide Web technology. A *hyperlink* is an object (either colored, underlined text or a graphic) you click to jump to a different location in the same document or to a different document.

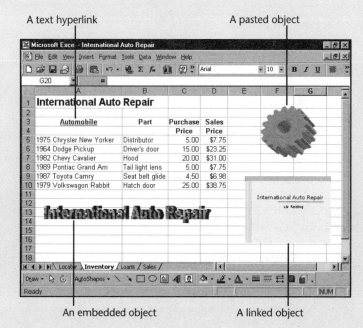

A text hyperlink

A pasted object

An embedded object

A linked object

Exporting and Importing Data

In cases where you don't need the data you are using from another source to be automatically updated if the source data changes, the most expedient way to get the data is to copy and paste it. In cases where you want to copy data from one program to another, you can convert the data to a format that the other program accepts. If you have text you want to include on your worksheet, you can import a text file in a workbook.

TIP

Excel can save a file to a format only with an installed converter. *If the format you want to save a file in does not appear in the Save As Type list, you'll need to install it by running Setup from the Microsoft Excel 2000 or Microsoft Office 2000 CD.*

Export Excel Data Using Copy and Paste

1. Select the cell or range that you want to copy.

2. Click the Copy button on the Standard toolbar.

3. Open the destination file, or click the program's taskbar button if the program is already open.

4. Position the insertion point where you want the data to be copied.

5. Click the Paste button on the Standard toolbar.

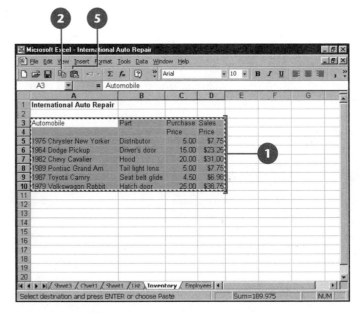

Export an Excel File to Another Program Format

1. Open the file from which you want to export data.

2. Click the File menu, and then click Save As.

3. Click the Save As Type drop-down arrow.

4. Click the file format you want.

5. Click Save.

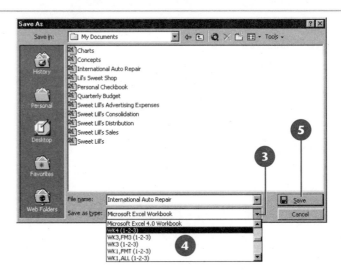

SEE ALSO

See "Selecting Cells" on page 27 and "Moving Cell Contents" on page 40 for information on working with cell ranges.

TRY THIS

Export Excel data to Access. *Export worksheet data into Access, and then examine the data in Access.*

Import an Text File

1. Open the workbook in which you want to insert text data.

2. Click the Data menu, point to Get External Data, and then click Import Text File.

3. Click the Look In drop-down arrow, and then select the folder where the text file is located.

4. Click the text file you want to import.

5. Click Import.

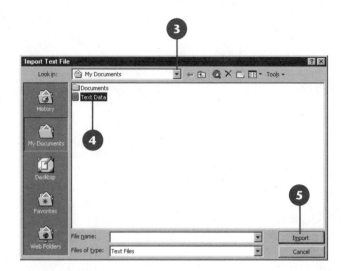

Linking and Embedding Files

Information created using other Office programs can be shared among them. This means that data created in an Excel workbook, for example, can be included in a Word document without being retyped. This makes projects such as annual or departmental reports simple to create. Information can be either linked or embedded. Data that is linked has the advantage of always being accurate because it is automatically updated when the linked document is modified.

TIP

Select multiple links. *You can select multiple links by holding down the Ctrl key while you click each link.*

Create a Link to Another File

1. Open the source file and any files containing information you want to link.

2. Select the information in the source file, and then click the Copy button on the Standard toolbar.

3. Click the insertion point in the file containing the link.

4. Click the Edit menu, and then click Paste Special.

5. Click Paste Link.

Modify a Link

1. Open the file that contains the link you want to modify.

2. Click the Edit menu, and then click Links.

3. Click the link you want to change.

4. Click Change Source.

5. Select a file from the Change Links dialog box, and then click OK.

6. Click OK.

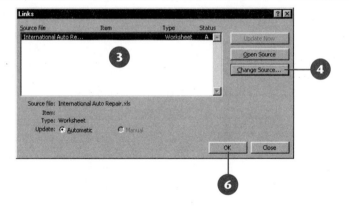

Embed a New Object

1. Click the Insert menu, and then click Object.

2. Click the Create New tab.

3. Click the object type you want to insert.

4. Click OK.

5. Follow the necessary steps to insert the object.

   The steps will vary depending on the object type.

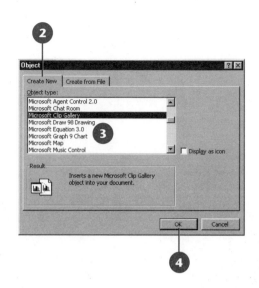

Embed an Existing Object

1. Click the Insert menu, and then click Object.

2. Click the Create From File tab.

3. Click Browse, and then locate the file that you want to link.

4. Click to select the Link To File check box.

5. Click OK.

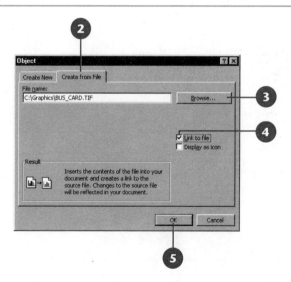

Linking Data

A *link* can be as simple as a reference to a cell on another worksheet, or it can be part of a formula. You can link cells between sheets within one workbook or between different workbooks. Cell data to be linked is called the *source data*. The cell or range linked to the source data is called the *destination cell* or *destination range*. If you no longer want linked data to be updated, you can break a link easily. Create links instead of making multiple identical entries; it saves time and ensures your entries are correct.

TIP

For static data, stick with copy and paste. *To use data from another source that you don't want updated, copy or move instead of linking.*

Create a Link Between Worksheets

1. Select the destination cell or destination range.

2. Click the = button on the formula bar.

3. Click the sheet tab that contains the source data.

4. Select the cell or range that contains the source data.

5. Click OK or click the Enter button on the formula bar.

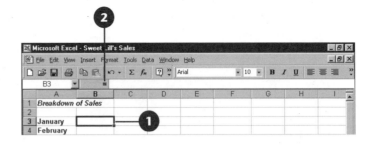

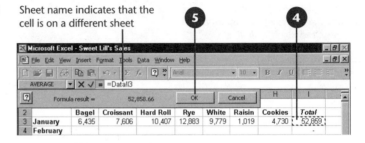

Sheet name indicates that the cell is on a different sheet

Break a Link

1. Click the cell containing the linked formula you want to break.

2. Click the Copy button on the Standard toolbar.

3. Click the Edit menu, and then click Paste Special.

4. Click the Values option button.

5. Click OK.

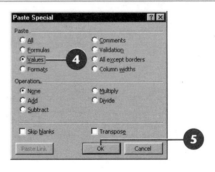

Arrange worksheet windows to make linking easier. *To arrange open windows, click the Window menu, click Arrange, and then click the option button for the window arrangement you want.*

Create a link between two workbooks, and then close the workbook that contains the link. *In the open workbook, change the cell containing the source data. When you open the other workbook, watch how Excel updates the link to reflect the most up-to-date data.*

To include a link in a formula, treat the linked cell as one argument in a larger calculation. *Enter the formula on the formula bar, and then enter the workbook, worksheet, and cell address of the data you want to link.*

See "Creating a Simple Formula" on page 48 for information about arithmetic operators.

Create a Link Between Workbooks

1. Open the workbooks that contain the data you want to link.

2. Click the destination cell or destination range.

3. Click the = button on the formula bar.

4. If the workbook that contains the data you want to link is visible, click anywhere within it to activate it.

5. If necessary, click the sheet tab that contains the source data.

6. Select the cell or range that contains the source data.

7. Click OK, or click the Enter button on the formula bar.

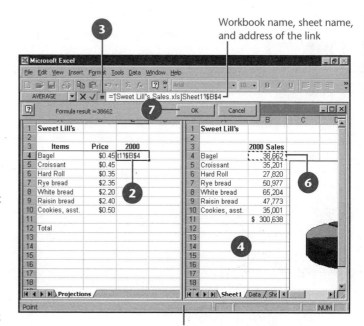

Workbook name, sheet name, and address of the link

To simplify your task, arrange the open windows for better visibility.

Consolidating Data

In some cases, you'll want to consolidate data from different worksheets or workbooks into one workbook rather than simply linking the source data. For instance, if each division in your company creates a budget, you can pull together—or *consolidate*—the totals for each line item into one company-wide budget. If each divisional budget is laid out in the same way, with the budgeted amount for each line item in the same cell addresses, then you can very easily consolidate all the information without any retyping. If data in individual workbooks change the consolidated worksheet or workbook will always be correct.

TIP

Include all labels. *Make sure you select enough cells to accommodate any labels that might be included in the data you are consolidating.*

Consolidate Data from Other Worksheets or Workbooks

① Open all the workbooks that contain the data you want to consolidate.

② Open or create the workbook that will contain the consolidated data.

③ Select the destination range.

④ Click the Data menu, and then click Consolidate.

⑤ Click the Function drop-down arrow, and then select the function you want to use to consolidate the data.

⑥ Type the location of the data to be consolidated, or click the Reference Collapse Dialog button and then select the cells to be consolidated.

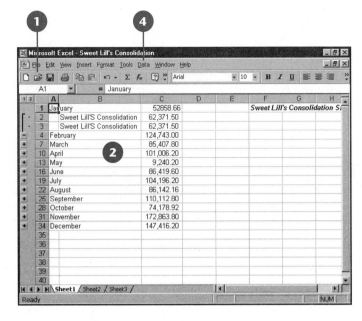

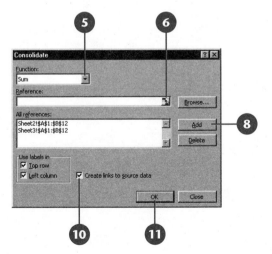

SEE ALSO

See "Linking Data" on page 232 for information on breaking links.

TIP

Consolidate worksheets even if they are not laid out identically. *If the worksheets you want to consolidate aren't laid out with exactly the same cell addresses, but they do contain identical types of information, select the Top Row and Left Column check boxes in the Consolidate dialog box so that Excel uses labels to match up the correct data.*

TIP

Arrange multiple workbooks. *Use the Window menu to move between workbooks or to arrange them so they are visible at the same time.*

7 Click the Expand Dialog button.

8 Click Add to add the reference to the list of consolidated ranges.

9 Repeat steps 6 through 8 until you have listed all references to consolidate.

10 Click to select the Create Links To Source Data check box.

11 Click OK.

The minus button indicates that consolidated data is displayed.

Consolidated data for March

Click the plus button to see consolidated data.

Getting Data from Queries

You can import data into Excel through database and Web queries and analyze data with formulas and formatting. You can insert columns within query tables and apply formulas and formatting. When data is refreshed, the formatting and analysis are retained. Excel helps you through the process of bringing data from a Web page to your worksheet. You can create a new Web query as you choose the URL and parameters for how you want to import the Web data. Once you save the query, you can run it again at any time.

TIP

Stop a query. *To cancel a query, click Stop Refresh.*

SEE ALSO

See "Understanding Excel Program Add-Ins" on page 220 for information on commonly used Microsoft Excel Add-Ins.

Get Data from a New Database Query

1. Click the Data menu, point to Get External Data, and then click New Database Query.

2. Double-click <New Data Source>.

3. Type a name for your data source.

4. Click the drop-down arrow, and then select the type of database you want to access.

5. Click Connect, select or create the database you want to access, and then click OK.

6. If you want, click the drop-down arrow, and then select the default table for your data source.

7. Click OK.

8. Click OK.

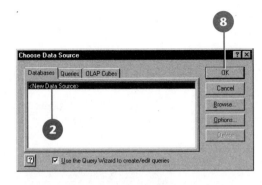

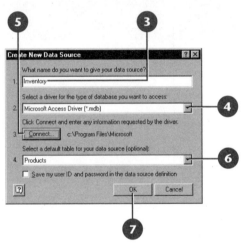

Get Data from a New Web Query

1. Click the Data menu, point to Get External Data, and then click New Web Query.

2. Type the address for the Web page that contains the data you want.

   If necessary, click Browse Web to help you locate a Web page on the Internet.

3. Click the option button to select the part of the Web page that contains the data you want.

4. Click the option button to select the formatting you want your data to keep.

5. If you want, click Save Query, type a name, and then click Save to save your query settings so you don't have to enter them again.

6. Click OK.

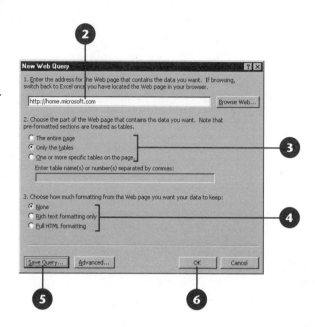

Getting Data from Another Program

Information you want to analyze may not always exist in an Excel workbook; you might have to retrieve it from another Office program, such as Access. Access table data can be easily converted into Excel worksheet data. Once the data is in Excel, you can use any of Excel's analytical tools (such as PivotTable and AutoFilter) on this data.

SEE ALSO

See "Displaying Parts of a List with AutoFilter" on page 178 for information on using the AutoFilter feature.

Export an Access Database Table into an Excel Workbook

1. Click Start on the taskbar, point to Programs, and then click Microsoft Access.

2. Open the database you want, and then click Tables on the Objects bar.

3. Click the table you want to analyze.

4. Click the OfficeLinks button drop-down arrow on the Database toolbar.

5. Click Analyze It With MS Excel to save the table as an Excel file, start Excel, and open the workbook.

6. Use Excel tools to edit and analyze the data.

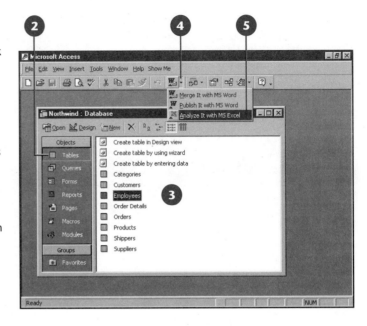

SEE ALSO

See "Analyzing Data Using a PivotTable" on page 182 for information on creating a PivotTable.

SEE ALSO

See "Getting Data from Queries" on page 236 for more information about importing data into Excel through database and Web queries.

Create an Excel Workbook PivotTable from an Access Database

1. Click the Data menu, and then click PivotTable And PivotChart Report.

2. Click the External Data Source option button.

3. Click Next.

4. Click Get Data.

5. Click Browse, and then locate and select the Access database you want to use.

6. Click OK.

7. Click Next.

8. Click a location option for the new PivotTable.

9. If you want, click Layout or Options to change the way the PivotTable looks or functions, and then click OK.

10. Click Finish.

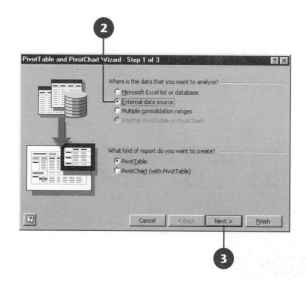

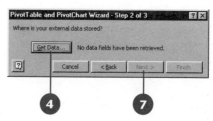

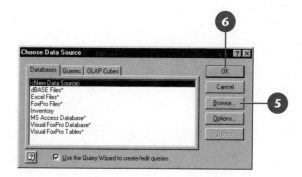

Converting Excel Data into Access Data

You can convert your Excel worksheet data into an Access table data using the File Conversion Wizard. This gives you the flexibility of using data created in Excel in Access, where you can take advantage of additional data management and manipulation features.

TIP

The AccessLinks add-in may not be installed. *If you don't see the Convert To MS Access command on the Data menu, install the AccessLinks add-in program from the Microsoft Excel 2000 or Microsoft Office 2000 CD.*

TIP

Bring Access data into Excel. *Convert an Access table to an Excel worksheet, and then create a PivotTable using the newly converted data.*

Convert Excel Data to Access Data

1. Select the Excel worksheet data you want to convert.

2. Click the Data menu, and then click Convert To MS Access.

3. Choose to create a new database or to open an existing one.

4. Click OK.

Access starts and creates a new table based on the Excel data in a new database or an existing one.

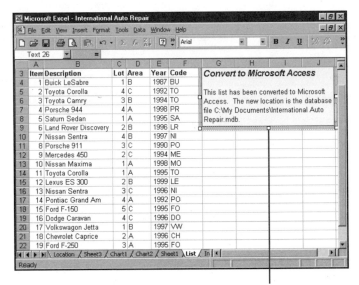

On completion of the conversion, a comment is embedded into Excel.

Linking Excel to the Internet

IN THIS SECTION

New2000 **Creating a Web Page**

New2000 **Opening a Workbook as a Web Page**

New2000 **Previewing a Web Page**

Inserting an Internet Link

Getting Data from the Web

New2000 **Copying a Web Table to a Worksheet**

New2000 **Understanding Office Server Extensions**

New2000 **Having a Web Discussion**

New2000 **Scheduling and Holding an Online Meeting**

New2000 **Sending Workbooks Using E-mail**

New2000 **Accessing Office Information on the Web**

Incorporating hyperlinks within your Microsoft Excel 2000 worksheet adds an element of connectivity to your work. Workbooks are now gateways to evolving information. By converting your Excel workbooks to Web pages, others can share your data on the Web. The improved functionality of Excel means others can use your workbooks with all their analytical tools intact. Excel is a now used as a "front end to data": this means you can collaborate with users on the Web and use rich analysis tools for better decision-making results.

Keeping in Touch

Using Excel's connectivity tools, you can easily maintain relationships with other professionals. A single worksheet can become a "window to the world" given Excel's ability to exchange information, analyze data, send files using e-mail, hold meetings, and have Web discussions. Any worksheet can easily be saved as a Web document and viewed in a browser while maintaining its Excel functionality. This same document can be a conduit for Web information, containing links to sites and obtaining data from other Web sources. In addition, Microsoft offers tips and general information through its Microsoft Office Web site.

Creating a Web Page

You can place an existing Excel worksheet on the Internet for others to use. In order for any document to be placed on the Web, it must be in *HTML (Hypertext Markup Language)* format. This format enables you to *post*, or submit, Excel data on a Web site for others. You don't need any HTML knowledge to save an Excel worksheet as a Web page. Dialog boxes lead you through steps needed to save an Excel worksheet as a Web page. A worksheet saved as a Web page retains all its spreadsheet, charting, or PivotTable functionality and formatting properties. This *interactivity* means that while your worksheet is on the Web, others can manipulate your data.

SEE ALSO

See "Previewing a Web Page" on page 245 for more information about seeing your Web pages in a Web browser.

Save a Workbook as a Web Page

1. Click the File menu, and then click Save As Web Page.

2. Click one of the icons on the Places bar to select a location to save the Web page.

3. If you want to save the file in another folder, click the Save In drop-down arrow, and then select the drive and folder in which you want to save the Web page.

4. Type the name for the Web page.

5. Click Save.

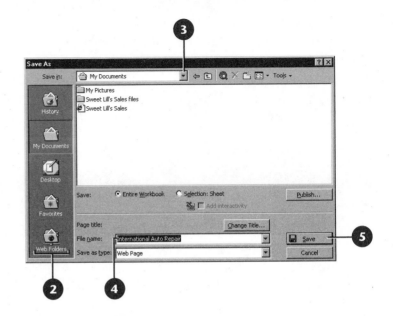

TIP

Your Web browser needs to support Office Web Components to interact with data. *Office Web Components—known as COM components—are used by Web browsers, such as Microsoft Internet Explorer 4.01 or later, to let users interact with spreadsheet, charting, and PivotTable data on the Web.*

TIP

Publish a Web page to an FTP site on the Internet. *In the Save As dialog box, click the Save In drop-down arrow, click Add/Modify FTP Locations, fill in the FTP site information, click Add, click OK, and then click the FTP location.*

TIP

What is a Web server? *A Web server is a computer on the Internet or intranet that stores Web pages.*

SEE ALSO

See "Understanding Office Server Extensions" on page 251 for information on publishing and viewing Office documents directly from a Web server with Office Server Extensions.

Save and Publish a Worksheet as an Interactive Web Page

1. Select the cell(s) you want saved as a Web page.

2. Click the File menu, and then click Save As Web Page.

3. If necessary, click the Selection: *range address* option button to convert the selected range.

4. To add interactivity to your Web document, click the Add Interactivity check box.

5. Click one of the icons on the Places bar to select a location for the Web page file.

   If you're connected to a Web server with Office Server Extensions, click the Web Folders icon to select a location on the Internet or your intranet.

6. Type the name for the Web page.

7. Click Publish.

8. Click the Add Interactivity With drop-down arrow, and then click Spreadsheet, PivotTable, or other Office Web Component.

9. Click Publish.

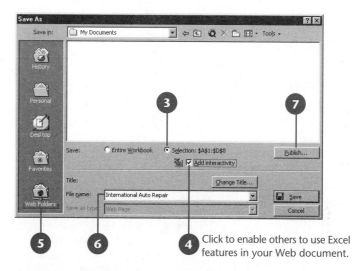

Click to enable others to use Excel features in your Web document.

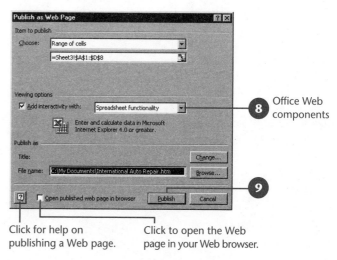

Office Web components

Click for help on publishing a Web page.

Click to open the Web page in your Web browser.

Opening a Workbook as a Web Page

After saving a workbook as a Web page, you can open the Web page, an HTML file, in Excel. This allows you to quickly and easily switch from HTML to the standard Excel format and back again without losing any formatting or functionality. For example, if you create a formatted chart in an Excel worksheet, save the workbook file as a Web page, and then reopen the Web page in Excel, the chart will look the same as the original chart in Excel. Excel preserves the original formatting and functionality of the workbook.

Open button

Open a Workbook as a Web Page in Excel

1. Click the Open button on the Standard toolbar in the Excel window.

2. Click the Files Of Type drop-down arrow, and then select Web Pages.

3. Click one of the icons on the Places bar for quick access to frequently used folders.

4. If the file is located in another folder, click the Look In drop-down arrow, and then select the folder where the file is located.

5. Click the name of the workbook file.

6. Click Open.

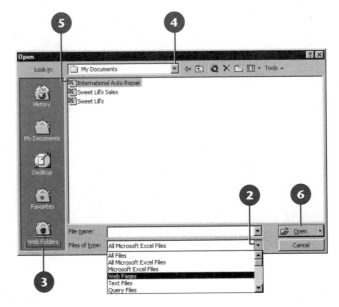

Previewing a Web Page

You can view any Excel worksheet as if it were already on the Web by previewing the Web page. By previewing a file you want to post to the Web, you can see if there are any errors that need to be corrected, formatting that needs to be added, or additions that need to be made. Just as you should always preview a worksheet before you print it, you should preview a Web page before you post it. Previewing the Web page is similar to using the Print Preview feature before you print a worksheet. This view shows you what the page will look like once it's posted on the Internet.

SEE ALSO

See "Creating a Web Page" on page 242 for information on saving a workbook as a Web page.

View the Web Page

1. Open the workbook file you want to view as a Web page.

2. Click the File menu, and then click Web Page Preview.

   Your default Web browser starts and displays the Web page.

3. Click any sheet tab you want to view.

4. Click the Close button to quit your Web browser and return to Excel.

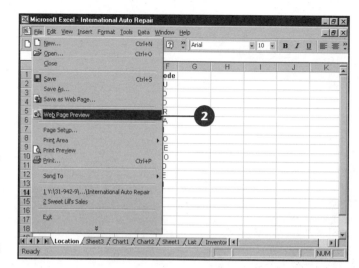

14

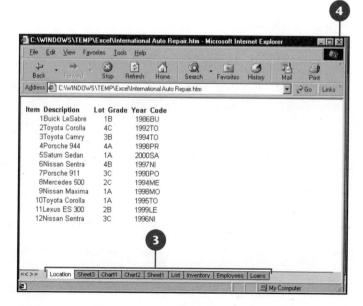

Inserting an Internet Link

With instant access to the Internet, your worksheet can contain links to specific sites so you and anyone else using your worksheet can access Web information. An Internet link that is embedded on a worksheet is called a *hyperlink*—because when it is clicked, you are instantly connected to the link's defined address on the Web. If your worksheet contains a hyperlink, the link appears in the worksheet as blue text. To connect to the Web site, just click the hyperlink.

Insert Hyperlink button

SEE ALSO

See "Sharing Information Among Documents" on page 226 for information on hyperlinks.

Create a Hyperlink

1. Select a cell where you want the hyperlink to appear.

2. Click the Insert Hyperlink button on the Standard toolbar.

3. Click one of the icons on the Link To bar for quick access to frequently used files, Web pages, and links.

   In addition, you can click an icon in the Or Select From List bar.

4. If the file or Web page you want to link is located in another folder, click File or Web Page.

5. If necessary, type the name and location of the file or Web page you want to link to.

6. Click OK.

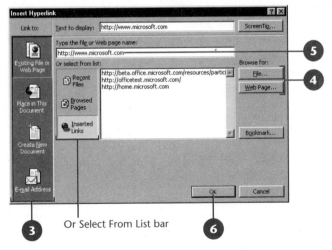

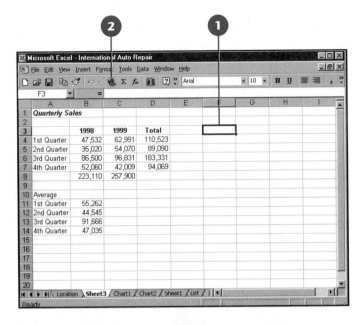

Or Select From List bar

Create a custom ScreenTip for a hyperlink. *Select the hyperlink you want to customize, click the Insert Hyperlink button on the Standard toolbar, click ScreenTip, type the ScreenTip text you want, click OK, and then click OK again.*

Web addresses and URLs. *Every Web page has a Uniform Resource Locator (URL), a Web address in a form your browser program can decipher. Like postal addresses and e-mail addresses, each URL contains specific parts that identify where a Web page is located. For example, the URL for Microsoft's Web page is* **http://www.microsoft.com/** *where "http://" shows the address is on the Web and "www.microsoft.com" shows the computer that stores the Web page.*

Jump to a Hyperlink

① Click the hyperlink on your worksheet.

Excel opens your Web browser.

② Establish an Internet connection.

The Web page associated with the hyperlink is displayed.

The mouse pointer changes to a hand when placed over a hyperlink.

Remove a Hyperlink

① Select a cell containing the hyperlink you want to remove.

② Click the Insert Hyperlink button on the Standard toolbar.

③ Click Remove Link.

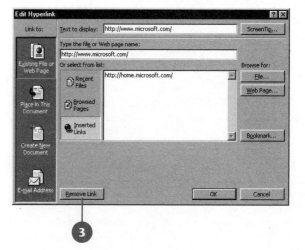

Getting Data from the Web

You can look up data on the Web and insert it into Excel using the Web toolbar. You can jump from Web site to Web site, gathering data to include on your own worksheets. You might, for example, want to include text from a Web site containing information relevant to your company, department, or research project. The Web is also a great source of free clip art. Using Microsoft's Clip Gallery Live or other online resources, you can illustrate a worksheet with almost any product, theme, or idea.

TIP

Hide and display other toolbars. *To help you see more information on the screen, you can show only the Web toolbar. To hide the other toolbars, click the Show Only Web Toolbar button on the Web toolbar. Click the button again to display the other toolbars.*

Get Data from the Web Using the Web Toolbar

1. Click the View menu, point to Toolbars, and then click Web.

2. Click the Search The Web button on the Web toolbar.

   Excel opens your Web browser.

3. Establish an Internet connection.

4. Follow the directions to search for Web sites that contain the data you want.

5. To get text data from a Web page, select the text, click the Edit menu, and then click Copy. Switch to Excel and then paste the text on your worksheet.

6. To download a file, click the download hyperlink, click the Save This File To Disk option button, click OK, select a location, and then click Save.

7. When you're done, click the Close button.

8. If necessary, close your Internet connection.

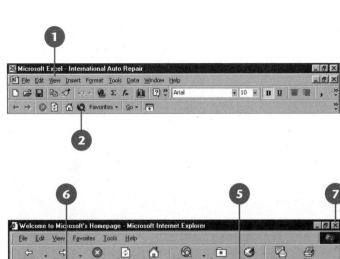

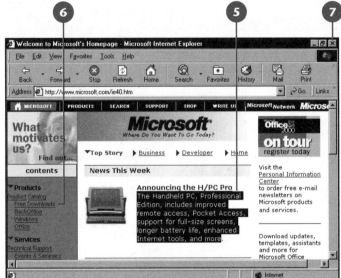

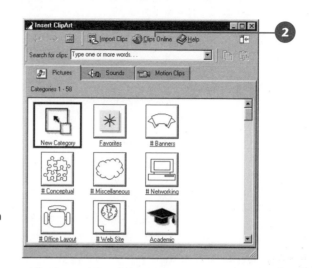

TIP

Change your search page.
Open the document you want as your search page, click the Go button on the Web toolbar, click Set Search Page, and then click Yes.

TIP

Jump to a favorite document or Web page.
Click the Favorites button on the Web toolbar, and then click the document or Web page you want.

SEE ALSO

See "Getting Data from Queries" on page 236 for information on importing data from the Web using a Web query.

SEE ALSO

See "Inserting Pictures" on page 104 for information on working with clip art.

Get Additional Clips from the Web

1. Click the Insert menu, point to Picture, and then click Clip Art.

2. Click the Clips Online button. Excel opens your Web browser.

3. Establish an Internet connection.

4. Click the appropriate hyperlinks as instructed on the Clip Gallery Live Web page to access and download clip art.

5. When you are finished, click the File menu, and then click Close.

6. If necessary, close your Internet connection.

14

Copying a Web Table to a Worksheet

You can copy tabular information on a Web page and paste or drag the information into an Excel worksheet. It's an easy way to transfer and manipulate Web-based table data using Excel. Excel simplifies access to table data by making it available to anyone with a browser.

TIP

Use copy and paste to transfer table data to Excel. *In your browser, select the table data you want, click the Edit menu, click Copy, switch to Excel, click the cell where you want to place the table data, and then click the Paste button on the Standard toolbar.*

Copy a Web Table to a Worksheet

1. Open your Web browser.

2. In the Address bar, type the location of the Web page with the table data you want to copy, and then press Enter.

3. Select the table data in the Web page you want to copy.

4. Open the Excel worksheet where you want to paste the table data.

5. Right-click the taskbar, and then click Tile Windows Vertically.

6. Drag the table data from the Web browser window to the location on the worksheet where you want the table data, and then release the mouse button.

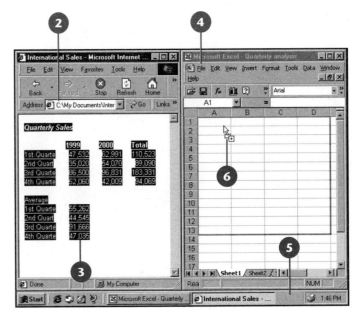

Understanding Office Server Extensions

Microsoft Office 2000 uses *Office Server Extensions* to provide a bridge between current Web technologies and the functionality needed to make the Web a friendly place to work with people and information. Office Server Extensions are a set of features that makes it easy to work with Office files and collaborate on the Web. Office Server Extensions allow you to publish and view Web documents directly from a Web server—a computer on the Internet that stores Web pages—with Office programs or Internet Explorer; to perform Web discussions and exchange information on documents located on the Web server; and to receive notification when a document on a Web server has been changed, which is known as *Web Subscription* and *Web Notification*.

Office Server Extensions are a superset of Microsoft FrontPage Extensions and other technologies that reside on an Windows NT–based Web servers to provide additional publishing, collaboration, and document management capabilities. Office Server Extensions do not replace existing Web server technologies. Rather, the extensions in Office 2000 are designed to enhance your experience with Office in a Web-based environment.

Office Server Extensions are included with Office 2000 Premium edition. To set up your computer with Office Server Extensions, you need a computer with Windows NT Workstation 4.0 or later running Personal Web Server 4.0 or later, or Windows NT Server 4.0 or later running Internet Information Server 4.0 or later. With the Server Extensions Configuration Wizard, you can set up and configure an existing Web server to use the Office Server Extensions.

Web File Management

Office Server Extensions make publishing and sharing documents on Web servers as easy as working with documents on file servers. Office 2000 enables you to create folders, view properties, and perform file drag-and-drop operations on Web servers just as you would on normal file servers. You can also perform these same Web server file operations directly from the Windows Explorer. In Internet Explorer, Office Server Extensions enable on-the-fly display of Web directory listings, files, and HTML views of Web folders.

Web Discussions

With the Office Server Extensions installed on a Web server, you can have online discussions in Web page (HTML) files and Office 2000 documents. A *Web discussion* is an online, interactive conversation that takes place within the Web page or document (also called "in-line") or that occurs as a general discussion about the Web page or Office document, which is stored in the discussion pane at the bottom of the page. A Web discussion can occur only through Internet Explorer or an Office program. Using the Discussions toolbar, users can insert new comments, edit and reply to existing comments, subscribe to a particular document, and view or hide the Discussion pane.

14

Having a Web Discussion

Unlike an online meeting, a Web discussion allows multiple users to discuss specific documents. The discussions are stored separately from their document counterparts and are merged later when you view the results. The documents can be on the Internet, an intranet, or on a network. The advantage to a Web discussion is that the context of your online collaboration is preserved in a file that can be viewed at a later date. You can, for example, discuss a worksheet at an online meeting, and then analyze not only the worksheet but the discussion with others later.

SEE ALSO

See "Understanding Office Server Extensions" on page 251 for information on what you'll need to have a Web discussion.

Select a Web Discussion Server

1. Open the workbook to which you want to add a Web discussion.

2. Click the Tools menu, point to Online Collaboration, and then click Web Discussions.

   If you are selecting a discussion server for the first time, skip to step 5.

3. Click the Discussions button on the Discussions toolbar, and then click Discussion Options.

4. Click Add.

5. Type the name of the discussion server provided by your administrator.

   The discussion server needs to have Office Server Extensions to hold a Web discussion.

6. If your administrator has set up security by using the Secure Sockets Layer (SSL) message protocol, click to select the Secure Connection Required (SSL) check box.

7. Type a name you want to use for the Web discussion.

8. Click OK.

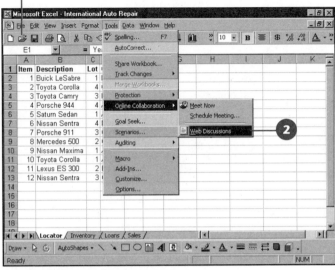

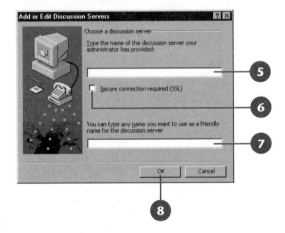

14

Hide the Discussion pane.
During a discussion, click the Show/Hide Discussion Pane button on the Discussions toolbar to show or hide the Discussion pane.

Print discussion remarks.
Start a discussion, click the Discussions button on the Discussions toolbar, click Print Discussions, and then select the print options you want.

Filter discussion remarks.
You can filter the discussion remarks on a worksheet so that you read only discussions inserted by a particular person or within a certain time frame. Start a discussion, click the Discussions button on the Discussions toolbar, click Filter Discussions, and then select the name of the person whose remarks you want to see in the Discussion pane and the time frame you want.

Start and Close a Web Discussion

1. Open the workbook for which you want to start a discussion.

2. Click the Tools menu, point to Online Collaboration, and then click Web Discussions.

3. Click the Insert Discussion About The Workbook button on the Discussions toolbar.

4. Type the subject of the discussion.

5. Type your comments.

6. Click OK.

7. Click Close on the Discussions toolbar.

Reply to a Web Discussion Remark

1. Open the workbook that contains the discussion you want to join.

2. Click the Tools menu, point to Online Collaboration, then click Web Discussions.

3. Click the Show A Menu Of Actions button, and then click Reply.

4. Type your reply, and then click OK.

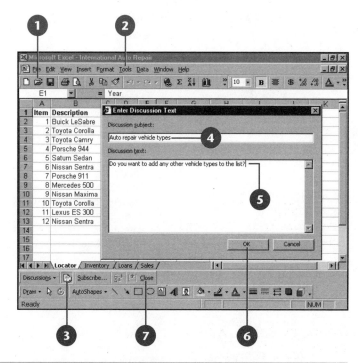

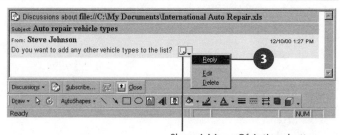

Show A Menu Of Actions button

Scheduling and Holding an Online Meeting

Excel 2000 helps you to collaborate with others online not only by sharing information but by scheduling and holding meetings online using a program called Microsoft NetMeeting. By scheduling a meeting online, attendees can check their schedules, determine if there are conflicts, and respond online whether or not they can attend. Holding a meeting online means that people across the country or across the world can meet on short notice without leaving their office or home.

TIP

Show attendee status. *Once a meeting is scheduled, you can check to see who has decided to attend. In the Meeting dialog box, click the Attendee Availability tab, and then click the Show Attendee Status option button.*

Schedule an Online Meeting

① Click the Tools menu, point to Online Collaboration, and then click Schedule Meeting.

② Click the To button to invite others to join the meeting.

③ Click the Directory Server drop-down arrow, select the directory server you want to use, and then enter the organizer's e-mail address, if necessary.

④ Click the Attendee Availability tab to determine who will be at the meeting.

⑤ Click the Show Attendee Availability option button to view when attendees are able to meet.

For Internet users, you need to post your calendar to an agreed upon Web server for the host to view your availability.

⑥ Click the Send button on the toolbar.

Names of meeting attendees appear here.

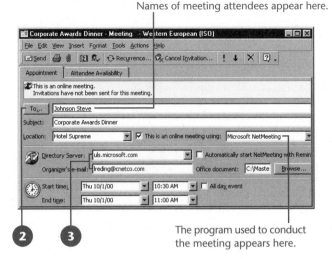

The program used to conduct the meeting appears here.

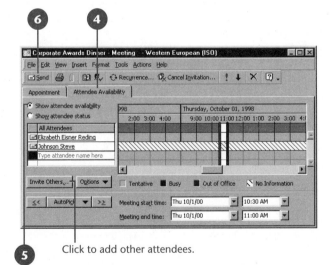

Click to add other attendees.

Receive an online meeting call. *You must have NetMeeting running on your computer to receive an online meeting call.*

Start NetMeeting using the Start button. *To start NetMeeting, click Start on the taskbar, point to Programs, and then click NetMeeting.*

Join an online meeting. *If you receive an online meeting call, click Accept in the Join Meeting dialog box. If you receive an Outlook reminder for the meeting, click Start This NetMeeting (host), or Join This NetMeeting (participant). To receive an Outlook reminder to join a meeting, you needed to accept the meeting from an e-mail message.*

See "Having a Web Discussion" on page 252 for information on having an online Web discussion about a specific Excel workbook.

Hold an Online Meeting

1. Open the document you want to share.

2. Click the Tools menu, point to Online Collaboration, and then click Meet Now.

3. If this is your first meeting, select a directory server and enter user information as instructed.

4. If you want, click the Directory drop-down arrow, and then select a directory server.

5. Select participants for the meeting, and then click Call.

Participate in an Online Meeting

◆ Use the buttons on the Online Meeting toolbar to participate in an online meeting.

Enter the names of the people you want to invite to the meeting.

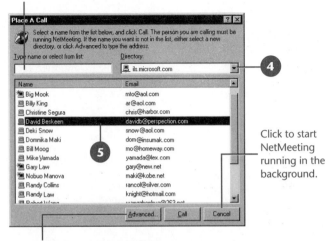

Click to start NetMeeting running in the background.

Click to enter the computer name or protocol address of the person you want to invite.

ONLINE MEETING TOOLBAR	
Button	**Description**
	Allows the host to invite additional participants to the online meeting
	Allows the host to remove a participant from the online meeting
	Allow participants to edit and control the presentation during the online meeting
	Allows participants to send messages in a Chat session during the online meeting
	Allow participants to draw or type on a Whiteboard during the online meeting
	Allows the host to end the online meeting for the entire group, or a participant to disconnect

Sending Workbooks Using E-Mail

E-mail is a great way to send timely information to friends and business colleagues. Often, however, either an e-mail message is just too short for all your information, or you may want someone to be able to read the actual document you're working on. You can send a worksheet in an e-mail message or an entire workbook as a file attachment using your favorite e-mail program. Nothing beats the immediacy of sending a file through e-mail. Route a workbook through e-mail, rather than send it, when you want others to review a copy of it online. As the workbook is routed, you can track its status. After all of the recipients have reviewed the workbook, it is automatically returned to you.

Send a Worksheet in an E-Mail Message

1. Open the worksheet you want to send.

2. Click the File menu, point to Send To, and then click Mail Recipient.

3. Click the To or Cc button. Select the contacts to whom you want the message sent, and then click OK.

4. Click the Send This Sheet button on the toolbar.

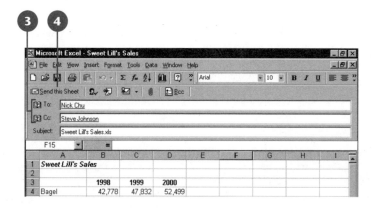

Send a Workbook as an E-Mail Attachment

1. Open the workbook you want to send.

2. Click the File menu, point to Send To, and then click Mail Recipient (As Attachment). Your default e-mail program opens, displaying a new e-mail message window.

3. Click the To or Cc button. Select the contacts to whom you want the message sent, and then click OK.

4. Type a related message.

5. Click the Send button on the toolbar.

Icons representing attached documents appear here.

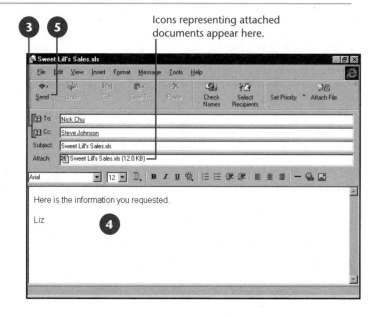

Change the order of the recipients. *You can change the order in which recipients will receive the routed workbook by changing the order of recipient names in the list. Select the name of the recipient you want to move up or down in the list, and then click the appropriate arrow.*

Select a group alias as the recipient. *You can select a group alias as the recipient. However, all members of the group alias are considered one recipient and receive one e-mail message.*

Route a workbook at a later time. *Open the workbook you want to route. Click the File menu, point to Send To, click Routing Recipient, click Addresses, select contact names, click the To or Cc button, click OK, and then click Add Slip. At a later time, click the File menu, point to Send To, and then click Next Routing Recipient.*

Route a Workbook in an E-Mail Message

1. Open the workbook you want to send.

2. Click the File menu, point to Send To, and then select Routing Recipient.

3. Click Addresses. Select the contacts to whom you want the message routed, click the To or Cc button, and then click OK.

4. Type the topic of the message.

5. If you want, type a related message.

6. Click to select other routing options you want.

7. Click Route.

   The workbook is sent as an attachment in an e-mail message.

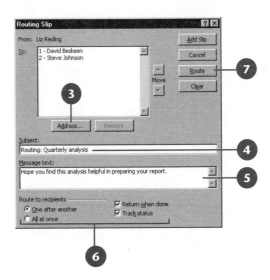

14

Accessing Office Information on the Web

New information about programs comes out with great frequency. You have access to an abundance of information from Microsoft about Excel and other programs in the Office 2000 suite. This information is constantly being updated. Answers to frequently asked questions, user forums, and update offers are some of the types of information you can find about Office. You can also find out about conferences, books, and other products that help you learn just how much you can do with your Office programs.

TRY THIS

Insert a hyperlink to the Microsoft Office site. *Since you'll probably want to check the Microsoft Office Update Web site often, create a hyperlink in a worksheet you use regularly.*

Find Online Office Information

1. Click the Help menu, and then click Office On The Web.

2. Establish an Internet connection.

3. Click a hyperlink of interest.

4. When you're done, click the Close button to quit the browser and return to Excel.

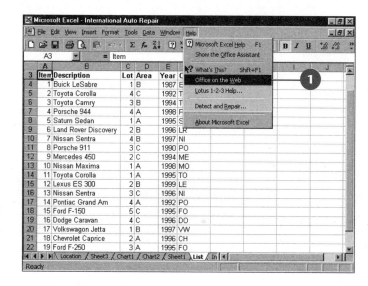

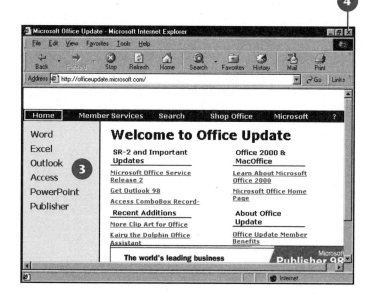

Index

SPECIAL CHARACTERS

' (apostrophe)
   macro comment prefix, 217
   numeric label prefix, 28
❣ (arrowhead, down-pointing
   double-headed), menu
   symbol, 14
▶ (arrowhead, right-pointing),
   menu symbol, 14
* (asterisk)
   multiplication operator, 48
   wildcard character, 175
✔ (check mark), menu
   symbol, 15
: (colon), range reference
   character, 27
$ (dollar sign), absolute cell
   reference prefix, 53
¼ (ellipsis), menu symbol, 14
= (equal sign)
   formula prefix, 48
   logical operator, 179
> (greater than sign), logical
   operator, 179
>= (greater than or equal to
   sign), logical operator, 179
< (less than sign), logical
   operator, 179
<= (less than or equal to sign),
   logical operator, 179

– (minus sign), subtraction
   operator, 48
< > (not equal sign), logical
   operator, 179
( ) (parentheses), changing
   precedence of operations
   with, 49
+ (plus sign)
   addition operator, 48
   by the mouse pointer, 39
   changing the mouse pointer
     from, 41
   mouse pointer, 7
? (question mark), wildcard
   character, 175
"" (quotation marks), macro
   code typed text delimiters,
   217
/ (slash), division operator, 48

A

abbreviations (initials), entering
   text with, 44
absolute cell references, 53,
   56, 57
Accept Or Reject Changes dialog
   box, 205
Access databases
   converting Excel data into,
     240

   creating PivotTables from,
     239
   importing tables, 238
AccessLinks add-in, 220
   installing, 240
actions, undoing and
   redoing, 35
active cell, 7
   navigating worksheets
     without changing, 12
Add Data dialog box, 158
add-in programs, 220
Add-Ins dialog box, 220
addition operator (+), 48
Add Report dialog box, 208
addresses. *See* Internet addresses;
   IP addresses; personal
   information; Web site
   addresses
Add View dialog box, 193
adjusting AutoShapes, 125
adjustment handles
   (Autoshapes), 124, 125
aligning
   cell contents, 88
   chart text, 166
   objects, 142, 143
   WordArt, 113
Align Left button (Formatting
   toolbar), 89
Alignment tab (Format Cells
   dialog box), 88

Align Right button (Formatting toolbar), 89
Alt key, drag-and-drop with, 39
Analysis Toolpak add-in, 220
analyzing worksheet data. *See* data analysis
AND condition, complex searches with, 179
apostrophe ('), macro comment prefix, 217
apostrophe ('), numeric label prefix, 28
applications. *See* programs
Apply Names dialog box, 57
area charts, 149
arguments (in formulas), 48
arithmetic operators, 48
    order of precedence, 49
Arrange Windows dialog box, 192
arranging workbook windows, 192, 233
Arrow button (Drawing toolbar), 122
arrowhead menu symbols
    down-pointing
        double-headed (⋎), 14
    right-pointing (▶), 14
arrowhead pointer, changing the mouse pointer to, 39, 41
arrow keys, navigating worksheets, 13
arrows
    double-sided
        (double-headed)
        mouse pointer arrow, 72, 73
    drawing, 123, 165
    formatting (editing), 123, 136, 165
asterisk (*)
    multiplication operator, 48

wildcard character, 175
auditing worksheets, 188
AutoCalculate feature, 59
AutoComplete feature, 28, 180
    entering labels, 29
    entering records, 180
AutoCorrect feature, 44
    adding entries, 44
    changing exceptions, 45
    deleting entries, 45
    editing entries, 44
    turning on, 46
AutoFill
    additional commands, 32
    entering data with, 32
AutoFilter feature, filtering lists, 178, 179
AutoFit feature, adjusting column width/row height, 72
AutoFormat dialog box, 96, 97, 185
AutoFormats
    formatting cell contents with, 81, 96
    formatting PivotTables with, 185
    modifying, 97
AutoSave add-in, 220
AutoShape command (Format menu)
    moving objects, 132
    resizing objects, 132, 133
AutoShapes, 121
    adjusting, 125
    drawing, 124
    finding in the Clip Gallery, 127
    inserting clips, 126
    replacing, 125
    reshaping, 124
    resizing, 124, 125
AutoSum button (Standard toolbar), 60

AVERAGE function, 61
axes. *See* chart axes

backgrounds, adding to worksheets, 66
Bold button (Formatting toolbar), 82
bold typeface, applying, 82
borders
    adding to pictures, 105
    See also cell borders
breaking links, 232
brightness (of images), changing, 120

calculating
    with AutoCalculate, 59
    with AutoSum, 60
    with the Conditional Sum Wizard, 220
    with functions, 61
    outcomes, 210–11, 212
        as goals, 213
calculations, order of precedence, 49
camera images, inserting, 107
canceling
    commands, 16
    drag-and-drop, 38
    selections, 36, 38, 39
cascading workbook windows, 192
cell borders
    adding, 94–95
    blue, 204
    formatting, 95
cell comments, 103, 118
    adding, 118

deleting, 34, 119
editing, 119
formatting, 119
showing, 118
cell contents
    aligning, 88
    clearing, 34, 43
    coloring, 91
    copying, 25, 26, 38–39
        canceling drag-and-drop, 38
        with drag-and-drop, 38, 39
        with the Windows Clipboard, 38
    cutting, 40
    data types, 26
        identifying, 91
    editing, 33
    editing options, 33, 190, 191
    entering. *See* entering data
    formatting, 31, 81–93, 96–102
        with AutoFormats, 96
        with styles, 98–99
    hiding/unhiding columns/ rows, 71
    moving, 25, 40–41
        canceling drag-and-drop, 38
        with drag-and-drop, 38, 41
        from rows/columns to columns/rows, 41
        with the Windows Clipboard, 38, 40
    orienting, 88
    outlining, 199
    overwrite alert, 191
    pasting, 36, 38, 51
        from rows/columns to columns/rows, 41
        selectively/using mathematical operations, 38, 39

cell contents, *continued*
  storing, 37
  See also data; formulas;
    labels; values
cell entries
  formatting, 31
  types, 26
  See also cell contents;
    formulas; labels;
    values
cell formats. *See* formatting (in
  cells)
cell names, 56
  applying to addresses, 57
cell notes. *See* cell comments
cell references (in formulas), 47
  absolute, 53, 56, 57
  entering, 48, 49
  labels as, 54–55
  relative, 52, 55, 57
cells, 7, 25
  active cell, 7
  adding, 25
  addresses, 7
  borders, 94–95, 204
  clearing, 34, 43
  coloring, 92–93
  deleting, 25, 34, 42, 43
  destination cells, 232
  entering data into. *See*
    entering data
  filling with patterns/colors,
    92–93
  formatting in. *See* formatting
    (in cells)
  inserting, 42
  linking, 232
  merging, 90
  naming, 56, 57
  navigating, 12–13
  pasting, 36
  selecting, 27
    redirecting selection
      following data
      entry, 191

tracing cell-formula relation-
    ships, 188
  See also cell comments; cell
    contents; cell refer-
    ences; ranges
Center button (Formatting
  toolbar), 89
characters
  printed, reducing/
    enlarging, 79
  WordArt
    adjusting spacing, 113
    making same height, 112
chart axes, 148
  adding titles to, 162
  formatting, 166
chart boxes (in org charts), 114,
  116
  adding, 116
  entering text into, 115
  modifying, 117
  rearranging, 117
Chart dialog box, changing
  chart types, 154
chart lines (in org charts),
  modifying, 117
Chart Object drop-down arrow,
  selecting/displaying
  selected chart objects,
  153, 159
chart objects
  adding, 162–63
  deselecting, 153
  displaying selected, 153
  formatting, 159, 160, 166
  identifying, 153, 157
  selecting, 152, 153, 159
charts, 147–66
  3-D charts, 149
  adding/deleting legends, 162
  adding gridlines to, 162, 163
  adding text annotations to,
    162, 163
  area charts, 149

combination charts, 149
  creating, 150–51
  drawing objects on, 164–65
  editing, 152
  embedded, 151, 155
  inserting pictures in, 160,
    161
  moving, 155
  pie charts, 149, 156, 157
  PivotCharts, 186
  resizing, 155
  selecting, 152, 153
  terminology, 148
  types, 149, 154
  updating, 152
  See also chart objects; chart
    text; maps; organiza-
    tion charts
chart text, 166
  adding shadows to, 164
  aligning, 166
  formatting, 166
  text annotations, 162, 163,
    164
  See also chart titles; legends
chart titles, 148, 162
  adding, 162, 163
  adding shadows to, 164
chart types, 149
  changing, 154
  choosing, 151
Chart Wizard, 150
  changing chart types, 154
  creating charts, 150–51
Chart Wizard button (Standard
  toolbar), 150
checking spelling, 46
check mark (✔), menu
  symbol, 15
circles, drawing, 124
clearing cells, 34
  vs. deleting cells, 36, 43
clip art
  displaying categories, 107

filling objects with, 136
inserting, 104
  from the Web, 107, 249
  See also pictures
clipboards. *See* Office Clipboard;
  Windows Clipboard
Clip Gallery
  finding AutoShapes in, 127
  importing pictures into, 127
  inserting AutoShapes from,
    126
  inserting clip art from, 104
  inserting sounds/motion
    clips from, 106
clips (AutoShapes), inserting,
  126
Close button
  Data Form dialog box, 172
  Excel window, 24
  toolbars, 197
closing workbooks, 24
Collapse Dialog buttons (dialog
  boxes), 62, 78
collating copies, 23
colon (:), range reference
  character, 27
coloring
  cell contents, 91
  cells, 92–93
  data series, 160
  fonts, 91
  objects, 136
  pictures, 120
  shadows, 138, 139
  WordArt text, 111
colors
  specifying, 136
  See also coloring; fill colors
column header buttons, 68, 69
column headers (letters)
  header buttons, 68, 69
  printing, 78, 79
column letters. *See* column
  headers

columns (in worksheets)
adjusting column width, 72–73
deleting, 70
freezing/unfreezing, 74
hiding/unhiding, 71
inserting, 69
printing as titles, 78, 79, 80
selecting, 68
See also column headers (letters)
column titles, printing, 78, 79, 80
combination charts, 149
commands
adding to menus, 198
canceling, 16
choosing, 14–15
order on menus, 15
Commands tab (Customize dialog box), 194, 197
COM components (Office Web Components), support requirements, 243
Comma Style button (Formatting toolbar), 82
comments
in macro code, 217
See also cell comments
complex searches, 179
conditional formatting, establishing/deleting, 84
Conditional Formatting dialog box, 84
Conditional Sum Wizard add-in, 220
Confirm Password dialog box, 206
consolidated data, displaying, 235
Consolidate dialog box, 234
consolidating data from worksheets/workbooks, 224–25, 234–35

contrast (of images), changing, 120
Convert To MS Access dialog box, 240
copies
collating, 23
printing more than one, 23
printing quick copies, 22
Copy button (Standard toolbar), displaying, 51
copying
cell contents, 25, 26, 38–39
canceling drag-and-drop, 38
with drag-and-drop, 38, 39
with the Windows Clipboard, 38
cell formats, 85, 92
formulas, 50–51
vs. linking, 232
Web tables to worksheets, 250
worksheets, 67
See also pasting
correcting spelling, 44–45, 46
COUNT function, 61
Create A Copy check box (Move or Copy dialog box), 67
criteria (for finding records), 174
logical operators/conditions, 179
wildcards, 175
Criteria button (Data Form dialog box), 172
cropping pictures, 120
Ctrl+End keys, navigating worksheets, 13
Ctrl+Home keys, navigating worksheets, 13
Ctrl key
constraining drawing objects, 123

nudging objects, 132, 133
currency formats, applying, 83
Currency Style button (Formatting toolbar), 82
curves
drawing irregular curves, 128–29
switching between open and closed, 129
Custom AutoFilter dialog box, 179
Customize dialog box
creating toolbars, 194
customizing menus, 195
customizing toolbar buttons, 197
customizing toolbars, 195, 196, 197
custom views (of worksheets)
creating, 193
creating reports with, 208
displaying, 193
Custom Views dialog box, 193
cutting cell contents, 40

D

Dash Style button (Drawing toolbar), 122
data
adding to the Template Wizard database, 225
calculating possible outcomes, 210–11, 212, 213
consolidating from other worksheets/workbooks, 224–25, 234–35
converting into Access data, 240
entering. *See* entering data
exporting

to other programs, 226, 228
to the Web, 242–43
finding records, 174, 175, 178, 179, 220
importing
from other programs, 226, 238
from queries, 236–37
in text files, 229
from the Web, 107, 237, 248–50
mapping geographic data, 167
protecting, 206
tracking, 204
validating, 181, 188
See also cell contents; data analysis; Data Forms; data series; records
data analysis, 169–88
Analysis Toolpak add-in, 220
See also filtering; PivotTables; sorting
databases
creating PivotTables from, 239
importing data from, 236
See also Access databases; lists
Data Form dialog box, 172
Data Forms, 169, 172, 173
entering records in, 173
managing records with, 174–75
data markers, 148
data points, 148, 158
deleting, 159
data ranges, editing, 152, 183
data series, 148, 158
adding, 158
coloring, 160
deleting, 158, 159

data series, *continued*
  editing data ranges, 152
  filling, 160–61
  inserting pictures in, 160, 161
  selecting, 152, 156
data tables, creating/deleting, 212
data tracking, 204
  creating form templates with, 220
data types, 26
  identifying, 91
data validation, adding, 181
Data Validation dialog box, 181
dates
  adding to worksheets, 77
  entering, 30
  formatting in cells, 31
debugging macros, 214, 218
decimal format, applying, 83
Decrease Decimal button (Formatting toolbar), 82
defaults
  column width/row height, 73
  fill color, 136
  line style, 136
  template, 202, 203
definition boxes, 18
Delete button (Data Form dialog box), 172
Delete Conditional Format dialog box, 84
Delete dialog box, 43
deleting
  AutoCorrect entries, 45
  buttons from toolbars, 196
  cell comments, 34, 119
  cell formatting, 34
  cells, 25, 34, 42, 43
    vs. clearing cells, 36, 43
  columns/rows, 70
  conditional formatting, 84

data points, 159
data series, 158, 159
data tables, 212
font attributes, 83
hyperlinks, 247
label ranges, 55
legends, 162
numeric formats, 83
page breaks, 75
pictures, 105
records, 175
reversing deletions, 159
styles, 101
vertices (in freeforms), 130, 131
worksheets, 65
depth, of 3-D objects, 141
deselecting chart objects, 153
destination cells/ranges, 232
destination files, 226
destination programs, 226
Detect and Repair feature, 17
detecting and repairing problems, 17
dialog boxes, 16
  selecting options in, 16
disk space, saving, 65
distributing objects, 142, 143
division operator (/), 48
documents
  discussing on the Web, 251, 252–53
  sharing information among, 226–27
  types, 5
dollar sign ($), absolute cell reference prefix, 53
double-headed arrowhead, down-pointing (Ꙩ), menu symbol, 14
double-sided (double-headed) arrow pointer, 72, 73
Down arrow key, navigating worksheets, 13

drag-and-drop
  with the Alt key, 39
  canceling, 38
  copying cell contents, 38, 39
  moving cell contents, 38, 41
drawing objects, 121–46
  arrows, 123, 165
  AutoShapes, 121, 124
  circles, 124
  control keys, 123
  formatting, 121, 136–39
  freeforms, 121, 128–29
  lines, 121, 122, 165
  outlines, 131
  ovals, 124
  rectangles, 124
  squares, 124
  types, 121
  See also objects
Drawing toolbar
  buttons, 122, 129, 135
  displaying (opening), 122, 164
  hiding, 164
  shared tools, 123
drawing tools
  Freeform tools, 128
  See also Drawing toolbar
drop-down lists, in dialog boxes, 16
drop shadows. *See* shadows

E

editing
  arrows, 123
  AutoCorrect entries, 44
  cell comments, 119
  cell contents, 33, 191
  charts, 152
  data ranges, 152, 183
  embedded objects, 231

formulas, 50–51
freeform objects, 130–31
lines, 122
macros, 219
records, 174
WordArt text, 110–11
Edit Report dialog box, 209
Edit Scenario dialog box, 210
Edit tab (Options dialog box), 191
Edit Text button (WordArt toolbar), 109
Edit WordArt Text dialog box, 111
editing options, changing, 33, 190, 191
ellipsis (...), menu symbol, 14
e-mail messages
  group aliases as recipients, 257
  routing workbooks in, 256, 257
  sending workbooks/worksheets in, 256
embedded objects
  charts, 151, 155
  editing, 231
embedding objects, 227, 231
End+arrow keys, navigating worksheets, 13
Enter button (formula bar), entering labels, 28
entering
  cell data. *See* entering data
  records, 171, 172
    with AutoComplete, 180
    in Data Forms, 173
    with the PickList, 180
  text
    into cells, 28, 29
    into org chart boxes, 115
    with abbreviations, 44
  See also inserting

entering data
applying styles before, 99
cell references, 48, 49
dates, 30
formulas, 48
functions, 61, 62
labels, 28–29
numbers
as labels, 28
as values, 25, 26, 30–31, 32
redirecting cell selection following, 191
times, 30
values, 25, 26, 30–31
repeating/series data, 32
Enter key
entering labels, 28
navigating worksheets, 13
equal sign (=)
formula prefix, 48
logical operator, 179
Esc key
canceling drag-and-drop, 38
canceling selections, 36
deselecting chart objects, 153
Excel (Microsoft), 5
add-in programs, 220
customizing the work environment, 189, 190–91
exiting, 24
installing, 2–3
linking to the Internet, 241–58
saving workbooks to a previous version, 21
starting, 6
Excel window, 8–9
Close button, 24
elements, 7
opening workbooks from, 10
See also workbook windows

exiting Excel, 24
Expense Statement template, 200
exploding pie charts, 156, 157
exporting data
to other programs, 226, 228
to the Web, 242–43

F

F1 key, getting Help, 18
F3 key, displaying named ranges, 58
F4 key, making cell references absolute, 53
favorite Web documents/Web pages, jumping to, 249
field names
in Data Forms, 172
in lists, 170, 171
fields (in list records), 170
index fields, 177
sorting on, 176–77
fields (in PivotTables and PivotCharts)
adding/removing, 184
changing settings, 185
hiding/displaying, 184
hiding/displaying PivotChart field buttons, 186
file formats, installing, 228
File menu
opening workbooks from, 10
starting workbooks from, 9
filenames, 20
files
destination files, 226
exporting, 226, 228
filenames, 20
finding, 11
importing. See importing data

inserting pictures from, 105
linking, 227, 230
source files, 226
Web file management, 251
See also workbooks
fill colors
coloring cells, 92–93
coloring objects, 136
fill effects, adding, 136, 160–61
fill handle
copying formulas with, 50
entering data with, 32
filling
cells, 92–93
data series, 160–61
objects, 136
filtering
lists, 169, 178, 179
Web discussions, 253
finding
records, 174, 175, 178, 179, 220
See also filtering, lists
workbook files, 11
Find Next button (Data Form dialog box), 172
Find Prev button (Data Form dialog box), 172
flipping objects, 134
floating toolbars, 15
folders, creating new, 21
font attributes
applying, 82
deleting, 83
fonts
coloring, 91
printer fonts, 87
specifying, 86–87
substitution for missing fonts, 86
TrueType fonts, 87
font size, specifying, 86–87
Font tab (Format Cells dialog box), 86

footers (for worksheets)
adding, 77
previewing, 77
form templates, creating, 220
Format AutoShape dialog box, 133, 135
specifying color and line options, 136
Format Cells dialog box
aligning cell contents, 88
applying borders, 94
coloring cell contents, 91
filling cells with colors/patterns, 92
formatting borders, 95
formatting dates/times, 31
formatting numbers, 83
modifying styles, 98, 100
opening quickly, 83
specifying fonts/font sizes, 86
vs. Formatting toolbar, 89
Format Cells option (shortcut menu), formatting cell entries, 31
Format menu, adjusting column width/row height, 73
format painting, 85, 92
formatting
arrows, 123, 136, 165
cell borders, 95
cell comments, 119
cell contents, 31, 81–93, 96–102
with AutoFormats, 96
with styles, 98–99
cell entries, 31
chart axes, 166
chart objects, 159, 160, 166
chart text, 166
dates, 31
drawing objects, 121, 136–39
labels, 82
lines, 136

formatting, *continued*
  numeric data, 31, 82, 83
  PivotCharts, 185, 186
  PivotTables, 185
  ranges, 97
  times, 31
  WordArt text, 111, 112–13
  worksheets, 81–102
  See also formatting (in cells)
formatting (in cells)
  conditional, 84
  copying (painting), 85, 92
  deleting, 34
Formatting toolbar, 14
  adding borders to cells, 95
  aligning cell contents, 89
  buttons, 82, 89
  coloring cell contents, 91
  filling cells with colors/
    patterns, 93
  specifying fonts/font
    sizes, 87
Format WordArt button
  (WordArt toolbar), 109
Format WordArt dialog box, 111
forms. *See* Data Forms
formula bar
  editing cell contents, 33
  editing formulas in, 50
  Enter button, 28
formula bar (Excel window),
  7, 26
formula prefix (=), 48
formulas, 26, 47–62
  aligning, 88
  arguments, 48
  cell insertion and, 42
  circling invalid data in, 188
  complex, 62
  copying, 50–51
  creating (entering), 48–49
  displaying, 48, 49
  editing, 50–51

evaluating with ranges of
    possible values, 212
  finding records with, 220
  including links in, 233
  listing formulas in
    PivotTables/
    PivotCharts, 185
  order of precedence of
    operations, 49
  tracing cell-formula
    relationships, 188
  using ranges/range names
    in, 58
  See also functions
freeform objects, 121, 128
  drawing, 128–29
  editing, 130–31
Freeform tools, 128
freehand drawing, 129
Free Rotate button (Drawing
  toolbar), 135
Free Rotate button (WordArt
  toolbar), 109
freezing columns/rows, 74
FTP sites, publishing Web pages
  to, 243
functions, 47, 61
  common, 61
  creating (entering), 61, 62

General tab (Options dialog
  box), 190
geographic data, mapping, 167
goals, calculating outcomes as,
  213
Goal Seek feature, 213
going to specific cells. *See*
  navigating worksheets
gradients
  filling data series with, 160

filling objects with, 136
graphics
  inserting, 103–20
  See also objects; pictures
graphs. *See* charts
greater than or equal to sign
  (>=), logical operator, 179
greater than sign (>), logical
  operator, 179
grid, snapping objects to, 143
gridlines
  on charts, 148, 162, 163
  on worksheets
    improving, 94–95
    printing, 79, 94
grouping data. *See* outlines (of
  worksheet data)
grouping objects, 144

handles
  adjustment handles, 124,
    125
  fill handle, 50
  selection handles, 148, 155
Header/Footer tab (Page Setup
  dialog box), 77
headers (for worksheets)
  adding/previewing, 77
  See also column headers; row
    headers
Help, 18–19
  for Lotus 1-2-3 users, 19
  online Office Help, 19, 258
  on Organization Chart, 115
Help pointer, getting help
  using, 18
Hide/Display Assistant button in
  wizards, 16
hiding
  columns/rows, 71

Drawing toolbar, 164
Office Assistant, 19
toolbars, 15, 197
  all but the Web toolbar,
    248
worksheets, 65
Highlight Changes dialog box,
  204
Home key, navigating
  worksheets, 13
HTML format, 242
hyperlinks, 227
  appearance, 246
  creating (inserting), 246
  creating ScreenTips for, 247
  jumping to, 247
  removing, 247

icons, on menus, 14
Ignore Relative/Absolute option
  (Apply Names dialog
  box), 57
images. *See* pictures
importing data
  from other programs, 226,
    238
  from queries, 236–37
  in text files, 229
  from the Web, 107, 237,
    248–50
Import Text File dialog box, 229
Increase Decimal button
  (Formatting toolbar), 82
index fields, protecting list
  order with, 177
initials (abbreviations), entering
  text with, 44
Insert Clip Art dialog box, 104,
  106
Insert dialog box, 42

Insert Hyperlink dialog box, 246
inserting
    AutoShapes (clips), 126
    camera images, 107
    cells, 42
    columns/rows, 69
    graphics, 103–20
    hyperlinks, 246
    media clips, 106–7
    motion clips, 106
    organization charts, 114
    page breaks, 75
    pictures, 104–5
        in data series/charts, 160,
            161
        scanner/camera images,
            107
    scanner images, 107
    sounds, 106
    vertices (in freeforms), 130
    WordArt text, 108–9
    worksheets, 65
    See also entering; importing
        data
Insert menu, command
    availability, 69
Insert Picture dialog box, 105
installing
    AccessLinks add-in, 240
    Excel, 2–3
    file formats, 228
    Microsoft Map, 167
    Template Wizard add-in, 225
Intellimouse
    wheel button, 12
    zooming on rolling, 13
interactivity of worksheets as
    Web pages, 242
Internet. See Web
Internet Explorer, Web file
    management, 251
Invoice template, 200
irregular curves, drawing,
    128–29

irregular polygons, drawing, 128
Italic button (Formatting
    toolbar), 82
italic typeface, applying, 82

keyboard
    drawing controls, 123
    navigating with, 13
keyboard shortcuts. See shortcut
    keys
keyword strings (initials),
    entering text with, 44

label prefix ('), 28
label ranges
    defining, 54
    deleting, 55
Label Ranges dialog box, 54, 55
labels (of cells), 26, 28
    aligning, 88
    as cell references, 54–55
    coloring, 91
    entering, 28–29
    entering numbers as, 28
    formatting, 82
    long, 29
    See also cell comments; cell
        contents; text
        annotations (charts)
languages, changing, 102
Left arrow key, navigating
    worksheets, 13
legends, 148, 162
    adding/deleting, 162
less than or equal to sign (<=),
    logical operator, 179
less than sign (<), logical
    operator, 179

light bulb, in the Office
    Assistant, 19
lighting, of 3-D objects, 141
Line button (Drawing toolbar),
    122
Line Color button (Drawing
    toolbar), 122
line patterns, creating, 137
lines, 121
    drawing, 122, 165
    editing, 122
    formatting, 136
Line Style button (Drawing
    toolbar), 122
line styles, setting the default
    style, 136
linking
    cells, 232
    Excel to the Internet, 241–58
    files (objects), 227, 230
    vs. copying, 232
    workbooks, 233
    worksheets, 232
    See also links
links, 232
    breaking, 232
    including in formulas, 233
    Internet links. See hyperlinks
    modifying, 230
    selecting multiple, 230
    updating, 231
    See also linking
Links dialog box, 230
List dialog box, 173, 175
list ranges, 170, 171
    Data Forms and, 173
lists, 170
    creating, 171
    displaying the top/bottom
        ten items, 178
    filtering, 169, 178, 179
    protecting list order, 177
    sorting, 169, 176–77
    terminology, 170

logical conditions, complex
    searches with, 179
logical operators, complex
    searches with, 179
logos
    creating, 108–9, 137
    inserting in data series/
        charts, 161
long labels, 29
Lookup Wizard add-in, 220
Lotus 1-2-3 users, help for, 19

macro code, 217
    comments, 217
    debugging, 214, 218
    editing, 219
    resources on, 217
macro comment prefix ('), 217
macro comments, 217
Macro dialog box, 214
    debugging macros, 218
    editing macros, 219
    running macros with, 216
macros, 214
    assigning buttons to, 197
    debugging, 214, 218
    editing, 219
    recording, 214, 215
    running, 214, 216
    storing, 214, 216
    vs. templates, 201
maintenance options for Office
    programs, 17
Map (Microsoft), installing, 167
maps, 147, 167–68
    creating, 167
    modifying, 168
    refreshing, 168
margins, setting, 76
Margins tab (Page Setup dialog
    box), 76

marquee, 38, 40
  removing, 36, 38, 40
mathematical operations,
    pasting cell contents
    using, 38, 39
MAX function, 61
media clips, inserting, 106–7
meetings (online), 254–55
  holding, 254, 255
  joining, participating, 255
  scheduling, 254
  showing attendee status, 254
menu bar, 7
menus, 14–15
  adding commands to, 198
  choosing commands
      with, 14
  creating, 198
  customizing, 195, 198
  expanding, 14
  menu symbols, 14
  order of commands/toolbar
      buttons on, 15
Merge And Center button
    (Formatting toolbar), 89
Merging
  cells, 90
  styles, 101
  workbooks, 224–25
Microsoft Access. *See* Access
    databases
Microsoft Excel. *See* Excel
    (Microsoft)
Microsoft Excel 2000 At a Glance,
    1–3
  approach, 1–2
  goals, 3
  overview, 2–3
Microsoft Map, installing, 167
Microsoft Map Control dialog
    box, 168
Microsoft Mouse, navigating
    with, 12

Microsoft Office. *See* Office
    (Microsoft)
Microsoft Office Language
    Settings dialog box, 102
Microsoft Organization Chart.
    See Organization Chart
    (Microsoft)
Microsoft Query, creating
    PivotTables with, 239
MIN function, 61
Minimize button, Excel
    window, 8
minimizing workbook
    windows, 8
minus sign (–), subtraction
    operator, 48
Module sheets
  debugging macros with, 218
  editing macro code, 219
More AutoShapes dialog box,
    displaying, 126
motion clips
  inserting, 106
  previewing, 107
mouse
  adjusting column width/row
      height, 73
  deselecting chart objects, 153
  navigating with, 12
  resizing objects with, 133
mouse pointer, 7
  changing to an arrowhead,
      39, 41
  for copying data, 39
  double-sided arrow, 72, 73
  Intellimouse, 12
  for moving data, 41
  plus sign by, 39
Move or Copy dialog box, 67
moving
  cell contents, 25, 40–41
      canceling drag-and-drop,
          38

  with drag-and-drop,
      38, 41
  from rows/columns to
      columns/rows, 41
  with the Windows
      Clipboard, 38, 40
  charts, 155
  objects, 132
  page breaks, 75
  pictures, 104
  toolbars, 15
  vertices (in freeforms), 130
  workbook windows, 8
  worksheets, 66, 67
  See also navigating
      worksheets
multiple columns/rows,
    inserting, 69
multiple page reports,
    generating, 208–9
multiple windows, arranging,
    192
multiple workbooks, viewing,
    192
multiplication operator (*), 48

Name box (Excel window), 7, 27
named cells/ranges
  applying names to addresses,
      57
  listing, 58
  selecting, 56
naming
  cells/ranges, 56, 57
  workbooks, 20
  worksheets, 64, 77
navigating keys, 13
navigating worksheets, 12–13
NetMeeting (Microsoft),
    opening, 255

networks, sharing workbooks
    on, 119, 221, 222–23
New button (Data Form dialog
    box), 172
New Database Queries,
    importing data from, 236
New dialog box, creating
    workbooks, 200
New Web Queries, importing
    data from, 237
New Workbook button
    (Standard toolbar), 203
not equal sign (<>), logical
    operator, 179
notes. *See* cell comments
Nudge command, 132
nudging objects, 132
  shadows, 139
numbers
  adding page numbers, 77
  entering
      as labels, 28
      as values, 25, 26, 30–31,
          32
  formatting, 31, 82, 83
  printing row numbers, 79
  See also values
Number tab (Format Cells
    dialog box), 31, 83
numeric formats
  applying, 31, 82, 83
  deleting, 83
numeric keypad, entering
    numbers with, 30
numeric label prefix ('), 28

Object dialog box, 231
objects
  adding shadows to, 138–39
  aligning, 142, 143

objects, *continued*
  arranging in the stack, 144
  coloring, 136
  creating 3-D objects from,
    140
  distributing, 142, 143
  drawing objects, 121–46
  drawing on charts, 164–65
  embedding, 227, 231
  flipping, 134
  grouping, 144
  linking, 227, 230
  moving, 132
  nudging, 132
  regrouping, 145
  resizing, 104, 132
    with the mouse, 133
    precisely, 132, 133
    retaining original
      proportions, 133
  rotating, 134–35
    around fixed points, 135
    in increments, 134, 135
    precisely, 135
  selecting, 104
  snapping to the grid, 143
  ungrouping, 145
  view settings, changing, 146
  See also 3-D objects; drawing
    objects
object views, changing settings,
  146
Office (Microsoft)
  accessing information on the
    Web, 258
  starting Excel from, 6
Office Art shared drawing tools,
  123
Office Assistant, 7, 18
  getting help from, 19, 182
  turning off/on, 16, 18
Office Clipboard
  copying/pasting data to/
    from, 37

  cutting data to, 40
  opening automatically, 41
  vs. Windows Clipboard, 37
Office documents
  opening, 11
  switching between, 8
Office programs, maintenance
  options, 17
Office Server Extensions (OSE),
  251
Office Shortcut Bar, starting
  Excel with, 6
Office Web Components,
  support requirements,
  243
online help. *See* Help
online meetings. *See* meetings
  (online)
Open dialog box
  changing templates, 202–3
  changing the default file
    location, 10
  creating new folders in, 21
  finding workbook files, 11
  opening templates, 202
  opening workbooks, 10–11
    as Web pages, 244
  performing management
    tasks, 21
opening
  Office documents, 11
  organization charts, 116
  templates, 202
  workbooks, 10–11
    files created in other
      spreadsheet
      programs, 11
    recently opened files,
      10, 11
    as Web pages, 244
operations, mathematical, order
  of precedence, 49
option buttons, in dialog
  boxes, 16

Options dialog box, customizing
  your work environment,
  190–91
Options tab (Customize dialog
  box), 195
OR condition, complex searches
  with, 179
order of precedence of operations, 49
Organization Chart (Microsoft),
  114
  getting help on, 115
organization charts
  adding text to, 115
  changing presets, 115
  creating (inserting), 114
  modifying, 116–17
  opening, 116
  restyling, 116
  See also chart boxes (in org
    charts)
orienting
  cell contents, 88
  pages, 76
OSE (Office Server Extensions),
  251
outcomes (of data), calculating
  possibilities, 210–11, 212,
  213
outlines (of objects), drawing,
  131
outlines (of worksheet data)
  collapsing/expanding, 199
  creating, 199
ovals, drawing, 124

page breaks (of worksheets),
  inserting/previewing/
  moving/removing, 75
Page Down key, navigating
  worksheets, 13

page numbers, adding to
  worksheets, 77
page orientation, specifying, 76
pages
  fitting worksheets on a
    specific number of, 79
  printing row and column
    titles, 78
  setting up for printing,
    76–80
  specifying number for
    printing, 23
Page Setup dialog box
  adding headers/footers, 77
  fitting worksheets on a
    specific number of
    pages, 79
  setting margins, 76
  specifying page orientation,
    76
  specifying worksheet
    features, 78, 79
  viewing changes made in, 76
Page tab (Page Setup dialog
  box), 76, 79
Page Up key, navigating
  worksheets, 13
painting cell formats, 85, 92
panes, splitting the screen into
  and freezing, 74
paper size, specifying, 76
parentheses (()), changing
  precedence of operations
  with, 49
passwords, protecting, 206
Paste Function feature, 47
  entering functions, 62
Paste Special command, 38, 39
Paste Special dialog box
  breaking links, 232
  linking files, 230
  pasting cell contents, 39, 51
    from rows/columns to
      columns/rows, 41

pasting
  cell contents, 36, 38, 51
    from rows/columns to
      columns/rows, 41
    selectively/using
      mathematical
      operations, 38, 39
  sharing information by, 226
Patterned Lines dialog box, 137
patterns
  axis patterns, 166
  filling cells with, 92–93
  filling data series with, 160
  filling objects with, 136
  line patterns, 137
percentage format, applying, 83
Percent Style button (Formatting toolbar), 82
Personal Macro workbook,
  storing macros in, 214,
  216
PickList feature, 28, 180
  entering labels, 29
  entering records, 180
pictures (images)
  adding borders to, 105
  changing brightness/
    contrast, 120
  coloring, 120
  cropping, 120
  deleting, 105
  importing into the Clip
    Gallery, 127
  inserting, 104–5
    in data series/charts, 160,
      161
    scanner/camera images,
      107
  moving, 104
  resizing, 104
  See also objects
Picture toolbar, displaying, 105
pie charts, 149, 156

exploding/undoing
  explosions, 157
  pulling out single slices, 156
PivotChart field buttons,
  hiding/displaying, 186
PivotCharts, 186
  creating
    from PivotTables, 186,
      187
    with PivotTables, 187
  editing data ranges, 183
  formatting, 185, 186
  listing formulas in, 185
  non-pivoting, 187
PivotTable And PivotChart
  Wizard, 182, 183, 187,
  239
PivotTables, 169, 182
  accessing functions, 184
  changing layouts, 184
  charting, 186, 187
  creating, 182, 183
    from databases, 239
    with PivotCharts, 187
  editing data ranges, 183
  formatting, 185
  listing formulas in, 185
  updating, 184
PivotTable toolbar, 184, 186
plus sign (+)
  addition operator, 48
  by the mouse pointer, 39
  changing the mouse pointer
    from, 41
  mouse pointer, 7
PMT function, 61
pointer. *See* mouse pointer
points (on freeforms), specifying
  vertex types, 131
points (text measurement unit),
  defined, 73
polygons, drawing irregular
  polygons, 128

precedence of operations, 49
Preview button (Standard
  toolbar), 93
previewing
  motion clips, 107
  Web pages (before posting),
    245
  worksheets, 22, 23, 93
    headers/footers, 77
    page breaks, 75
print area
  clearing, 80
  setting, 23, 80
Print dialog box
  previewing worksheets
    from, 23
  specifying print options,
    22, 23
printed characters, reducing/
  enlarging, 79
printer fonts, 87
printers
  selecting, 23
  specifying properties, 23
printing Web discussions, 253
printing worksheets, 22–23
  centering worksheet titles, 89
  changing print area, 23
  with column/row headers, 79
  fitting on a specific number
    of pages, 79
  with gridlines, 79, 94
  with headers/footers, 77
  more than one copy, 23
  page setup, 76–80
  with print titles, 78, 79, 80
  quick copies, 22
  specifying number of
    pages, 23
print previews, 22
print scaling, specifying, 76
print settings, 63
  customizing, 76–80, 193

print titles, printing, 78, 79, 80
problems, detecting and
  repairing, 17
programs
  add-in programs, 220
  destination programs, 226
  exporting files to other
    programs, 226, 228
  importing files from other
    programs, 226, 238
  Office program maintenance
    options, 17
  source programs, 226
protecting data, 206
Protect Sheet dialog box, 206
Publish as Web Page dialog box,
  243, 254
publishing Web pages, 243
Purchase Order template, 200

queries, importing data from,
  236–37
question mark (?), wildcard
  character, 175
quick copies, printing, 22
quotation marks (""), macro
  code typed text delimiters, 217

range names, 56
  applying to addresses, 57
  using in formulas, 58
range references, 27
ranges (of cells), 27
  AutoSum range,
    modifying, 60
  calculating automatically,
    59, 60

ranges (of cells), *continued*
   destination ranges, 232
   editing data ranges, 152, 183
   formatting, 97
   list ranges, 170, 171, 173
   naming, 56, 57
   pasting, 36
   selecting/deselecting, 27
   using in formulas, 58
recording macros, 214, 215
Record Macro dialog box, 215
records (in lists), 170
   deleting, 175
   displaying all, 174
   editing, 174
   entering, 171, 172
      with AutoComplete, 180
      in Data Forms, 173
      with the PickList, 180
   finding and displaying, 174,
      175, 178, 179, 220
   See also lists, filtering
   sorting, 169, 176–77
rectangles, drawing, 124
Redo button (Standard
   toolbar), 35
redoing actions, 35
refreshing. *See* updating
regrouping objects, 145
relative addressing/cell references, 52, 55, 57
repairing problems, 17
repeating data, entering, 32
replacing AutoShapes, 125
Report Manager add-in, 208,
   220
reports
   creating, 208
   reordering sections, 209
reshaping
   AutoShapes, 124
   toolbars, 15
   WordArt text, 110

resizing
   AutoShapes, 124, 125
   charts, 155
   objects, 104, 132
      with the mouse, 133
      precisely, 132, 133
      retaining original
         proportions, 133
   pictures, 104
   workbook windows, 8
Restore button
   Data Form dialog box, 172
   Excel window, 8
restoring workbook windows, 8
Reviewing toolbar, adding/
   modifying cell comments
   with, 118
revisions of worksheets, keeping
   track of, 205
Right arrow key, navigating
   worksheets, 13
rotating
   objects, 134–35
      around fixed points, 135
      in increments, 134, 135
      precisely, 135
   WordArt text, 110
Routing Slip dialog box, 257
routing workbooks in e-mail
   messages, 256, 257
row header buttons, 68, 69
row headers (numbers)
   header buttons, 68, 69
   printing, 78, 79
row numbers. *See* row headers
rows (in worksheets)
   adjusting row height, 72–73
   deleting, 70
   freezing/unfreezing, 74
   hiding/unhiding, 71
   inserting, 69
   in lists, 171
   printing as titles, 78, 79, 80

   selecting, 68
   sorting lists in, 177
   See also row headers
      (numbers)
row titles, printing, 78, 79, 80
running macros, 214, 216

S

Save As dialog box
   creating new folders in, 21
   creating templates, 201
   exporting files, 228
   performing management
      tasks, 21
   saving workbooks
      with different names in
         different formats,
         21
      for the first time, 20
      to a previous version of
         Excel, 21
      as Web pages, 242
   saving worksheets as Web
      pages, 243
saving
   disk space, 65
   scenarios, 211
   shared workbook changes,
      222–23
   workbooks, 20–21
      automatic feature, 220
      with different names in
         different formats,
         21
      on exiting, 24
      for the first time, 20
      to a previous version of
         Excel, 21
      as templates, 201
      as Web pages, 242
   worksheets, as Web pages,
      242, 243

scaling worksheets, 79
scanner images, inserting, 107
Scenario Manager, 210, 211
scenarios
   creating, 210, 213
   creating reports with, 208
   saving, 211
   showing, 211
   "What If" scenarios, 213,
      220
Scenario Values dialog box, 210
screen, splitting, 74
ScreenTips
   creating for hyperlinks, 247
   displaying, 14, 153, 157
Scribble button (Drawing
   toolbar), 129
search criteria. *See* criteria (for
   finding records)
Select Changes to Accept or
   Reject dialog box, 205
selecting
   cells, 27, 56
      redirecting selection
         following data
         entry, 191
   chart objects, 152, 153, 159
   charts, 152, 153
   columns/rows, 68
   data series, 152, 156
   links, 230
   ranges, 27, 56
   worksheets, 68
selection handles, of charts,
   148, 155
selections, canceling, 36, 38, 39
series data, entering, 32
Setup Wizard, 2
shadows
   adding to chart text, 164
   adding to objects, 138–39
   coloring, 138, 139
   nudging, 139
   relocating, 138

shadows, *continued*
  turning on/off, 139
  vs. 3-D effects, 141
shaping. *See* reshaping
Share Workbook dialog box,
  222–23
"[Shared]" status alert, 205, 223
sharing information among
  documents, 226–27
sharing workbooks (on networks), 119, 221, 222–23
  enabling, 222
  save options, 222–23
  "[Shared]" status alert, 205,
  223
Sheet tab (Page Setup dialog
  box), 78, 79
sheet tabs (on worksheets), 7, 64
  displaying, 12
Shift key
  constraining drawing
  objects, 123, 124
  drawing lines, 165
  resizing objects retaining
  original proportions,
  133
  rotating objects in
  increments, 135
Shift+Tab keys, navigating
  worksheets, 13
shortcut keys, 14
  choosing commands
  with, 15
  getting help with, 18
  for navigation, 13
  running macros with, 216
slash (/), division operator, 48
snapping objects to the grid,
  143
social security numbers,
  entering, 28
Solver add-in, 220
Sort dialog box, 177
sorting lists, 169, 176–77

in rows, 177
sounds, inserting, 106
source data, 232
source files, 226
source programs, 226
spelling
  checking, 46
  correcting, 44–45, 46
spin boxes, in dialog boxes, 16
spinning 3-D objects, 140
squares, drawing, 124
stacks, arranging objects in, 144
Standard toolbar, 14
  buttons, 35, 51, 60, 93, 150,
  159, 203
starting
  Excel, 6
  Web discussions, 253
  workbooks, 9
Start menu
  opening Office Documents
  from, 11
  opening recently opened
  workbooks from, 11
  starting Excel from, 6
status bar, 7
step mode, debugging macros
  in, 218
storing cell contents, 37
storing macros, 214, 216
Style dialog box, 98–101
styles
  applying, 99
  creating, 98, 99, 101
  deleting, 101
  merging, 101
  modifying, 100
submenus, displaying, 14
subroutines (in macros),
  beginning and ending,
  217
subtotals, calculating, 59, 60
subtraction operator (–), 48
SUM function, 61

T

Tab key, navigating
  worksheets, 13
table data (Web-based),
  importing, 250
tabs
  in dialog boxes, 16
  See also sheet tabs
taskbar (Windows), switching
  between Office
  documents, 8
telephone numbers, entering, 28
templates, 189, 200
  built-in, 200
  changing, 202–3
  creating, 201, 220
  creating workbooks with,
  200
  customizing, 203
  default, 202, 203
  folder for, 203
  form templates, 220
  opening, 202
  testing, 201
  vs. macros, 201
Template Utilities add-in, 220
Template Wizard add-in, 220
  adding data to the database,
  225
  installing, 225
  merging workbooks with,
  224–25
text
  entering
  into cells, 28, 29
  into org chart boxes, 115
  with abbreviations, 44
  flow control, 90
  formatting, 82–83
  See also cell comments; chart
  text; labels; spelling;
  titles; WordArt text
text annotations (charts)

adding, 162, 163
  adding shadows to, 164
text attributes. *See* font
  attributes
text boxes
  in Data Forms, 172
  in dialog boxes, 16
text files, importing, 229
textures, filling data series with,
  160
three
  3-D charts, 149
  3-D effects, 140, 141
  vs. drop shadows, 141
  3-D objects
  creating, 140
  setting lighting/depth/
  surfaces/direction,
  141
  spinning, 140
tiling workbook windows, 192
times
  adding to worksheets, 77
  entering, 30
  formatting in cells, 31
tips
  from the Office Assistant, 19
  See also ScreenTips
title bar, 7, 8
  "[Shared]" status alert, 205,
  223
titles
  charts, 148, 162, 163, 164
  org charts, 115
  rows and columns, 78,
  79, 80
  worksheets, 89
toolbar buttons, 7
  adding to toolbars, 15, 35,
  51, 196, 197
  assigning to macros, 197
  choosing commands
  with, 14
  deleting from toolbars, 196

toolbar buttons,
   Drawing toolbar, 122, 129, 135
   Formatting toolbar, 82, 89
   order on menus, 15
   restoring originals, 197
   running macros with, 216
   Standard toolbar, 35, 51, 60, 93, 150, 159, 203
   WordArt toolbar, 109
toolbar icons, on menus, 14
toolbars, 7, 14
   adding buttons to, 15, 35, 51, 196, 197
   creating, 194–95
   customizing, 195, 196
   deleting buttons from, 196
   displaying, 15
   hiding, 15, 197
      all but the Web toolbar, 248
   moving, 15
   PivotTable toolbar, 184, 186
   reshaping, 15
   Reviewing toolbar, 118
   Web toolbar, 248
   WordArt toolbar, 109
   See also Drawing toolbar; Formatting toolbar; Standard toolbar; toolbar buttons
Toolbars tab (Customize dialog box), 194, 196, 197
tools
   drawing tools
      Freeform tools, 128
      See also Drawing toolbar
   for specialized projects, 207–13
   for working efficiently, 189–206, 207, 214–20
   for working together, 221–40
   See also toolbar buttons

Top 10 command (AutoFilter), 178
totals, calculating, 59, 60
tracing cell—formula relationships, 188
Track Changes feature, 204, 205
tracked changes (in worksheets)
   accepting or rejecting, 205
   viewing, 204
trends, data, calculating, 210–11, 212
TrueType fonts, 87
typefaces, specifying, 86–87

Underline button (Formatting toolbar), 82
underlining, applying, 82
Undo button (Standard toolbar), 35, 159
undoing actions, 35
ungrouping objects, 145
Uniform Resource Locators (URLs), 247
Up arrow key, navigating worksheets, 13
updating
   charts, 152
   links, 231
   PivotTable reports, 184
URLs (Uniform Resource Locators), 247
Use row and column names option (Apply Names dialog box), 57

validating data, 181
   circling invalid data in formulas, 188

validation rules, adding, 181
values (in cells), 26
   aligning, 88
   calculating goals by adjusting inputs, 213
   calculating outcomes of possible inputs, 210–11, 212
   coloring, 91
   entering, 25, 26, 30–31
      with AutoFill, 32
   formatting, 82, 83
   See also cell contents; data
vertices (in freeforms), 130
   deleting, 130, 131
   inserting, 130
   modifying vertex angles, 131
   moving, 130
   specifying point types, 131
viewing
   multiple workbooks, 192
   tracked changes, 204
   See also previewing
views
   changing object view settings, 146
   changing worksheet views, 193
Village Software template, 200

Web (Internet)
   accessing Office information on, 258
   changing options, 237
   getting help from, 19, 258
   importing data from, 107, 237, 248–50
   linking Excel to, 241–58
   links to. *See* hyperlinks
Web addresses, 247

Web browsers, system requirements, 243
Web discussions, 251, 252–53
   filtering, 253
   printing, 253
   replying to remarks, 253
   selecting a server, 252
   starting, 253
Web documents
   jumping to favorites, 249
   worksheets as, 241
Web file management, 251
Web pages
   creating, 242–43
   jumping to favorites, 249
   opening workbooks as, 244
   previewing before publishing, 245
   publishing, 243
   workbooks as, 241, 242
   worksheets as, 242, 243
Web servers, 243, 251
   selecting a discussion server, 252
Web tables, importing, 250
Web toolbar, importing data from the Web, 248
"What If" scenarios, 213, 220
wheel button (Intellimouse), 12
wildcards, as search characters, 175
windows. *See* Excel window; workbook windows
Windows Clipboard, 39, 40
   copying cell contents with, 38
   copying formulas with, 50, 51
   moving cell contents with, 38, 40
   pasting cell contents from, 36, 38
   vs. Office Clipboard, 37

Windows Explorer, Web file management, 251
wizards, 16
  add-ins, 220
  making choices in, 16
  PivotTable and PivotChart Wizard, 182, 183, 187, 239
  Setup Wizard, 2
  Template Wizard, 220, 224–25
  See also Chart Wizard
WordArt (Microsoft), 108
  closing, 110
  See also WordArt text
WordArt Alignment button (WordArt toolbar), 109
WordArt button (WordArt toolbar), 109
WordArt Character button (WordArt toolbar), 109
WordArt Gallery button (WordArt toolbar), 109
WordArt Same button (WordArt toolbar), 109
WordArt Shape button (WordArt toolbar), 109
WordArt text
  coloring, 111
  creating (inserting), 108–9
  editing, 110–11
  formatting, 111
    text effects, 112–13
  printing samples, 113
WordArt toolbar buttons, 109
WordArt Vertical button (WordArt toolbar), 109
workbook windows
  arranging, 192, 233
  moving, 8
  resizing, 8
  switching between, 8
  See also Excel window

workbooks, 5
  adding data to the Template Wizard database, 225
  arranging multiple views of one workbook, 192
  closing, 24
  consolidating data from, 224–25, 234–35
  creating, 25
    with templates, 200
  finding, 11
  linking, 233
  merging, 224–25
  modifying, 63–67
  naming, 20
  opening, 10–11
    files created in other spreadsheet programs, 11
    recently opened files, 10, 11
    as Web pages, 244
  protecting, 206
  routing in e-mail messages, 256, 257
  saving, 20–21
    automatic feature, 220
    with different names in different formats, 21
    on exiting, 24
    for the first time, 20
    to a previous version of Excel, 21
    as templates, 201
    as Web pages, 242
  sending in e-mail messages, 256
  sharing. See sharing workbooks (on networks)
  starting, 9
  storing macros in, 214, 216

viewing multiple, 192
  as Web pages, 241, 242
  See also files; workbook windows; worksheets
work environment, customizing, 189, 190–91
working together, 221
  tools for, 221–40
worksheets, 5
  activating, 64
  adding backgrounds to, 66
  adding graphics to, 103–20
  adding headers/footers to, 77
  auditing, 188
  basic skills, 25–46
  consolidating data from, 234–35
  copying, 67
  creating reports with, 208
  customizing views, 193
  deleting, 65
  discussing on the Web, 251, 252–53
  entering data in. See entering
  formatting, 81–102
  hiding, 65
  importing Web tables into, 250
  inserting, 65
  keeping track of revisions, 205
  linking, 232
  modifying, 63–67
  moving, 66
  naming, 64, 77
  navigating, 12–13
  outlining data, 199
  page breaks, 75
  previewing, 22, 23, 93
  printing. See printing worksheets
  protecting/unprotecting, 206

saving as Web pages, 242, 243
  scaling, 79
  selecting, 68
  sending in e-mail messages, 256
  switching, 12
  titles, centering, 89
  tracing cell—formula relationships, 188
  tracking changes, 204–5
  as Web documents/Web pages, 241, 242, 243
  See also workbook windows; workbooks
worksheet titles, centering, 89
worksheet windows. See workbook windows
World Wide Web. See Web
Wrap text feature, 90

x-axis, 148
  adding a title to, 162
  formatting, 166

y-axis, 148
  adding a title to, 162
  formatting, 166
year 2000 dates, formatting in cells, 31

zooming on rolling with an Intellimouse, 13

Elizabeth Eisner Reding has authored many computer books since 1992. Some of the topics include HTML, and Microsoft's Excel, PowerPoint, and Publisher products. She has worked for many publishers in the capacities of author, technical editor, and development editor. In her copious spare time, she collects fine art, renovates her home, and is working on a MBA degree.

Author's Acknowledgments

The task of creating any book requires the talents of many hard working people pulling together to meet impossible deadlines and untold stresses. Having said that, I'd like to thank the outstanding team responsible for making this book possible: my editor, MT Cozzola; the copyeditor, Jane Pedicini; and Steve Johnson and David Beskeen at Perspection. What a great team!

I'd also like to thank my wonderful husband, Michael, for putting up with me when I was at my worst. What a sweetheart—and to think I was lucky enough to meet you on the "T"!

The manuscript for this book was prepared and submitted to Microsoft Press in electronic form. Text files were prepared using Microsoft Word 97 for Windows 95. Pages were composed in PageMaker for Windows, with text in Stone Sans and display type in Stone Serif. Composed pages were delivered to the printer as electronic files.

Cover Design
Tim Girvin Design

Graphic Layout
David Beskeen

Compositors
Gary Bellig
Tracy Teyler

Proofreader
Jane Pedicini

Indexer
Michael Brackney
Savage Indexing Service

Master
Microsoft Office 2000
in a hurry!

Microsoft Press Quick Course® books offer you streamlined instruction in the form of no-nonsense, to-the-point tutorials and learning exercises. The core of each book is a logical sequence of straightforward, easy-to-follow instructions for building useful business skills—the same skills that you use on the job.

- QUICK COURSE® IN MICROSOFT® EXCEL 2000
- QUICK COURSE IN MICROSOFT ACCESS 2000
- QUICK COURSE IN MICROSOFT OFFICE 2000
- QUICK COURSE IN MICROSOFT POWERPOINT® 2000
- QUICK COURSEIN MICROSOFT WORD 2000
- QUICK COURSEIN MICROSOFT FRONTPAGE® 2000
- QUICK COURSEIN MICROSOFT INTERNET EXPLORER 5
- QUICK COURSE IN MICROSOFT PUBLISHER 2000
- QUICK COURSE IN MICROSOFT OUTLOOK® 2000

mspress.microsoft.com

Stay in the *running*
for maximum *productivity.*

These are *the* answer books for business users of Microsoft® Office 2000. They are packed with everything from quick, clear instructions for new users to comprehensive answers for power users—the authoritative reference to keep by your computer and use every day. THE RUNNING SERIES—learning solutions made by Microsoft.

- RUNNING MICROSOFT EXCEL 2000
- RUNNING MICROSOFT OFFICE 2000 PREMIUM
- RUNNING MICROSOFT OFFICE 2000 PROFESSIONAL
- RUNNING MICROSOFT OFFICE 2000 SMALL BUSINESS EDITION
- RUNNING MICROSOFT WORD 2000
- RUNNING MICROSOFT POWERPOINT® 2000
- RUNNING MICROSOFT ACCESS 2000
- RUNNING MICROSOFT INTERNET EXPLORER 5.0
- RUNNING MICROSOFT FRONTPAGE®
- RUNNING MICROSOFT OUTLOOK® 2000

mspress.microsoft.com

Step up!

STEP BY STEP books provide quick and easy self-training—to help you learn to use the powerful word processing, spreadsheet, database, presentation, communication, and Internet components of Microsoft Office 2000—both individually and together. The easy-to-follow lessons present clear objectives and real-world business examples, with numerous screen shots and illustrations. Put Office 2000 to work today, with STEP BY STEP learning solutions, made by Microsoft.

- MICROSOFT® OFFICE PROFESSIONAL 8-IN-1 STEP BY STEP
- MICROSOFT WORD 2000 STEP BY STEP
- MICROSOFT EXCEL 2000 STEP BY STEP
- MICROSOFT POWERPOINT® 2000 STEP BY STEP
- MICROSOFT INTERNET EXPLORER 5 STEP BY STEP
- MICROSOFT PUBLISHER 2000 STEP BY STEP
- MICROSOFT ACCESS 2000 STEP BY STEP
- MICROSOFT FRONTPAGE 2000 STEP BY STEP
- MICROSOFT OUTLOOK 2000 STEP BY STEP

Microsoft Press® products are available worldwide wherever quality computer books are sold. For more information, contact your book or computer retailer, software reseller, or local Microsoft Sales Office, or visit our Web site at mspress.microsoft.com. To locate your nearest source for Microsoft Press products, or to order directly, call 1-800-MSPRESS in the U.S. (in Canada, call 1-800-268-2222).

Prices and availability dates are subject to change.

mspress.microsoft.com

Register Today!

Return this
Microsoft® Excel 2000 At a Glance
registration card today

Microsoft®Press
mspress.microsoft.com

OWNER REGISTRATION CARD   **1-57231-942-9**

Microsoft® Excel 2000 At a Glance

_____   _____   _____
FIRST NAME   **MIDDLE INITIAL**   **LAST NAME**

_____
INSTITUTION OR COMPANY NAME

_____
ADDRESS

_____

_____   _____   _____
CITY   **STATE**   **ZIP**

                                                                                      ( )
_____   _____
E-MAIL ADDRESS   **PHONE NUMBER**

U.S. and Canada addresses only. Fill in information above and mail postage-free.
Please mail only the bottom half of this page.

For information about Microsoft Press® products, visit our Web site at **mspress.microsoft.com**

Microsoft®*Press*

BUSINESS REPLY MAIL
FIRST-CLASS MAIL   PERMIT NO. 108   REDMOND WA

POSTAGE WILL BE PAID BY ADDRESSEE

MICROSOFT PRESS
PO BOX 97017
REDMOND, WA 98073-9830

NO POSTAGE
NECESSARY
IF MAILED
IN THE
UNITED STATES